South France Pilot
LA CORSE

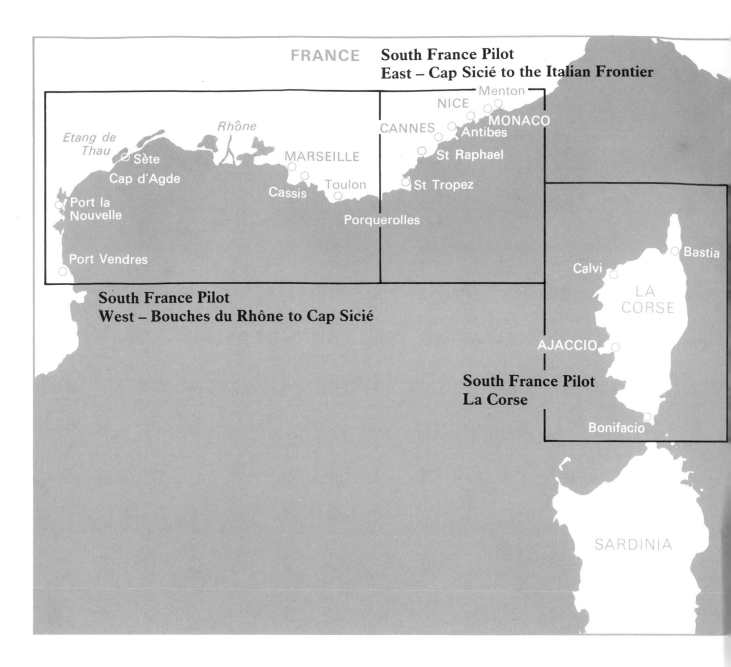

FRANCE **South France Pilot**
East – Cap Sicié to the Italian Frontier

Etang de Thau

Rhône

Ø Sète

Cap d'Agde

MARSEILLE

Cassis

Toulon

NICE

Menton

MONACO

CANNES

Antibes

St Raphael

St Tropez

Port la Nouvelle

Porquerolles

Port Vendres

South France Pilot
West – Bouches du Rhône to Cap Sicié

Calvi

Bastia

LA CORSE

AJACCIO

South France Pilot
La Corse

Bonifacio

SARDINIA

South France Pilot

South France Pilot
LA CORSE
(Corsica)

Robin Brandon

Imray Laurie Norie & Wilson Ltd
St Ives Cambridgeshire England

Published by
Imray, Laurie, Norie & Wilson Ltd
Wych House, St Ives, Huntingdon,
Cambridgeshire, PE17 4BT, England.

© Robin Brandon 1991
Part I
First published as *South France Pilot I*
1974
2nd edition 1983
3rd edition 1989

Part II La Corse
First published as *South France Pilot VI* 1976
2nd edition 1983

British Library Cataloguing in Publication Data

Brandon, Robin
  South France Pilot.
  Chapter 3.
  1. Southern France. Coastal Waters. Pilots' Guides
  I. Title
  623.89 29449

  ISBN 0 85288 145 2

This work has been corrected to January 1991 and amendments will be issued periodically after that date. A subscription form is enclosed at the end of the book.

IMPORTANT
While every effort has been made to check and crosscheck the data and information given in this book, the Author and Publishers cannot accept responsibility for any accidents, injury or damage occasioned by the use of this information or data.

Readers should use this book with prudence and in a seamanlike manner. Their attention is directed to the many changes, both man-made and natural, that are certain to occur subsequent to publication. Furthermore reference should always be made to any amendments issued by the Publishers as well as the latest Admiralty *Notices to Mariners, List of Lights Volume E* and *Lists of Radio Signals*.

In addition, users of this guide themselves are asked to report any changes, omissions or corrections to the Publishers or Author. A correction reported immediately when noted, briefly on a postcard or by rough sketch, may subsequently avoid another yachtsman getting into difficulties. Your cooperation in this matter therefore, is gratefully requested.

Printed in Great Britain at the Bath Press, Avon.

Contents

Preface

The original reconnaissance of La Corse was undertaken in 1974/5 and the first edition was published in 1976. The second edition was published in 1983 after further visits to bring it up to date. During the intervening fifteen years there have been many changes to the harbours and coast but in general they have neither been so large nor widespread as those which have taken place on the mainland coast. The great change has been the vast increase in the number of yachts visiting the island, its harbours and anchorages. This factor has encouraged us to replan the layout of the book to include more anchorages and to undertake a virtual rewrite of its contents. The original *South France Pilot Chapter I Introduction*, suitably amended, has been added to the rewritten *Chapter VI Corsica* so that all the necessary data is in one volume. The planning guide has been expanded to include the 174 anchorages which are described in this book. The details given for the 22 harbours have been increased considerably and, above all, a large number of new photographs, many taken from the air, have been included. The welcome improvements in the quality of the printing and reproduction of the photographs, thanks to modern printing equipment, will also be noted.

It is hoped to keep up the production of an annual list of corrections and in this context I would once again appeal to anyone finding an error, change or a correction necessary to let me or the publisher know as soon as possible.

In conclusion may I wish all readers a pleasant voyage and visit to this delightful island.

ACKNOWLEDGEMENTS

It is difficult for an author to know how to acknowledge those who helped with the earlier editions when drafting the acknowledgements for the 3rd. My thanks to them are still given but life has moved on so I will concentrate on the present due to lack of space!

The harbour masters and their staff have continued to be most helpful and I am indebted to them for many corrections and details of future changes that they know about. I have continued the close two-way cooperation with the Royal Cruising Club which has been very helpful.

Help from those individuals who, in a seaman-like way, have sent in reports on errors and changes which have been invaluable and have been a sound basis for the annual corrections sheets. I would especially like to thank M. Wilfrid Polome for his help with the area of the Bouches de Bonifacio and the port of Bonifacio also Mr D. Le Franc and Mr M.

H. Waller for their reports. Robert Quintaña who flew a light aircraft so that I could take the photographs deserves a special mention for his skills.

Without a small crew it would have been very difficult to carry out an efficient reconnaissance, my thanks go to Robert and Faith Cox, my friends and crew for many years and David Broughton for their assistance during fair and foul weather. Not forgetting my wife, Jan, who crewed, cooked, cleaned and finally put all the new information onto a PC disk for the publishers.

Willie Wilson, Ettie Wilson and their excellent staff should also be mentioned with thanks, for without them there would be no end product. Their work has been detailed and difficult which they have carried out with considerable skill.

R. J. Brandon
Grimaud, France
November 1990

PART I
Introduction and general information

About this pilot book

Aim

This pilot book has been written with the intention of providing a simple and safe guide for the skipper who has not had a vast amount of pilotage experience, so that by following the series of instructions given he can visit the many pleasant harbours on this coast with the greatest ease and least risk. Those who are very experienced may find that the obvious has been stated too frequently for their need, but nevertheless they will find a large amount of useful and sometimes vital information for their use.

Amendments

It is important that readers finding any errors, omissions, additions or amendments necessary should notify the publishers. A postcard will be sufficient, just give the title, page and line numbers and details of the amendment, but for large corrections a sketch and/or photograph would be of assistance. Your help in doing this will be much appreciated.

This book can be kept up to date to an extent by extracting the relevant corrections from the weekly *Notices to Mariners* which are issued by the Admiralty. The French equivalent, the *Avis aux Navigateurs* published by the Service Hydrographique de la Marine can be obtained but it is expensive to have them sent to the UK. A better alternative is to obtain the annual list of corrections which is issued each May by the same office (address page 6) entitled *Corrections apportées aux Cartes Marines des Côtes de France et des Côtes Voisines.*

Layout

The layout of this book has been specially planned in a natural order of progression. *Part I* is concerned with the general background information necessary to equip the skipper and his crew with the knowledge and material items which will be needed for the voyage out and on arrival in France.

Under the heading *Preparation* are listed and discussed the major items of equipment, clothing, documents, medical supplies, etc., which may have to be provided or obtained before leaving Britain.

Under the heading *Technical information*, outline details of the French coast are given for planning purposes together with details of weather, radio signals, buoyage, special hazards to be found, etc.

The heading *France* covers a very brief introduction to the country and important facts that a visiting yachtsman should know. Finally there is an outline guide covering the various routes to the area, and a list of reference books.

Part II has its own introduction for detailed planning and includes special information such as radiobeacons, weather forecasts, harbours of refuge, health services, etc. There is a valuable planning guide which lists harbours, anchorages, headlands and passages, showing the distances between important places and including the direction of the winds which can enter the anchorages.

Finally comes the important *Pilotage* section which is dealt with in geographical order and includes the ports, harbours, headlands, passages and anchorages.

The part dealing with the ports and harbours is laid out as follows. The first few lines answer the questions: Can I take my yacht into the harbour? How easy is it to enter? How big is it and its nearest town? Is it a nice place? What facilities does it have? There follows a short description of the harbour to confirm these points.

Next is a list of technical data necessary for the approach and entrance, and a paragraph about any possible problems. The approach by day and night from various directions is now discussed, followed by instructions on how to enter, again by both day and night.

Having entered the harbour, advice is given about berthing and where to report to complete formalities.

A list of facilities, both in the harbour and area, are detailed with a note about future developments. Finally where possible a short extract on local history is given.

The whole of the pilotage section is backed up by plans and photographs. The skipper/navigator will find that the information required to approach and

1

enter a harbour is collected together onto one or two pages for ease of reference and the type and headings have been selected for easy reading under poor conditions.

Types of yacht

The pilotage and sailing directions have been written for yachtsmen with either power or sailing yachts drawing up to 2m (6·6ft) and of normal design. Mention is made of many smaller harbours that can be used by yachts drawing about 1m (3·3ft) and anchorages outside harbours have been described where larger yachts drawing more than 2m can lie.

Types of harbour

A port in this book is considered to be of large size and primarily concerned with commerce, a harbour on the other hand is small, often with a commercial and fishing quay. A yacht harbour (normally misnamed a marina in Britain) is a harbour mainly devoted to yachts but may have a small fishing section. A marina is a complex of yacht harbour, shops, habitations and facilities especially designed for yachtsmen. In France the term *port* can cover the largest commercial port down through a normal harbour to a small cove or bay without any facilities whatever.

Pontoons

Some yacht harbours are equipped with long narrow pontoons, jetties, catwalks, landing stages and piers to which yachts secure. There are very many different types of design but for the purposes of this pilot book they have all been referred to as pontoons.

Plans

The plans that are provided for every harbour are of a simplified nature for the express use of yachtsmen. All irrelevant data such as depths over 5m have been excluded in most cases and extra data such as yacht clubs have been added. These have been produced from detailed surveys but in view of the great changes that are taking place and are planned they should be used with care and prudence. Plans labelled 'Sketch plan. Not to scale' should only be used as a guide and not for navigation.

Soundings

Soundings shown on the plans and mentioned in the text are in metres (m) and are based on the local datum which is the Lowest Astronomical Tide (LAT). The water levels will only fall below this datum under extreme meteorological conditions.

Bearings

All bearings in this pilot book are given 360° notation, are from seaward, and are true.

Magnetic variation

The local magnetic variation for each harbour is given together with the amount by which it decreases each year.

Times

Normal winter time in France is UT + 0100 and summer time is UT + 0200. These times are referred to as *l'heure locale* (local time). UT is sometimes referred to as *temps universel* (universal time) or TU and is the same as UT and GMT.

Where times are used in this book they are given for UT. A note is made if local time is to be used.

Photographs

The majority of photographs were taken under some difficulty, for instance when the yacht was being navigated short-handed into a strange harbour. Others were taken under conditions of poor light and visibility, therefore the quality of the results is not always as good as would have been preferred. Many photographs inside the harbours were taken with wide-angle lenses and show some distortion.

Classification of harbours

Each harbour has been classified by a three-digit code and this number is given in the planning section of each chapter and also at the top of the first page of the harbour concerned. The three numbers refer to attractiveness, ease of approach and entrance, and facilities available, the key being given below.

In selecting a code number every effort has been made to keep a constant standard throughout, but it will be appreciated that the code number selected for a particular harbour is naturally a personal opinion and may have been influenced by weather conditions, the reception encountered, the numbers and behaviour of tourists and other yachtsmen in the area, just to mention a few factors concerned. Comparisons have not been made between large and small ports but like has been compared with like. A preference for a large port with all its facilities or for a small harbour with its simpler arrangements must remain the decision of the reader.

Attractiveness – First number
1 Very attractive, make every effort to visit
2 Attractive, go a little out of your way to visit
3 Normal, visit if convenient
4 Not attractive, expect to be disappointed
5 Most unattractive, only visit if really necessary

Ease of approach – Second number
1 Possible to enter under almost any condition
2 Possible to enter under almost any condition except with strong winds from one direction
3 Possible to enter in strong winds except those from several directions
4 Possible to enter in medium winds only
5 Possible to enter in light winds only

Facilities – Third number
1 All possible facilities for yachtsmen
2 Many facilities but no major repairs possible, a large number of shops
3 Limited facilities, only simple repairs of a minor nature possible, many shops
4 Very limited facilities, a few shops and no repairs
5 Virtually nothing except perhaps a water supply point

Key to symbols

Where practical, symbols are used in the plans and French terms are applied where the meaning is obvious. Users are referred to the comprehensive glossary.

	English	French
⚓	harbourmaster/ port office	*Capitaine de Port/ Bureau de Port*
⚓	water	*eau*
🛢	fuel	*gas-oil/carburant*
🅰	yacht chandler	*Chandler*
	crane	*grue*
♪	telephone	*telephone*
	travel-lift	
Ⓥ	visitors' berths	*visiteurs*
🆈	yacht club (initials)	*Club Nautique*
	showers	*douche*
i	information	*syndicat d'initiative*
✉	post office	*P & T PTT*
⚡	mechanic	*mechanique*
	ship/yacht yard	*chantier naval*
⊖	customs	*douanes*
❋	ice	*glace*
	swimming pool	*pisine*
▬	slip	*cale*
⚓	anchorage	*mouillage*
⚓	anchoring prohibited	*mouillage interdit*
	yachts prohibited	*yachts interdit*
⚓	yachts	*yachts*
WC	water closet (WC)	*toilettes*
	laundrette	*laverie*

Preparation

Preferred design of yacht

It is beyond the scope of a pilot book to discuss in detail the type of craft most suited to the area and in any case the reader may already possess a yacht. However, for those about to purchase one and for those who can have their yacht adapted, the following may be of use.

Hull

The choice of material should be carefully considered. Steel is strong, can be repaired almost anywhere but even if insulated it tends to be hot below decks and needs constant attention against rust. Aluminium has an electrolysis problem in addition to those of steel. Wood has many advantages provided it is looked after continually by a crew on board. GRP has fewer problems than other materials, but fibreglass repairs of any significance can only be undertaken in major harbours.

Engine power

A good reliable engine is essential because, due to calms, the engine will be used more frequently than in British waters. On occasions it may have to be used to drive the yacht against a Force 8 (+) *tramontane* or *mistral* wind into a harbour, so it should be powerful enough to make to windward in adverse conditions.

Space and ventilation

In the very hot conditions that prevail in the area during the summer months, adequate space and ventilation are essential for comfort. The 'well corked bottle' type of yacht which is ideal for the English Channel soon becomes uncomfortably stuffy. Deck insulation, extra cabin skylights and hatchways are of value.

Cockpit

Most of the time on board will be passed in the cockpit, therefore adequate space and comfortable seats are essential.

Decks

Good deck space for the crew to relax or sunbathe is also advisable.

Shower

A shower on board is well worth having if there is space but it may require extra water tanks, a pressurised hot and cold water system and pump-assisted drainage. An alternative is to have a special plastic container, preferably dark coloured, that can be pressurised by hand and has a pipe and rose. This water-filled can placed in the sun will soon give hot water for showering.

Mast steps

Permanent mast steps, or a special ladder which can be hoisted, are well worth having to deal with mast problems when at sea. This also enables a crew member to climb aloft easily to 'con' the yacht into a shallow anchorage. When 'conning' a yacht the use of Polaroid glasses are of great value in spotting underwater dangers.

Ice box

An ice box or refrigerator is almost essential and the larger the better. Large blocks of ice one metre long are obtainable at most harbours and if there is space for several of these blocks they last much longer. The most effective yacht refrigerators are those with engine-driven compressors.

Equipment for yacht

A yacht fully equipped for extensive cruising around the shores of the British Isles should require very little extra for a cruise in the Mediterranean but the following items are useful to have on board:

Awnings

The sun in summer can be very hot around midday and awnings make life much more pleasant. If they are so designed that they throw a shadow onto the whole deck then the cabins will remain much cooler. Side curtains are also of value as they will keep the side decks cool and keep out the low evening sun. Awnings should be made of heavy canvas type material; light nylon or *Terylene* type materials flap in the breeze and make a considerable noise.

The actual design is naturally dependent on the type of yacht concerned but by using strong points such as standing rigging, booms, wheelhouse roofs, etc., coupled with battens in pockets in the awnings and suitable lashings, an effective shelter can be made. Due to expense and the time factor it is best to have this awning made in England though there are many places in the Mediterranean where it could be made. A large cowl made of canvas which can be suspended over the forward hatch to direct air below is well worth having.

Mosquito nets

Mosquitoes are prevalent in most areas of the western Mediterranean and house flies can at times be most annoying. It is well worth constructing mosquito nets to fit all hatchways and other openings. The alternative is to rely on the various chemicals, available from supermarkets and chemists, which can be sprayed around the cabin or rubbed on the skin.

Gangplanks

Most yachts that are kept in the Mediterranean have stern gangplanks (*passerelles*) which vary from an old bit of rough timber to the most complicated and elaborate affairs in stainless steel and beautifully varnished mahogany with stanchions and rope rails.

For the visiting yacht all these are quite unnecessary provided the skipper and crew are agile enough to jump a metre wide gap to the pontoon; they are also very awkward and difficult to stow on small and medium sized yachts when not in use. For yachts that are going to spend weeks, months or even years in port without going to sea they have obvious advantages. They may be essential to some modern yachts with sloping sterns which project a long way aft.

Cockpit tables

Most meals will be taken on deck and in the cockpit during spring, summer and autumn and a folding table is well worth having. A simple camping table will suffice.

Gas cylinders

If the yacht is equipped with a gas system for cooking etc., and uses *Calor Gas* type bottles it will be necessary to make alterations because refills for *Calor Gas* are not obtainable in France. On the other hand *Camping Gaz* refills are obtainable in the very smallest harbours and are comparatively cheap.

There exists an adaptor which fits *Camping Gaz* cylinders and will take the reverse thread union of the *Calor Gas* equipment. This can be bought in Britain along with *Camping Gaz* cylinders and a refund obtained when the cylinders are returned after the cruise.

Water hose

A length of hose some 25m long is of great value for refilling water tanks from standpipes that are to be found on most pontoons and quays. There are several types and sizes of taps in use at the various harbours and suitable connectors can usually be bought at a local shop.

Water filters and chemicals

Water from public supply is usually safe to drink, but should the tanks be filled with contaminated water the 'bugs' will breed well in the warm environment and affect anyone drinking unboiled water. The installation of modern water filters is one practical solution. The frequent use of various chemicals, specially prepared to sterilise the water, is another. The foolproof alternative is to always use bottled water which can be bought everywhere and is guaranteed to be pure.

Due to the excessive demand for water during the summer, many wells become contaminated with salty (brackish) water which is unpleasant to drink and to wash in.

Electric cable

Virtually every harbour provides electrical outlet sockets on the pontoons and quays, usually 220v AC. Some of the large harbours also have 385v AC 3-phase sockets for use by the bigger yachts. About 20m of 3-core heavy duty outdoor electric cable to bring a supply to the yacht will be invaluable. It can then be used with a trickle charger to keep the yacht's batteries charged up or it can be used with a separate mains voltage system for lights etc.

Unfortunately there are many different types of electrical sockets to be found in the various harbours and it will be necessary to buy several types of plug. To save continually having to change the plug on the long cable fit a normal male plug to it and have a series of female plugs of the same type, each with a very short length of cable, one for each type of the harbour plugs.

Charging engines

If an electric refrigerator or other extra electrical apparatus has been installed it may be considered essential to have a small petrol or diesel driven battery charger aboard. These engines can be very noisy when running so do not run them in anchorages and yacht harbours where and when it will annoy your neighbours.

Flags

The courtesy flags of the various countries through whose waters it is planned to pass must be carried and it is worth remembering that there is a Monégasque flag which should be flown when visiting Monaco. The Corsican flag is the moor's head and it is considered polite to fly it below the French courtesy flag. A full set of international code flags will be needed if intending to dress the yacht overall in company with most other yachts on days of celebration. On these days a number of yachts go to the trouble of dressing overall with lights at night usually powered with the supply from the quay. Spare ensigns and burgees should be taken as due to the sun, salt and strong winds they wear out much more quickly than in British waters.

Varnishes and paints

Though a good selection of paints and varnishes is available in the shops, they are more expensive than in Britain so a supply should be taken. Repainting and varnishing is important because in the hot sun with very salty spray, brightwork and paint deteriorate rapidly. However, in the Mediterranean the excellent painting conditions give a good chance to bring shabby yachts up to the high standard of most of those to be found in the harbours there.

Spares and expendables

If only to save time and money a comprehensive supply of spares and expendables should be carried. Spares for internationally known engines and equipment may be available at the larger ports. Equivalent replacement yacht parts of a non-specialist nature and normal yacht chandlery are usually available at the large yachting harbours, but in general are more expensive than they would be in Britain. The problem is to find the correct shop or agent that has the part required and this search can take some time. Large and heavy replacement parts sent from Britain may take several weeks before they arrive and they have to be cleared with the customs. Good reserves of special batteries, oils, etc. for British equipment should be carried. See also under *Customs*, page 22.

Toolkit and manuals

A comprehensive tool kit which includes tools to fit the engine is a must, to which should be added the relevant manuals for all equipment on board. A large filing book with transparent pockets is ideal for keeping the manuals separate and immediately available.

Anchors

Much of the seabed near the coast in the Mediterranean where anchoring is possible is of hard-packed sand covered with a thick layer of fine grass-type weed. Anchors of the CQR and Danforth type which are so good elsewhere have difficulty penetrating the weed and getting into the sand because as they drag they collect a mass of weed and then cannot dig in at all.

The best anchor for this type of bottom is the old fisherman-type or 4-pronged Mediterranean anchor (a folding version can now be obtained) of a good size and weight which will cut through the weed and get into the sand. Although awkward to stow, they are worth having should the yacht be caught in a blow. Anchors without points are hopeless.

Two anchors are essential and a third advisable. The largest anchor should have 60m (197ft) of heavy chain. The others can have 10m (33ft) chain and 50m (164ft) nylon line. Anchors with sharp points, e.g. CQR, Danforth, etc., are strongly advised; again a 4-pronged Mediterranean type is ideal but very difficult to stow. Some popular harbours and anchorages have a bottom of loose sand due to the thousands of anchors which have been dropped and weighed; a pointed anchor is vital in this situation.

Anchor weight

A heavy anchor weight and chain saddle, sometimes called a 'chum', should be carried and used if caught by a *mistral* when at anchor. It will take most of the jerk away when snubbing at the chain.

Berthing lines

Yachts that are kept in the Mediterranean for a long period and especially over the winter months need a pair of very strong stern lines for use when securing stern-to pontoons. These lines should have a loop of chain at the outer end of similar weight to that used for the anchor, these loops are used to connect to the ring or bollard on the pontoon; they often incorporate large metal springs or snubbers to smooth out any jerks. A similar line is sometimes used at the bow.

Materials for the construction of these lines should be taken on board and made up when a more accurate assessment of the length of each line can be made after practical experience in the Mediterranean. Extra-strong berthing lines should be taken for everyday use because during gales, very heavy surges will be encountered in some harbours and those normally used at home will not be strong enough unless doubled. See diagram on page 20.

Cleats

Strong cleats and large fairleads are required and they must be securely bolted through the deck. Extra cleats and fairleads may have to be fitted amidships to take holding-off and spring lines.

Charts

Admiralty charts of the area can be obtained from normal Admiralty chart agents and in addition the following can also obtain French and Spanish charts: Imray, Laurie, Norie & Wilson Ltd., Wych House, St Ives, Huntingdon, Cambs PE17 4BT ☎ (0480) 62114. Kelvin Hughes, 145 The Minories, London, EC3 1NH ☎ 071 709 9076

At least three month's notice should be given to enable these agents to obtain foreign charts.

In France, Admiralty charts are available from Lt Commander M. Healy, 10 rue Jean Brucco, 0631 Beaulieu sur Mer, and official chart agents.

French charts can be bought at the major ports from large ships' chandlers and bookshops. They are also obtainable from Imrays as above or the Etablissement Principal du Service Hydrographique et Océanographique de la Marine (EPSHOM), Section Délivrances, BP426, 29275 Brest Cedex. ☎ (98) 02 09 17. Telex 940568 HYDRO.

The *ECM Navicarte* series of charts are also available from most ships' chandlers and bookshops or direct from Editions Cartographic Maritimes, 7 Quai Gabriel Péri 94340, Joinville-le-Pont, France ☎ (1) 48 85 77 00.

It should not be necessary to purchase large scale harbour charts as they are covered by the plans in this pilot; the medium scale coastal charts are useful to have.

The old French and Spanish charts do not have compass roses so the use of a Douglas protractor or similar instrument is necessary in order to obtain or use bearings. The new specification charts have compass roses.

The French charts are probably the best for this section of coast though those who are more familiar with the Admiralty issues may find these easier to use. The obsolete charts are best for anchorages.

The figure following the title of each chart or plan denotes its natural scale.

British Admiralty charts

Chart	Title	Scale
South coast France		
149	Rade de Toulon	12,500
	Rade de Villefranche – Monaco and Port of Nice	15,000
150	Marseille	20,000
1506	Plans on the South Coast of France	
	Port Vendres	5,000
	Port La Nouvelle	15,000
	Approaches to Port Vendres	50,000
1705	Cape St Sebastien to Iles d'Hyères	300,000
1780	Barcelona to Naples	1,000,000
2164	La Rhône to Cap Sicié	75,000
	Port de la Ciotat	20,000
2165	Cap Sicié to Cap Camarat	75,000
2166	Cap Camarat to Cannes	60,000
	Saint Raphaël	20,000
2167	Cannes to Menton	60,000
	Cannes: Antibes	15,000
2606	Approaches to Sète	50,000
	Port de Sète	10,000
2607	Marseille to Agay Road	145,600
2609	Rade d'Agay to San Remo	145,500
3498	Golfe de Fos	25,000
Corsica		
1213	Bonifacio Strait	50,000
1424	Ports on the south and west coasts of Corsica	
	Bonifacio	7,500
	Ajaccio: Propriano	10,000
	Golfe d'Ajaccio and Golfo de Valinco	60,000

Chart	Title	Scale
1425	Ports on the north and east coasts of Corsica	
	Macinaggio	10,000
	Bastia	15,000
	Calvi	17,500
	Porto Vecchio	25,000
	Approaches to Calvi	50,000
1985	Ajaccio to Oristano inc. the Bonifacio Strait	300,000
1992	Parts of Sardegna and Corse with Bonifacio Strait	300,000
1999	Livorno to Civitavecchia inc. Northern Corse	300,000

French charts
General area charts

Chart	Title	Scale
7014	Des îles Baléares à la Corse et à la Sardaigne	1,000,000
5017	Bassin Ouest de la Méditerranée (3e feuille) du méridien de La Calle au méridien de Messine. Côtes d'Italie et de Tunisie, Corse, Sardaigne et Sicile	1,070,000

Coastal charts

Chart	Title	Scale
1248	Du cap Creux aux îles des Mèdes	50,800
5151	Rade d'Hyères	25,000
5175	Parages de Toulon, golfe de Giens	25,000
5255	Golfe de St Tropez	14,400
5266	Baies de Briande, de Bon-Porte et de Pampelonne	25,000
5325	Du Bec l'Aigle à la presqu'île de Giens	50,100
5329	De la presqu'île de Giens au cap Camarat	50,100
5477	Du Cap Sicié au Cap Bénat, rades de Toulon et d'Hyères	50,200
6610	De Bandol au Cap Sicié Rade de Brusc	20,000
6612	De Cassis à Bandol, baie de la Ciotat	20,000
6615	Iles de Port Cros et du Levant (Iles d'Hyères)	25,000
6616	Du Cap Bénat au Cap Lardier, rade de Bormes, baie de Cavalaire	25,000
6632	De Marseille à Menton. Côte Nord-Ouest de Corse	285,000
6684	Golfe et Port de Fos	25,000
6693	Des Saintes-Maries-de-la-Mer à Port-Saint-Louis du Rhône	49,900
6713	Côte Nord-Est de la Corse, canal de Corse	152,000
6739	Golfe de Marseille	17,000
6767	De Fos sur Mer à Marseille	49,900
6821	Côte Ouest du Corse, du cap Corse au Golfe d'Ajaccio	152,000
6822	Abords, Nord de Bastia	50,300
6823	Abords Sud de Bastia	50,600
6850	St-Florent, Centuri, Macinaggio	10,000, 15,000
6851	Ports d'Ajaccio et de Propriano	75,000, 10,000
6855	Du phare d'Alistro à Solenzara	51,000
6856	Abords et port de Bastia	15,000
6838	Abords de Saint-Raphaël. De la Pointe des Issambres à la Pointe d'Anthéor	20,000
6839	Etang de Thau	30,000
6843	Du Cabo Creus à Port Barcarès	50,000
6844	De Port Barcarès à l'embouchure du l'Aude	50,000
6863	Du Cap Ferrat au Cap Martin	20,000
6873	Du phare du Titan au Cap Roux	50,000
6881	Abords de Monaco. Ports de la Condamine, de Fontvieille et de Cap d'Ail	7,500
6882	De l'île de Planier à la Ciotat	50,000
6907	Etang de Berre	25,000
6911	Golfe de Porto-Vecchio	15,000
6929	Abords de Porto Vecchio, de l'anse de Favone aux îles Lavezzi	51,200
6942	De Punta d'Orchino au Cap Muro	50,000

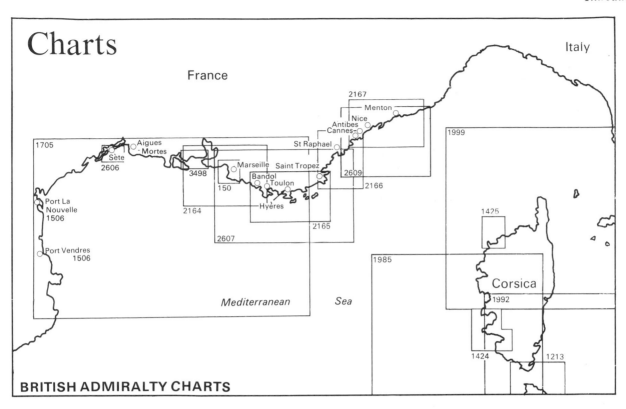

Charts

BRITISH ADMIRALTY CHARTS

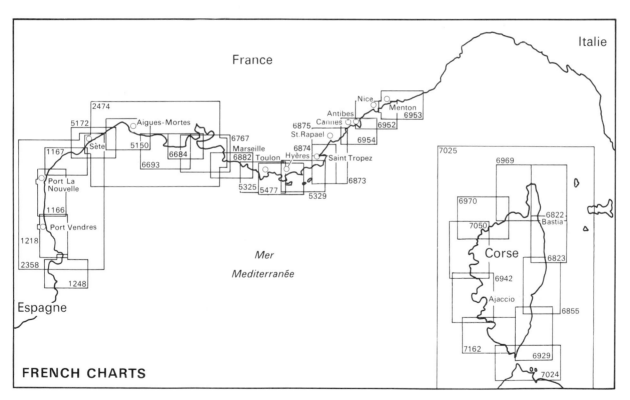

FRENCH CHARTS

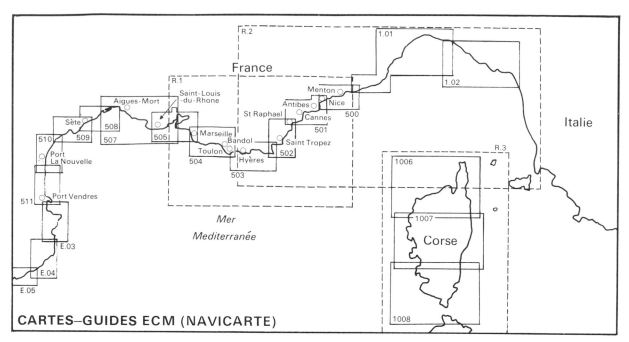

CARTES–GUIDES ECM (NAVICARTE)

Cartes-Guides ECM

Chart	Title	Scale
6951	De Fos-sur-Mer à Capo Mele	250,000
6952	D'Antibes à Menton	49,600
6953	De Monaco à San Remo	49,600
6954	Du Cap de Drammont au Cap d'Antibes	50,000
6969	Du Cap Corse à la pointe de l'Acciolu Golfe de St Florent	50,300
6970	De Punta di l'Acciolu à Capo Cavallo	50,500
6980	L'Ile Rousse, Sant'Ambrogio, Calvi	15,000
7002	Ports de Banyuls-sur-Mer, Port Vendres, Collioure, Saint-Cyprien, Port-la-Nouvelle	10,000
7003	Le Cap d'Agde – Embouchure de l'Hérault	15,000
7004	Golf d'Aigues-Mortes Ports de Palavas-les-Flots, Carnon-Plage et des Saintes-Maries-de-la-Mer	15,000
7017	Du Cap Ferrat à Capo Mele	100,000
7024	Bouches de Bonifacio	50,000
7025	Ile de Corse	250,000
7050	De Calvi à Cargèse	50,000
7053	De Sète à la pointe de l'Espiguette	50,000
7054	De l'embouchure de l'Aude à Sète	50,000
7072	Port de Sète	15,000
7008	Du Cabo de San Sébastian à Fos-sur-Mer	25,000
7093	Rade de Toulon	10,000
7096	Port de Bonifacio	5,000
	Baie de Figari	10,000
7162	Du Cap Muro au Cap de Feno	50,000

Spanish charts

49	Golfo de León. De punta del Llobregat a cabo d'Antibes	400,000
121	Golfo de Génova. De las islas d'Hyères a la isla Elba y costa N de Córcega	400,000

Chart   **Title**

Navicarte

Carte-Guides Navigation Côtière & Routiers, published by Editions Cartographiques Maritimes (ECM). General scale 1:50,000 with enlarged insets.

South coast France

500	Nice – San Remo
501	St-Raphael – Nice
502	Cavalaire – St-Raphael
502	Toulon – Cavalaire – Iles d'Hyères
504	Marseille – Toulon
505	Port-Saint-Louis – Marseille
507	Port de Bouc – Port Camargue
508	Port-Camargue – Sète
509	Sète – Valras
510	Valras – Port Leucate
511	Port Leucate – Banyuls

Corsica

1006	Calvi – Bastia
1007	Porto – Ajaccio
1008	Propriano – Bonifacio – Maddalena

Routiers (1:250,000)

R1	Marseille – San Remo
R2	Golfe de Gênes (Hyères – Calvi – l'Elbe)
R3	Corse

Provisions

In addition to the normal stock of food required to cover the voyage out to the Mediterranean, it is also advisable to carry stocks of the following which are more expensive in France and La Corse: coffee powder, tea or preferably tea bags, tins of meat, breakfast cereals and any special types of British food required by skipper or crew. Visit the manager of the local cash and carry warehouse and explain what you want and what you plan to do, he may allow you to stock up at wholesale prices as you will be buying in commercial quantities.

Drink

Visit the local customs officer several weeks before you set sail and explain your plan for the voyage, he may allow you to take duty free drink in bond. Make sure that he explains the necessary procedure to be followed and the requisite forms to be completed. When in the Mediterranean duty free goods can be bought at any of the major ports and harbours, all that is required is to find out which shop sells duty free goods and to place your order. The manager of the shop will contact the customs for you and arrange for a customs officer to be present when the goods are delivered on board. Stores in bond must naturally be consumed on board and never taken on shore, neither should they be taken out of bond through the inland waterways. When deciding the amounts of the various types of drink to buy, bear in mind if you expect to have foreign visitors on board, they will almost invariably drink whisky.

Medicines

Specially prescribed or branded drugs should be bought in Britain in sufficient quantity to cover the length of the cruise. Medicines are very expensive in France and often have different brand names from those used in Britain. Your doctor will probably be able to advise you of the continental name for any particular drug.

Inoculations

It is advisable though not essential to have a series of two typhoid injections and a smallpox vaccination well in advance of the date of departure and in addition some doctors advise cholera and tetanus inoculations as well.

Urgent medical treatment

Medical treatment in France is very expensive and has to be paid for directly the treatment has been concluded. You are strongly advised to obtain *Certificate E111* from the local offices of the Department of Health and Social Security before leaving Britain. This certificate enables overseas medical expenses to be reclaimed under international agreement.

Documents

Ship Under the current French regulations for visiting yachts the original Certificate of Registration, radio licence, etc. must be on board at all times; photo-copies are not accepted. These documents may be inspected on arrival in any harbour and are sometimes inspected at sea.

Crew Passports are essential and are frequently checked. These are also required as a means of identification when cashing cheques, etc. at a bank.

Insurance

It is unlikely that any yacht insurance policies held extend cover beyond the normal British cruising areas and extra cover will have to be arranged for the Mediterranean with the insurance company concerned. At the same time separate cover for the voyage out can be negotiated. Check that personal insurances are valid outside Britain.

Clothing

Normal hot-weather yachting clothing including bathing wear are needed and should include a good supply of items that can be washed easily and dried without ironing. Bathing costumes and bikinis (which can be topless) can be worn on most beaches without restrictions but are not permitted on the streets in shops and cafés. In smaller places which are less frequented by tourists, abbreviated shorts may also cause offence if worn on the village street. Normal common sense should prevail in the choice of clothes to wear at official functions in restaurants and away from the coast. On many secluded beaches it is now quite usual not to wear any clothes.

For those not used to the very hot sun in summer, some form of light head gear is required preferably with a good brim to shield the eyes and the neck. If the cruise is planned to extend through the winter then warm sweaters, shirts, trousers, socks, etc. are required because it can become quite cold at night, and also during the day out of the sun especially if there is a strong wind blowing. Oilskins which might not be used in the summer will be essential in winter.

Banking and Money

Eurocheque card and cheques should be obtained from the bank so that cheques can be cashed at virtually any bank or money exchange office. The usual internal British bank card is no longer valid. A limited number of places accept well known international credit cards, such as *Visa*, alternatively traveller's cheques can be used to obtain money or a transfer can be made to a French bank.

The British banks have no branches in La Corse but they are represented by the French bank – Société General which has branches at Ajaccio (three branches), Bastia, Bonifacio, Calvi, Propriano and Saint Florent.

It is worth noting that most items and services in France are more expensive than in the UK if the exchange rate is less than 10 Francs to £1.00, the converse holds true. Areas where there are a lot of visitors and tourists are more expensive than country areas.

Technical information

Outline description of the coast

The coast of Mediterranean France stretches from her boundaries with Spain at the east end of the Pyrénées chain of mountains, along a varied coastline to the Italian border some 330 miles to the northwest. It also includes the island of La Corse, 100 miles offshore, which has a coastline of some 200 miles, and a number of other large islands near the mainland.

The first 10 miles of coast from the Spanish frontier is rugged and indented where the high mountains come down to the sea, it is very similar to the Spanish Costa Brava which adjoins it and is called *la Côte Vermeille* (the Vermilion Coast) after the reddish colour of the rocks. Quite suddenly just beyond Collioure the coast becomes flat with miles of straight sandy beaches and a few very low rounded hills near La Nouvelle and Sète; this type of coast stretches as far as the Golfe de Fos on the east side of the mouth of the River Rhône, some 70 miles in all. There are no offlying dangers with the exception of the delta of the River Rhône which should be given a good berth because of extending shoals. There exists just inland from this coast a series of very large lagoons, most of which are connected to the sea and are navigable.

From Cap Couronne on the E side of the Golfe de Fos, the coast becomes high and rugged with very bare white rock cliffs; this stretch is called *la Côte Bleue* (the Blue Coast) because of the colour of the sea over these rocks. This high spectacular rocky coast extends in general to Cap Sicié some 40 miles eastwards, there being a series of bare rocky islands offshore of similar nature to the mainland, some of which are quite large.

From Cap Sicié to Cap Ferrat 80 miles further along *la Côte d'Azur* (the Azure Coast), mountains which are some miles inland march with the coast which is only reached by an occasional spur and headland. Between the headlands are large open bays with sandy beaches and some smaller inlets; offlying dangers consist of the Iles d'Hyères, a group of large islands, and the Iles de Lérins, a smaller group, together with a number of tiny islands close inshore.

From Cap Ferrat the high mountain ranges of the Alps now come down to the sea and stretch along the Riviera as far as the border with Italy 15 miles distant, producing a coast of spectacular beauty.

Some 100 miles off the mainland lies the island of La Corse which is mountainous with a number of very high peaks, the coast being in general rock-cliffed and steep-to. There is in all some 200 miles of coast, the west being more indented than the east, and the north of the island is the most spectacular.

Meteorology

General

The weather pattern in the West Mediterranean is affected by the interaction of many differing systems around the basin which it forms and is largely unpredictable, being quick to change and often very different at places only a short distance apart. Due to the high surrounding land masses and the latitude, the climate can at times be extreme, but on average it is very pleasant, especially in the summer months.

Winds

The prevailing winds in this area of the Mediterranean are from a NW and SE direction, as will be seen from the diagram. The directions of these winds are altered to some extent by the local topography (see diagram) and have special names in different areas. See also page 31.

NW mistral – tramontane

This wind is the most frequent, especially in winter when it blows for over 50% of the time in some areas and over 10% at Force 8 or more. It is most danger-

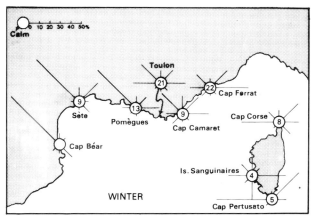

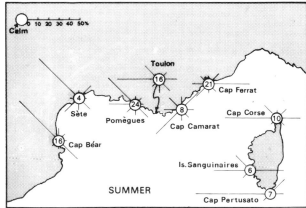

Percentage wind diagrams. Winds blow towards the centre of the rose

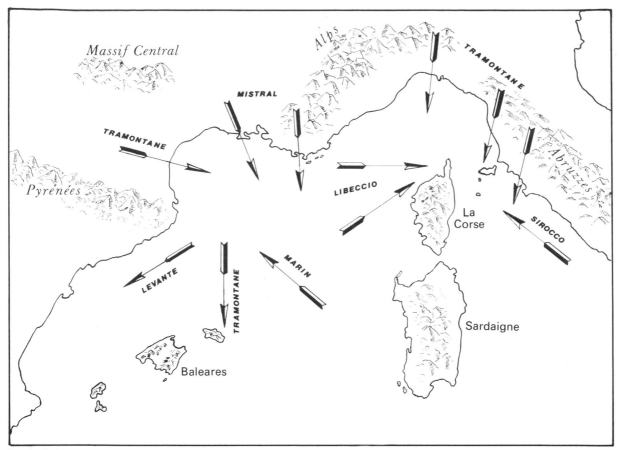

Local winds

ous because it can arrive out of a clear blue sky on a calm day and in a matter of minutes can blow at a full gale. The warning signs are very clear visibility, very dry air, virtually no clouds, any that do appear are cigar-shaped, and a stationary or slightly rising barometer; if away from the coast a swell from the north-westerly direction and a line of white on the horizon may provide a few minutes warning. If a warning of a deep depression crossing France is received it is advisable to proceed directly to a safe harbour. This steady powerful wind can blow for up to a week without slackening although it normally only lasts two to three days raising a very nasty sea. Its domain extends from the French coast as far as the Balearics and Sardinia and it is advisable to keep listening watch H+01 and H+33 on Marseille or Grasse Radio for gale warnings when far from a safe harbour or anchorage.

Only a really bad *mistral* affects the coast from Cannes eastwards and on many occasions a *mistral* blowing in the Golfe du Lion only reaches as far east as Toulon.

In winter a strong NW wind with high stratus cloud is sometimes referred to as a white *mistral* and a similar wind with lower and thicker layer cloud is referred to as a black *mistral*.

A strong NW wind of Force 4 to 6 sometimes creates a secondary depression in the Golfe de Gênes and about 4 to 6 hours after it commenced to blow, a true *mistral* suddenly develops.

E-levant and SE-ceruse

A strong wind accompanied by dull wet weather and bad visibility. Low clouds forming on top of hills and the air becoming damp are warning signs. These winds cause heavy seas on E and SE facing coasts.

S-marin

This is a wind which can blow from SE-S-SW raising a heavy sea on coasts facing these directions. It is a warm and wet wind and though strong does not rival the *mistral*.

Vent du Midi, Vent Solaire

This is the normal sea breeze caused by the convection currents rising over the land on a hot day and drawing air from over the cooler sea, it is more noticeable in calm conditions and usually blows towards the land following the sun by about 15°. It can add to or subtract from the strength of another wind already blowing, depending on this wind's own direction and strength. In summer it commences around 1000 hours increasing in strength until about 1500 hours when it can sometimes reach almost gale force. It then starts to fall away and by 1800 hours it has ceased altogether.

Other winds

There are other winds which blow from different directions on occasions and some only on certain parts of the coast. They all have special names but

BULLETIN POUR LE LARGE

CAPITAINERIE

Here is the weather forecast for sea areas

SEA WEATHER FORECAST

VOICI LE BULLETIN MÉTÉOROLOGIQUE POUR LES ZONES DU LARGE

still in force   expected

1 - AVIS DE   Warning of .... N° .... néant   None ..., en cours ...., prévu ....

T.U.

| Jour de la semaine   Day | Date | Heure   Time |

Zones : ....   Zones affected
Zones menacées

Vent de : ....   Wind from .... Force .... Speed in knots
Direction   Beaufort   Vitesse en nœuds

2 - SITUATION GÉNÉRALE LE ....   General situation .... A .... HEURES   ET ÉVOLUTION

Time and forecast

Forecast

2 - PRÉVISION   pour la journée du ......   for the day of ....
pour la nuit du ......   for the night of .... au ....

ZONES	CARACTÈRE GÉNÉRAL DU TEMPS Type of weather	VENT Wind	ÉTAT DE LA MER Houle (facultatif) Sea/swell state	VISIBILITÉ Visibility

4 - PROBABILITÉS   pour la nuit du ......   Further forecast for the night of .... au ....
pour la journée du ......   for the day of ....

5 - TENDANCE GÉNÉRALE ULTÉRIEURE DU TEMPS   Future tendency

6 - A .... HEURES 6 ON OBSERVAIT : Hours station reports were

A	à	à	à	à
un temps	: weather			
un vent de	: wind			
une visibilité de	: visibility			
une mer	: sea state			

French weather forecast format

there is no agreement among the various sources of information as to what these names are, when the winds blow, how frequently they blow and how they can be predicted. It can only be advised that very occasionally winds can blow from other directions but they are normally weak and short lived.

Clouds

This area is remarkably free of clouds and in winter the average cloud cover is only 4/8th and in summer 2/8th (English Channel 6/8ths and 5/8ths).

Precipitation

The rainfall on average varies from between 450mm to 1300mm (18 to 51 ins) a year (English Channel 540mm to 835mm) which is surprising considering the lack of cloud cover, but when it does rain it is usually very heavy and visibility is seriously reduced. October and November are the wettest months. Thunderstorms occur most often in summer and autumn but only with a frequency of 15 to 20 days a year (English Channel 24). Snow is very rare with an appearance of only two or three times a year (English Channel 8 to 12).

Visibility

Fog rarely exceeds a day a month (English Channel 24 to 28 days a year) and is more common in winter and around dawn, clearing by mid-morning. Smoke haze often causes poor visibility near large towns of which Marseille is an example. Winds from the sea also tend to reduce visibility. Mirages form on calm days particularly near the shore in the morning.

Temperature

January to February are the coldest months but the mean average temperature of 1°C to 11°C (34°F to 54°F) is relatively mild (English Channel -2°C to 12°C). July and August are the hottest months with a mean average temperature of 17°C to 29°C (63°F to 84°F) (English Channel 11°C to 27°C).

Humidity

The humidity is moderate and around 75%. It is highest at dawn and in the winter(80%) and lowest at midday and in the summer (53%). Winds from the land reduce these values and from the sea increase them (English Channel 88%, 75%).

Ocean

Sea temperature

The mean sea temperature varies from 12°C (54°F) in February to 23°C (73°F) in August (English Channel 8°C, 16°C).

Swell

Due to the shortness of the fetch the swell can never reach the proportions it reaches on the Atlantic coast. Nevertheless when strong winds have been blowing from the E-SE-SW for some time a large swell develops which can be dangerous in shallow water.

Water spouts

Water spouts occur occasionally off the Riviera coast and sometimes in the Golfe du Lion and off La Corse.

Currents

There is a basic one knot circulatory current that runs in a NE to SW direction along this coast with sometimes a weaker current in the opposite direction close inshore. NW winds may reduce and sometimes reverse this flow, onshore winds will increase the flow in the W-SW direction and this increased rate often appears in advance of the wind and may reach 4 knots. Details of local variations are given in the introduction to each chapter.

Tides – See also page 34

Tidal range

The tidal range in the area covered by the pilot reaches a maximum of 0.15m(0.5ft) at springs and is hardly detectable at neaps.

Tidal streams

The tidal streams caused by these tides can for all practical purposes be neglected.

Sea levels

The sea level can rise as much as 1m (3ft) during strong winds from the SE and fall 0·5m (1·5ft) in winds from NW. The mean sea levels can be 0·5m (1·5ft) lower in winter as compared with summer.

Radio – See also page 34

Marine radiobeacons

The following radiobeacons operate in the area in groups or singly:

South France Group 287·3 kHz
Cap Béar BR (— ··· / — ·) 50M every 6 mins Seq. 1, 2
Sète SÉ (··· / — — ··) 50M every 6 mins Seq. 3, 4
Ile du Planier PN (· — — · / — ·) 100M every 6 mins Seq. 5, 6

East Corsica Group 308 kHz
Ile de la Giraglia GL (— — · / — · ·) 60M every 4 mins Seq. 1, 2
Pointe de la Chiappa CP (— · — · / — — ·) 100M every 4 mins Seq. 3, 4
West Corsica Group 294·2 kHz
Pointe Revellata RV (· — · / · · · —) 100M every 6 mins Seq. 3,

La Garoupe GO (— — · / — — —) 100M every 6 mins Seq. 5, 6
Other stations
Cap Couronne CR (— · — · / — ·) 305·7 kHz 50M Continuous

West Mediterranean Group 313·5 kHz
Cap Bon (Tunisia) BN (—···/—·) 200M every 6 mins Seq. 1, 2
Ras Caxine (Tunisia) CX (—·—·/—··—) 200M every 6 mins Seq. 3, 4
Porquerolles PQ (·——·/———·) 200M every 6 mins Seq. 5, 6

Air radiobeacons

The following air radiobeacons operate in the area but may not transmit continuously:

Istres, Le Tubé ITR (··/—/·—·) 390·5 kHz 43°31'·6N 4°55'·8E

Hyères, Palyvestre HYE (····/—·——/·) 322 kHz 70M 43°02'N 6°09'·1E

Nice, Mont Leuza LEZ (·—··/·/·———·) 398·5 kHz 75M 43°43'·53N 7°19'·37E

Ajaccio, Campo del'Oro IS (··/···) 341 kHz 50M 41°54'N 8°36'·9E

Ajaccio CT (—·—·/—) 387·5 kHz 41°47'·42N 8°43'·29E
Ajaccio RO (·—·/———) 365 kHz 41°56'·95N 8°49'·10E
Calvi, St Catherine CV (—·—·/···—) 404 kHz 42°34'·7N 8°48'·5E

Pointe de Senetosa SNE (···/—·/·) 394·5 kHz 15M 47°33'·50N 8°47'·90E

Solenzara SZA (···/———·/—) 349·5 kHz 80M 41°55'·9N 9°23'·8E. Bearings may be unreliable 080° to 120°.

Bastia, Poretta BP (—···/·———·) 369 kHz 50M 42°25'·7N 9°32'·2E

Coast radio stations – See also page 34

St Lys (FFL-FFS-FFT)
R/T watch on 8284·9, 12407·5, 16543·7 kHz Continuous (0700–2230 UT). The above coast radio station operates on this coast but it is normally only used for commercial purposes. Traffic lists on 4366·7, 8808·8, 13178·3, 17316·6, 22673·5 kHz at H+03, and when necessary at H+30 (0700–2230). See Admiralty List of Radio Signals Vol 1 Part I for full details also WT(MF) service of stations listed below.

Perpignan
VHF Ch 02, 16 Continuous. Call Marseille Radio.

Marseille (FFM)
R/T 1906, 1939, 2182, 2628, 3722, 3795 kHz, 1kW. VHF Ch 16, 24, 26 Continuous. Traffic lists on 1906 kHz at every odd H+10.
VHF Ch 16, 24, 26 Continuous. Call Marseille Radio.

Martigues
VHF Ch 16, 27, 28 Continuous. Call Marseille Radio.

Sète
VHF Ch 16, 19. Continuous. Call Marseille Radio.

Toulon
VHF Ch 16, 25, 62. Continuous. Call Marseille Radio.

Grasse (TKM)
R/T Transmits 1834, 2182, 2649, 3722 kHz Receives 2182 kHz. Continuous. Traffic lists on 2649 kHz every even H+33 (0633–2033). VHF Transmits Ch 02, 04, 05, 16 (0630–2100)

Monaco (3AC, 3AF)
R/T Transmits 4363·6, 6509·5, 8728·2, 13172·1, 17251·5, 22651·8. Receives 4069·2, 6203·1, 8204·3, 8257, 12392, 12401·3, 16478·6, 16522, 22055·8, 22062 kHz. Traffic lists on 4363·6, 8728·2, 13172·1, 17251·8 every H+00

(0700–2300). VHF Ch 16, 20, 22, 86. Continuous. Traffic lists Ch 16 every H+03 (0700–2300) UT

Ajaccio Transmits Ch 16, 24. Receives Ch 16, 24. Continuous
Bastia Transmits Ch 16, 65. Receives Ch 65. (0630–2200[1]).★
Porto Vecchio Transmits Ch 05, 16, 25. Receives Ch 05, 25. (0630–2200[1])★

Port radio stations

All of the large ports and many of the yacht harbours have port radios and details are given in the section dealing with the port concerned. These radios all operate on low power in the VHF band, normally Ch 9 and 16.

Radio weather forecasts

Details of radio weather forecasts for a particular area are given in the introductory section of Part II that deals with that particular length of coast. The most important forecasts are given by Marseille and Grasse Radio which are transmitted in French at dictation speed, being repeated twice, and at the end the whole forecast is read through at normal speed. With a little practise even non-French speaking listeners can understand. France Inter covers a very large area and the forecast is read fast. A tape recorder is advisable.

Perpignan In French VHF Ch 02 (0633, 1133)★
Agde (CROSS) In French VHF Ch 09 (0730, 1715)★
Sète In French VHF Ch 19 (0633, 1133)★
Marseille (FFM) In French on 1906 kHz at 0103★ (areas W of Ile d'Hyères only), 0705, 1220, 1615★ and on request. VHF Ch 28, 26 at 0633, 1133★
Toulon In French VHF Ch 62 (0633, 1133)★
La Garde (CROSS) In French VHF Ch 09 at 0810, 1730★
Grasse (TKM) In French on 2649 kHz at 0733, 1233, 1645★ and on request. VHF Ch 02 at 0633, 1133★
Monaco (3AC, 3AF) In French on 4363·6, 6509·5, 8728·2kHz at 0803, 1303, 1715 and 0715, 1715★ VHF Ch 22, 23 at 0803, 1603, 1715 and 0600-2200★. Continuous in French and English.
Radio Monte Carlo In French on 218, 1466 kHz at 0800, 1900★
Corse (CROSS) In French VHF Ch 09 at 0745, 1745★
Ajaccio In French VHF Ch 24 0633, 1133★
Bastia In French VHF Ch 24 0633, 1133★
Porto Vecchio In French VHF Ch 25 at 0633, 1100★

Storm warnings are transmitted on receipt and at the end of the next two silence periods.

Radio Riviera 104·1, 106·5 MHz at 0730, 1930 in English.★ Coastal waters between St Tropez and Italian frontier.

France Inter (Allouis) On 164 kHz at 0555 and 1905.

Radio France
Marseille 675 kHz at 0555, 1905★ 150 miles
Nice 1350 kHz at 0555, 1905★ 300 miles

Minitel weather forecast
Service giving detailed weather reports and forecasts on ☎ 36/15 + METEO in French or English.

★ 1 hour earlier when daylight time (DST) is in force.

Lights – See also page 35

Details of major lights are given in subsequent sections. The bearings given are towards the light (from sea) in 360° true notation, the range is the nominal range a light can be seen under normal conditions of 10M visibility. Lights are illuminated 15 minutes after sunset until 15 minutes before sunrise.

Minor lights are listed under each port. These minor, low-power lights are at times difficult to see against a background of lights emanating from the shore establishments nearby. The characteristics of lights are sometimes changed and others added, it is therefore advisable to check the data given against an up-to-date official light list before leaving Britain.

Lights occasionally fail or become faulty in that the period is not correct, and attention should be paid to the navigational warnings that are broadcast each day by the coast radio stations.

Buoyage

The area covered by this pilot book was changed to IALA System 'A' (red to port) in 1980. In addition there are special coastal buoys.

Beacons

Use is made of beacon towers on isolated dangers and headlands, these often carry topmarks and are coloured in accordance with IALA System A. The paintwork of some beacons and the topmarks of others have been washed away, this is noted in the text but may have been rectified since publication.

Signals

Signal stations

Signal stations are maintained on the mainland and inshore islands at Cap Béar, Sète*, Cap Couronne*, Ile de Pomègues, Bec de l'Aigle (La Ciotat), Cap Cépet*, Ile de Porquerolles*, Cap Benat, Cap Camaret, Dramont, La Garoupe and Cap Ferrat.

On La Corse at Cap Corse, Ile Rousse, Pointe de la Parata, Cap Sagro and Pointe de Chiappa.

Communication with these stations may be made by telephone, by the international code of signal flags, by using Morse code or by VHF Ch 16 or 9.

Not all stations are open 24 hours a day. New stations are planned for Outre Allistro, Leucate and L'Espiguette.

*24 hour service. Others normally 0600–1800.

Storm and weather signals

Storm signals are flown from the signal stations listed above and from the Bureau de Port in many harbours. See diagram.

Many of the smaller yacht harbours may fly their own special signals and in certain cases verbal announcements are made by public address system or a

Buoyage

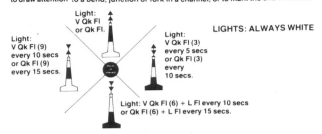

IALA buoyage system A

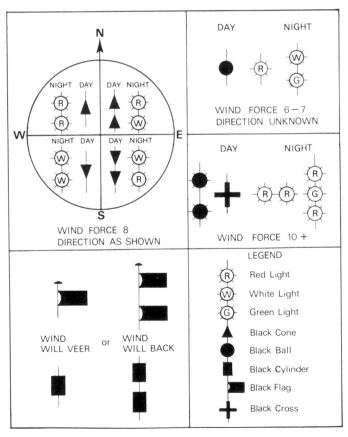

Storm signals

runner. These variations are detailed in the section dealing with the harbour concerned.

Traffic signals

The current and new traffic control systems are given with their meanings in the diagram. These signals are usually shown near the entrance of major ports and must be obeyed by yachts.

Any local variation from these general rules are given in the section dealing with the harbours concerned. The new International Port Traffic Signals are being adopted.

MEANING	DAY	NIGHT
PORT CLOSED ABSOLUTELY FORBIDDEN TO ENTER	● ● ●	R R R
FORBIDDEN TO ENTER (EXIT PERMITTED)	● ▲ ● or ◗R	R W or R R
FORBIDDEN TO LEAVE (ENTRANCE PERMITTED)	▼ ▲ ▼ or ◗G	G W or G G
FORBIDDEN TO ENTER OR LEAVE	▼ ▲ ● or ◗R ◗G	R W or R G · R
PORT OPEN NAVIGATE WITH CAUTION THERE MAY BE OBSTRUCTIONS OR NO RESTRICTION	APPROPRIATE INTERNATIONAL CODE FLAGS	G G G
	NO SIGNALS	NO SIGNALS

Current French signals

MAIN SIGNALS	MAIN MESSAGES	REMARKS
1 R R R Flashing	SERIOUS EMERGENCY — ALL VESSELS TO STOP OR DIVERT ACCORDING TO INSTRUCTIONS	Some ports may use an Exemption Signal with Signal 2 see 2a
2 R R R Occulting	VESSELS SHALL NOT PROCEED	Some ports may not use the full range of main signals, e.g. they may use only Signals 2 and 4, or only Signal 1
3 G G G	VESSELS MAY PROCEED. ONE-WAY TRAFFIC	
4 G G W Fixed or Slow	VESSELS MAY PROCEED. TWO-WAY TRAFFIC	The uncoloured circle in Signals 4, 5 and 5a represents a white light
5 G W G	A VESSEL MAY PROCEED ONLY WHEN IT HAS RECEIVED SPECIFIC ORDERS TO DO SO	Used when a vessel or special group of vessels must receive specific instructions in order to proceed. All other vessels must not proceed. Specific instructions may be given by Auxiliary Signal or by other means such as radio, signal lamp or patrol boat. Some ports may use an Exemption Signal with Signal 5 see 5a.

EXEMPTION SIGNALS	EXEMPTION MESSAGES	REMARKS
2a Y R R R Occulting	Vessels shall not proceed, except that vessels which navigate outside the main channel need not comply with the main message.	
5a Y G W G Fixed or Slow-Occulting	A vessel may proceed only when it has received specific orders to do so; except that vessels which navigate outside the main channel need not comply with the main message.	Some ports may use the additional yellow light (always displayed to the left of the top main light) to allow smaller vessels to disregard Messages 2 and 5.

AUXILIARY SIGNALS	AUXILIARY MESSAGES	REMARKS
Normally white and/or yellow lights, displayed to the right of the main lights.	Local meanings: e.g. added to Signal 5 to instruct a vessel to proceed; to give information about the situation of traffic in the opposite direction; or to warn of a dredger operating in the channel.	Special messages may apply at some ports with a complex layout, or complicated traffic situation. Nautical documents should be consulted for the details.

. New international signals

Lifeboats

Lifeboats are stationed at all the major ports and many of the smaller harbours on this coast. These are listed below. Lifeboats are grouped in three classes depending on their size, the first class being the largest.

Inshore rescue craft are either all weather pneumatic boats, pneumatic dinghies or runabouts.

Charges may be made if the lifeboat is called out to assist unnecessarily.

Port	Type	Département	☎
Cerbère	RA	Pyr. Orient	68 38 41 60
Port Vendres	AW	Pyr. Orient	68 82 11 46
			68 82 02 54
San Cyprien	2	Pyr. Orient	68 21 07 98
Canet en Roussillon	3	Pyr. Orient	68 80 20 66
Le Barcarès	2	Pyr. Orient	68 86 07 35
Leucate	2	Aude	
Port La Nouvelle	1	Aude	64 48 01 81
Gruissan	1	Aude	67 45 04 42
Valras Plage	2	Hérault	67 93 00 23
Agde	RA	Hérault	67 94 53
Mèze	2	Hérault	67 43 80 13
Sète	AW	Hérault	67 74 40 00
Palavas les Flots	2	Hérault	67 68 03 45
La Grande Motte	2	Hérault	67 56 03 01
Port Camargue	1	Gard	66 51 43 09
Stes Maries	2	Bouches du Rhône	90 97 83 07
Carro	RA	Bouches du Rhône	42 80 71 53
			42 80 74 04
Port St Louis de Rhône	RA	Bouches du Rhône	
Martigues	2	Bouches du Rhône	42 42 14 35
Marseille	1	Bouches du Rhône	42 95 91 70
La Ciotat	AW	Bouches du Rhône	42 08 47 63
Bandol	3	Var	
Toulon	1	Var	94 65 58 59
Hyères	2	Var	94 65 05 46
Porquerolles	1	Var	94 58 30 57
Le Lavandou	3	Var	94 71 13 09
Saint Tropez	AW		94 97 02 72
Ste Maxime	RA	Var	94 96 00 35
Théoule sur Mer	3	Alpes Maritimes	93 90 31 00
Cannes	3	Alpes Maritimes	93 39 28 39
Antibes	1	Alpes Maritimes	93 33 65 00
Cros de Cagnes	3	Alpes Maritimes	93 31 72 28
Nice	3	Alpes Maritimes	93 89 50 85
Menton	1	Alpes Maritimes	93 35 75 06
Ajaccio	1	Corse	95 22 39 18
			95 21 44 45
St Florent	2	Corse	95 30 00 51
			95 37 00 68
Bastia	AW	Corse	95 31 50 95
			95 31 62 24
Macinaggio	AW	Corse	95 35 43 20
Bonifacio	AW	Corse	95 73 00 33
Propriano	2	Corse	95 76 06 11

Legend

1 = 1st Class, 2 = 2nd Class, 3 = 3rd Class, AW = All weather, D = Dinghy, RA = Runabout.

In addition to the lifeboats listed above, the following services and organisations have their own seagoing craft and helicopter which are sometimes employed in a back-up role: *Affaires Maritimes, Gendarmerie National, Douanes CROSS* and *Protection Civile*.

Coastal security

The Centres Régionaux Opérationnels de Surveillance et de Sauvetage, (CROSS) assist in the coordination of maritime rescue on the French coasts. They have eight stations of which the following are located on the Mediterranean coast.

- CROSS MED Fort Ste Marguerite, 83130 La Garde (☎ 94 27 27 11) near Toulon
- CROSS MED AGDE Mont Saint-Loup 34300 Agde (☎ 67 94 12 02)
- CROSS MED CORSE 20184 Ajaccio (☎ 95 20 13 63) Call VHF Ch 16 Work Ch 9 or telephone for assistance etc. These centres also transmit weather forecasts, storm and navigational warnings. They make a call on VHF Ch 19 and transfer to Ch 9 at 0845 and 1845 local time.

Fishing

Commercial fishing boats

The number of commercial fishing boats on this coast is not great nor are the boats large, but they should be given a wide berth when encountered as they may be:

- Trawling either singly or in pairs with a net between the boats,
- Laying a long net, the top of which is supported by floats,
- Picking up or laying pots either singly or in groups or lines,
- Trolling with one or more lines out astern,
- Drifting trailing nets up wind.

Tunny nets

Tunny nets are laid at places along the coast during the summer to autumn, these nets can be up to 1 mile long and are laid as far out as 20 miles from the coast but are normally laid inshore in depths of 15–40m. It is usual for the outer end to be indicated by a red flag by day and a white light by night. If the net does not reach the coast a similar light or flag is shown at the other end. These nets are made with very strong rope and therefore care must be taken to avoid them. The lights and flags are also used on smaller and shorter nets.

Small fishing boats

The shallow waters of this coast have been heavily fished in the past and average catches are very small compared with those obtained on the Atlantic coasts, nevertheless many thousands of small fishing craft put to sea daily. They should be avoided as far as possible as they too can be using nets or trolling with lines astern. At night many put to sea and use very powerful electric or gas lights to attract fish to the surface and when seen from a distance these lights appear to flash as the boat moves up and down in the waves giving the appearance of a lighthouse.

It is not advisable to follow any fishing boat which appears to be taking a short cut because the skipper

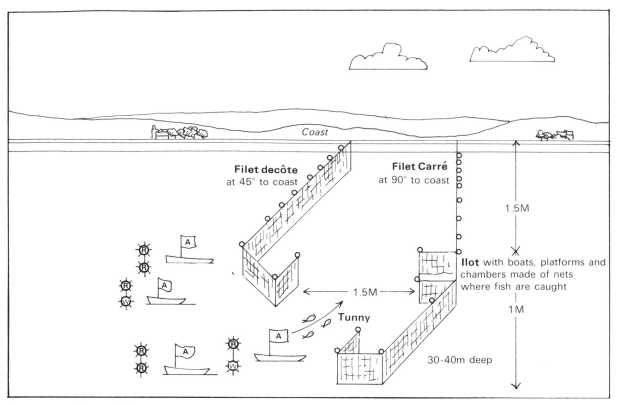

Arrangement of tunny fishing nets

Small fishing boat with powerful lamps to attract fish

probably knows the area in great detail and may be following a narrow and twisting channel between rocks and sandbanks which are not shown on the chart.

Charter

In recent years some 50 charter fleets or agencies have been established in La Corse or on the mainland offering yachts for hire. Most of the fleets are small with 3 or 4 yachts, others have a large number which are used for flotilla sailing. Many charter yachts will be encountered in harbours and popular anchorages.

Hazards

Motor and ski boats

One of the hazards encountered in the summer on this coast are the many small motor craft and water scooters which are driven at speed by unskilled and thoughtless drivers. These frequently approach far too close to yachts for safety and often cause annoyance by their noise and wash. They are not allowed to exceed a 5 knot speed limit within 300m of the coast. In recent years the use of large very fast power craft in the hands of inexperienced helmsmen has been an additional hazard and there have been many accidents.

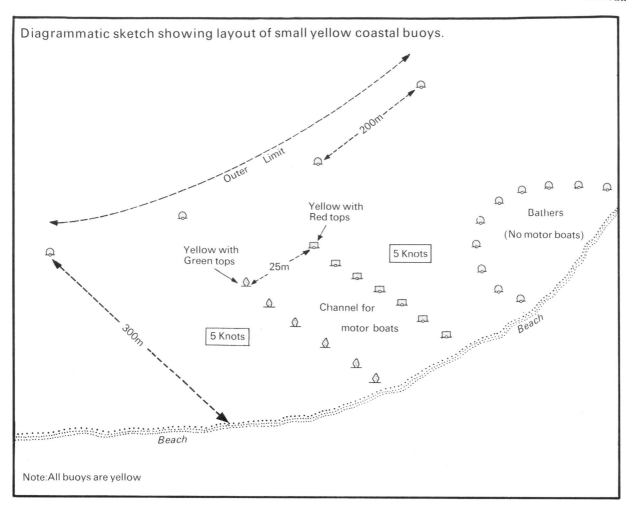

Diagrammatic sketch showing layout of small yellow coastal buoys.

Outer Limit

200m

Yellow with
Red tops

Yellow with
Green tops

25m

5 Knots

Bathers

(No motor boats)

300m

5 Knots

Channel for

motor boats

Beach

Beach

Note: All buoys are yellow

Layout of buoys off beaches

Subaqua swimmers

A good lookout must be kept at all times for the many amateur subaqua and snorkling swimmers who may stray well away from the coast and into the entrance channels to harbours, thereby offering another hazard to yachtsmen. Many professional and teaching groups of subaqua swimmers will be seen but these usually have an attendant boat with the special diving flag displayed.

Speed limits

All harbours have speed limits, usually 3 knots or less and there is a blanket speed along the whole coast of 5 knots within 300m of the shore. Most harbour masters and their staff enforce these speed limits especially against any yacht who, by virtue of its design and speed, creates a heavy wash.

Coastal buoys

Small buoys are placed in a series off many beaches where in summer there are numerous swimmers, as follows:

Yellow spherical buoys, 0·96m diameter, are placed every 200m at a distance of 300m offshore. Speed limit inside them is 5 knots.

Small yellow conical or can buoys, 0·64m high, mark the S side of a channel 25m wide from the beach out to sea, for use by water-skiing boats, etc.

Large can buoys painted red above yellow and conical buoys, green above yellow, 1·28m high, mark the outer ends of this channel; for water-skiing boats, etc.

Small yellow spherical buoys, 0·64m high, close together, mark an area for swimmers only.

See diagram above.

Anchorages – See also page 31

Harbour anchorages

In almost every harbour anchorage is forbidden except in emergency or for a very short period while selecting a berth or mooring. However in a few harbours anchors have to be used to hold the yacht away from the quay or pontoon. Always use a sinking type of anchor tripline without a buoy attached when anchoring in a harbour or near moorings.

Coastal anchorages

The quality of the bottom in shallow water varies considerably on this section of the coast and in many cases on the Côte d'Azur, Riviera and Côte Vermeille it is steep-to and rocky. In the bays and creeks it is usually sandy and on the coast of Languedoc-Roussillon it is sand and mud covered with a thick layer of fine grass-like seaweed but there are often large areas of bare sand where the current and swell is strong enough to prevent the growth of this weed.

Suitable places to anchor off each harbour have been given in the harbour section concerned but the actual selection or the place to drop an anchor should be made at the time. Due to the clarity of the water it is usually possible to see the bottom and to be able to select a suitable patch of bare sand. It should be remembered that CQR and Danforth type anchors tend to drag and fail to dig into hard packed sand when it is covered with heavy weed, anchors without points are hopeless. Fisherman and Mediterranean type anchors are better for this type of bottom. If possible try to snorkel over the anchor to check that it is holding.

If anchoring in rocky areas an anchor trip line is advisable as the flukes can easily become caught in the jagged broken rocks. When anchored off the coast a watch should be maintained on the radio for storm warnings and contingency plans made in advance in case a gale should blow up.

Calanque anchorages

There are many delightful anchorages to be found in the *calanques*, (narrow creeks) and little bays on this coast, some of which are detailed in Part II.

Approach these anchorages with care with a lookout forward who should be stationed as high as possible, preferably up the mast where the bottom can be seen and any obstruction will be very evident. The use of polarised spectacles is advised.

Anchor in an area of bare sand and if necessary take a line ashore but make sure that its position will not obstruct the fairway.

When entering or leaving under sail remember that the wind may be very fluky if the sides of the *calanque* are high. This type of anchorage should only be used in good weather and if there is a warning of bad weather or should the wind or swell rise they should be left at once as it may later become impossible due to the wind funnelling through the narrow entrance. These winds can even become dangerous when they blow down the creek from a landwards direction.

It is unwise to leave a yacht unattended in such an anchorage and advance plans for a hurried exit should be made. In recent years the sandy bottoms of popular anchorages and harbour berths where anchors have to be used have been so dug up that the sand is now loose. CQR-Danforth type of anchors hold fairly well if used with a long chain but Fisherman and Mediterranean 4-pronged types are better.

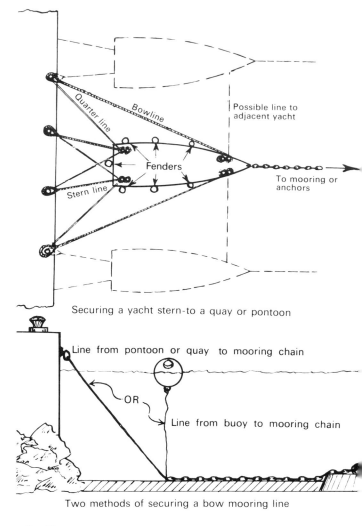

Securing a yacht stern-to a quay or pontoon

Two methods of securing a bow mooring line

Berthing

Berthing

Due to the vast numbers of yachts and limited space available, berthing stern-to the quays and pontoons is the normal method used in the Mediterranean. For greater privacy or because the design of the yacht prevents berthing stern-to, it may be desirable to berth bow-to the quay or pontoon.

The manoeuvres to bring a yacht stern first into a narrow berth between two other yachts sometimes with a cross wind blowing is a skill which has to be acquired and it is most advisable that some practise at manoeuvring astern should be undertaken in advance. The only advice offered is:

● Have plenty of fenders out especially near the stern.
● Approach the berth slowly from some distance off.
● If not fully satisfied with the approach draw off and try again.
● Warping the yacht or pulling her in by hand when close in is better than using the engine.

It is better to make several attempts in slow time and to berth quietly in a seamanlike manner than to go rushing around with engines roaring and endangering nearby yachts.

The yacht is usually secured to the quay or pontoon by two stern lines leading from the quarters. In order to hold the yacht away from the quay or pontoon, a bow mooring of some kind will have to be picked up. These take several different forms as follows:

- A small buoy with line or light chain attached to it which leads to a heavier chain which must be pulled in, brought aboard and secured.
- A line or light chain that has one end attached to the quay or pontoon and the other to the heavy mooring chain. This light chain has to be picked up from near the quay or pontoon and followed along to the heavy chain which has to be pulled in, taken on board and secured.
- Finally there are the mooring posts or piles located either side of the berth which sometimes have chains running out to them from the quay or pontoon. In this case it is necessary to secure the bow lines to the posts (see diagram).

In many cases the chains are heavy and dirty and gloves are advisable when handling them because they are often covered with small sharp barnacles. Where no mooring chains are provided yachts have to use their own anchors which should be dropped at least 50m from the berth and should have an un-buoyed sinking type of anchor trip line attached to facilitate recovery should they become foul.

In winter and stormy weather these securing lines will have to be doubled and extra lines such as quarter lines, cross-stern lines and bow lines laid out. Extra fenders may be necessary especially where the stern (or bow) could ride up to and touch the quay or pontoon (see diagram for details).

Winds of gale force can arise with great speed and if the yacht has to be left unattended even for a short period it is wise to lay out extra lines. In the few places where it is possible to lie alongside, holding-off lines are usually employed especially by fishing boats and can present an unexpected obstruction when approaching a berth. Harbours in the Mediterranean are subject, during gales, to exceptionally strong surges of water much more powerful than encountered in British harbours and berthing lines should be stronger than those usually used at home.

Moorings

Virtually all moorings are privately owned and if one is used it will have to be vacated should the owner return. There are often no markings to give any indication as to the weight and strength of the mooring so they should be used with caution.

Harbour facilities

Slipways

Because there is very little tide in the Mediterranean it is impossible to dry out to scrub or to carry out underwater repairs or painting, as is normal on other coasts, yachts therefore have to be hauled out. Slipways and travel-lifts are to be found at most harbours. Outline details of these have been given in the

section dealing with the harbours concerned. The cost of hauling out and relaunching varies considerably, and quotations should be obtained from several places.

Repairs

Many of the large harbours and ports have good repair facilities and numbers of self-employed artisans exist at all the harbours. These can carry out repairs though the quality of their work and their charges vary enormously. It is recommended that local advice be taken in the selection of a yard or craftsman to undertake any repairs and that a clear and firm quotation should be obtained first making sure that all extras such as travelling time and taxes have been taken into account. During the high season the demand on all repair services is considerable and a visitor will have to wait his turn.

Cranes

All harbours have small cranes and some have travel lifts and large cranes capable of lifting small and medium-sized yachts out of the water. Details are given for the harbour concerned.

Laying up

Many owners may wish to lay up their yachts for the winter in the Mediterranean so that they can use the boat the following year without the long outward passage.

Arrangements can be made with the yards or yacht harbours at many places for yachts to be looked after afloat or hauled out. The facilities and services provided vary considerably as does the cost, it is therefore advisable to get several quotations and to find out exactly what will be provided. Local advice is also worth taking as to the quality of the services provided.

The employment of another yachtsman often living on his own yacht in the same harbour to look after a yacht is fraught with risk as there is no guarantee that he will not be called away for some personal matter or just sail away for reasons of his own. Again local advice and the recommendation of others is essential.

The NW *mistral-tramontane* can be frequent and severe in winter and early spring and this should be borne in mind when selecting the area and site to lay up. The power of the sun which shines on most days and the dryness of the air must also be considered by those with yachts that have wood decks and superstructure and arrangements must be made for these to be watered daily and if possible covered by awnings. Varnish work also will deteriorate quickly if exposed without protection to these conditions.

Information – France

General

It is beyond the scope of this pilot to go into any detail about the characteristics of the area and its occupants but there are some important points of note which are detailed below and which will be of value to visiting yachtsmen.

Behaviour

The French have been subject to an annual avalanche of international tourism for many years and are not strangers to the outrageous behaviour of a small section of foreigners on holiday. However, if the visiting yachtsman wants to obtain the friendly cooperation and help of the local inhabitants and officials all he has to do is to approach them in a pleasant manner and to make every possible use of what little knowledge he has of their language no matter how bad his accent. Any rude or boorish behaviour will immediately result in an atmosphere of non-cooperation which will be difficult to overcome.

Tourists

The annual influx of tourists of all nations and all walks of life is an event that has been taking place for generations. The older resorts of the Côte d'Azur and the Riviera are well adjusted to receive this invasion and though the area becomes jam-packed in July and August it is usually possible to obtain goods and services without waiting too long. The new resorts of Languedoc-Roussillon and places where packaged tourism is being developed present a different picture because the facilities have not yet caught up with the tremendous expansion of the tourist industry.

You are strongly advised to try to avoid this coast in July and August and to visit the area in May and June or September and October or during the winter months.

Special rules and regulations for foreign yachts

On arrival in France

Take the yacht's papers and a photocopy of the owner's passport to the nearest customs office. A *Titre de Séjour* (visa) will be issued and the yacht's papers returned to the owner.

There are large numbers of foreign yachts kept either permanently or temporarily in the harbours on the south coast of France. In the past, many of the owners of these yachts have failed to comply with the existing rules and this has resulted in the regulations being strengthened and more severely enforced. The customs who are responsible for seeing that these laws are complied with have very considerable power to investigate and take action as necessary.

Owners of visiting yachts are cautioned to make certain that these rules and regulations are meticulously observed.

Group 'A'

Yachts registered in the following EC countries or in countries which have special financial arrangements with France.

Algeria, Austria, Belgium, Benin (ex-Dahomey), Burkina Faso, Cameroon, Central African Republic, Chad, Congo, Czechoslovakia, Denmark, Finland, Gabon, Germany, Greece, Iran, Ireland, Italy, Ivory Coast, Lebanon, Luxembourg, Madagascar, Malawi, Mali, Mauritania, Monaco, Morocco, Netherlands, Niger, Norway, Pakistan, Poland, Portugal, Romania, Singapore, Spain, Sweden, Switzerland, Thailand, Togo, Tunisia, United Kingdom, United States of America, Yugoslavia, Zambia.

Yacht

Must have the original Certificate of Registration on board at all times unless it is being taken to the custom's office. (See below). Photocopies are not valid.

Skipper/owner

The yacht can only be used or lived on when the skipper/owner is on board. His passport must agree with the name etc. of the skipper/owner as shown in the yacht's Certificate of Registration. A yacht can never be let or loaned to anyone with the exception of the owner's immediate family.

Company yachts

An official document is required from the company specifying the directors with a photocopy of their passports, list showing the allocation of shares, copies of the Articles and Memoranda of Association and a photocopy of the yacht's Certificate of Registration. With these documents the director with the majority shareholding must visit the custom's office and fill in the appropriate form. Approval comes from Paris which takes several months.

Maximum period of use in French waters

Having obtained a *Titre de Séjour* (visa) from the customs, a foreign yacht may be used in French waters for six months in any twelve without paying import duties and *TVA* (VAT). At the end of the six months period the yacht must either be laid up or it must leave French waters. The six months period of use need not be continuous but could be, for example, three months use followed by three months laid up etc., always provided that the yacht is only in use for a total of six months in any consecutive twelve months. When the yacht is laid up, no one may live on board.

Renewal of Titre de Séjour

At the end of the twelve month period the documents and the visa must be taken to the customs office for renewal.

Possible changes

When the EC rules are changed in 1992 it is expected that VAT/TVA will have to be paid on all yachts which have made use of the above mentioned concessions.

Group 'B'
Yachts registered in countries that do not have a special financial arrangement with France have to pay the customs a charge of 3 francs (1988) a registered ton per day while in French harbours, in addition to the normal charges. They can remain in French waters for six months only.

Formalities

The officials on this part of the French coast carry out their duties with more care than those on the other coasts but will normally adapt their rules with Gallic common sense to meet a particular situation. If on the other hand they feel that they are being imposed upon they will enforce the rules with severity.

On arrival in any harbour the skipper is expected to report at once, having regard to the time of day, to the *Bureau de Port* (harbour office, sometimes called *La Capitainerie*) or occasionally to the yacht club where he must complete a form giving particulars of his yacht and crew and his intention regarding the proposed length of stay.

Instructions for large yachts
Many of the harbours described in this pilot are too small for a large yacht which must anchor outside whilst its crew visit the harbour by tender. It is essential that the skipper of a large yacht, who wishes to enter a harbour, telephones or radios the *Bureau de Port* well in advance to reserve a berth if practicable and receive necessary instructions.

Customs
The first port of call in France from a foreign port should be a major one, and on arrival the yacht must fly the yellow Q flag by day or show one red over white light by night. This requirement is not enforced at present. The skipper must visit the customs with ship's papers and his crew's passports as soon as possible. They will then complete a *Titre de Séjour* (visa), a copy of which must be kept on board. There is normally no restriction on going ashore before clearance, provided someone is left on board with the papers. On occasions the various officials may make a visit to the yacht and have been known to carry out searches on board; sometimes a yacht may be stopped at sea by the customs and searched. See also pages 21 and 35.

Harbour dues
Harbour dues are now charged in every harbour on the south French coast and these charges can vary from the very modest to the exorbitant, they are levied in very many ways and to many different scales which are constantly changing. It is impossible to list dues for any particular harbour because by the time this pilot is printed many would be out of date.

In some harbours the first day or two days are free, but beware, because if a yacht stays beyond the free period it is possible that payment will have to be made for all the back dues with no free period. In some harbours there is a sliding scale and the rate becomes greater as the days pass, in others a large sum of money has to be paid on arrival to cover a stay of several weeks with no reduction for a shorter period. Some scales are calculated on the overall length of the yacht, some on length multiplied by breadth and others on net or gross tonnage registered. In almost every case there is a sliding scale that varies with the time of year, but the charges in July and August are much greater than those made during the winter. The payment of these charges also varies from harbour to harbour, sometimes payment must be made on arrival, sometimes before leaving or even from day to day. The time of day from which these dues are calculated is also different and it can be either from midday, midnight or any other hour. The only recommendation therefore is to visit the *Bureau de Port* on arrival and find out exactly how much it costs and when and where the dues have to be paid.

There are unfortunately a number of yachtsmen in the Mediterranean who, after using all the facilities of a harbour, take pleasure in trying to cheat their way out of paying their dues by leaving in a hurry thereby getting the harbour staff into trouble with their employers. Visitors should therefore appreciate the reason for rather peremptory demands for harbour dues that they may occasionally experience.

Yacht clubs
A yacht club will be found in nearly every harbour and these can be large modern buildings with every facility, old or adapted buildings with only a bar, lounge and a shower, or at the other extreme a small wooden hut for an office only. Yacht clubs in general cater for practising yachtsmen and the vast majority do not have large social memberships as do the *Club Náuticos* in Spain. Visiting yachtsmen are welcome within reason to make use of the facilities available and should make themselves known to the secretary and fill in the visitors' book where one is provided. Many yacht clubs have a sailing school incorporated with the club and in some places it is difficult to find out where one ends and the other begins.

The Touring Club de France (TCF) has a number of clubhouses and other facilities for yachtsmen along the coast and some foreigners join this organisation in order to be able to use these facilities. Information can be obtained from their head office at 65 avenue de la Grande Armée, 75 Paris 16e (☎ 727 89 89) or from the French Government Office in London at 178 Piccadilly, W1V 0AL (☎ 071 493 3171).

Fuel

Diesel
This is available at most harbours usually from pumps on the quayside as follows:
• Diesel (*gasoil or mazout*) is taxed and may be used in yachts and vehicles. It is normally available at most harbours usually near the entrance.
• Diesel (*gasoil*), untaxed, in special pumps in fishing harbours may only be used in fishing boats.

● *Fuel-oil domestique (FOD)* which is heating oil and also a form of diesel oil that carries only a small tax and cannot be supplied to yachts.

For those yachts that require large amounts of fuel, bunkering arrangements exist at the major ports, details of these and of the credit card system should be obtained from the fuel company in Britain.

Petrol

Low grade petrol is supplied in almost every harbour from a pump labelled *Essence or Normal*. Pumps with high grade petrol labelled *Super* are only available in the major yachting harbours. Petrol/oil mixture may be obtained from many harbours from a pump labelled *mélange* or *2 temps*.

Oil

Many grades of oil are available at most harbours or from garages nearby.

Paraffin

This is available under the name *pétrole*. A better quality product, *pétrole raffiné*, often called *kerdane*, is more suitable for use on a yacht and available from *drogueries*, *épiceries* and ships' chandlers at most harbours. Methylated spirits called *alcool à brûler* may also be bought from *drogueries* and *épiceries*.

Water

Water is available almost everywhere and in most harbours water taps are established along the quays and pontoons. With a few exceptions the water from these taps is clean and can be drunk but the careful may prefer to boil their drinking water or buy bottled mineral water instead. The latter is advised because the water tank of a yacht can become foul.

Due to the very salty water and the hot dry air and sun, any object subjected to sea spray rapidly becomes impregnated with salt crystals, rope and sails become heavy and stiff, difficult to use and harsh to handle. These salt crystals do in time weaken and damage the materials and should be removed as soon as possible. On arrival in harbour it is quite normal to hose down all sails and cordage that have been exposed to salt water and to hang them up in the rigging where they will dry in a surprisingly short time.

Water is expensive and in short supply along the south coast of France and should not be wasted. No one will object to tanks being filled, decks and sails being washed to get the salt out of them or wooden decks being swilled down to keep them leak proof, but taps should be turned off directly these tasks are finished and they should never be left running unnecessarily. In recent years due to the huge increase in the number of people visiting and living on the coasts of the Mediterranean the demand for water has exceeded the supply and wells have run dry or only supply brackish water. Always test water before using or before filling tanks.

Ice

Ice for ice boxes is available in the summer season at most harbours and can be bought in blocks of about one metre long by 20 centimetres cross section. The best way to carry these heavy slippery blocks is in a towel until they can be broken into smaller portions by using a sharp instrument such as a pointed marlin spike. This ice should not be used in drinks as it is sometimes made from impure water. It is possible to buy special ice in most harbours from the bars that is clean and has been prepared for drinking purposes.

Food – See also page 36

At first, food may be found to be somewhat expensive in France but the quality is usually excellent. Much cheaper food is to be obtained in the larger ports especially in the markets and the back street shops. Cuts of meat will on first experience seem to be very expensive, but the type of cut is different and the weight does not normally include fat and bone as in England. Fruit or vegetables which are in season are usually very cheap.

By careful shopping and the choice of local foods it is possible to keep down the cost of feeding to British levels. Imported and special foods will be found to be very expensive.

Drink

Milk (*lait*) is obtainable at most harbours in glass bottles or paper or plastic cartons. Unless remaining in the area for some time, milk supplied in glass bottles should not be bought as these bottles will not be exchanged at another harbour. It is advisable to buy *lait stérilisé* as it is safer and keeps better.

Local wines (*vin du pays* or *vin ordinaire*) of excellent quality can be obtained by shopping around but spirits and château wines will be found to be relatively expensive, by buying duty free stores however this expense can be kept down. The cheaper wines are usually supplied in glass bottles with a ring of small stars around the base of the neck which are returnable for a refund, although many wines today are being supplied in non-returnable plastic bottles.

Shopping

The price of goods in the shops varies considerably from street to street and from town to town and the difference in price of an item bought in the main street of a smart resort and exactly the same item bought from a back street shop or supermarket in a large commercial port is considerable in winter and even greater in the summer season.

Most shops open by 0900 hours but some food shops open as early as 0700, with very few exceptions close at 1200 hours and do not reopen until 1400 or later. Some shops close for the day around 1730 while others stay open as late as 2100. Many food shops open on Sunday mornings.

Restaurants

Restaurants, cafés and bars will be found around every harbour, the quality of food and drink is in almost every case of a high order and the price is reasonably low considering the cost of the actual food in the shops. The charges made in a high class restaurant are considerable as merits the standard of cuisine.

The French as a rule eat out more frequently than the English and have their main meal at midday so that by twelve-thirty it will be difficult to find a table. Despite this early meal their evening meal is usually taken later than the English and the restaurants will not start to fill up until after eight. Menus are always displayed outside the establishment and a tour to study these is recommended. It is unwise to choose a restaurant by its location, décor or state of repair, the best quality and often the best value is to be found in an unpretentious restaurant in the back streets. Try to find out or see where the local people feed, this is bound to be one of the best places to visit. Some idea of the numbers of restaurants has been given for every harbour but details have not been included because many change so quickly.

Hotels

Hotels have been listed by numbers by classes under each harbour. This classification by the local Syndicat d'Initiative is similar to that used in Britain by the AA and RAC and gives some idea of what is available.

Holidays

There are a number of official holidays in France in addition to the normal weekend and these are listed below. Many places have local holidays on special feast days, but when these fall in the 'season' many shops including food shops remain open, especially in the morning.
1st January, New Year's Day; Easter Monday; 1st May, Labour Day; Ascension Day; 8th May, Liberation Day; Whit Monday; 14th July, Fête Nationale; 15th August, Feast of the Assumption; 1st November, All Saints' Day; 11th November, Armistice Day; 25th December, Christmas Day. Good Friday and Boxing Day are not holidays in France.

Laundrettes

Laundrettes (*laveries*) will be found near the larger harbours and ports usually situated in the back streets. In certain cases these establishments are not of the 'do it yourself' type common to Britain as the actual placing of the clothing in the machines and their removal is carried out by staff.

Garbage and pollution

The extent of the pollution of what was one of the fairest and cleanest seas in the world is frightening to behold. It is impossible when coasting on a calm day to find a stretch of sea free of floating rubbish, usually plastic, and the beaches and coves that are not cleaned daily are covered with flotsam of every conceivable kind of man made material. The French authorities are becoming aware of this menace and are taking steps to improve the situation but the deplorable behaviour of many of the tourists, the local fishermen, the crews of commercial vessels and

the occasional yachtsman in disposing of their rubbish into the sea nullifies their effort. Many bags and containers for rubbish are to be found on all quays and pontoons, collect your rubbish when at sea and on return to port put it in one of the containers provided, never put it in the sea.

Information offices

The information offices provided by the local Syndicat d'Initiative near every harbour should always be visited on arrival and free brochures and maps of the area obtained. These will make the visit more interesting as they usually contain a detailed history of the area with a list of places to visit, hotels, restaurants and many other items.

Before leaving Britain much information of a background nature can be obtained from the French Government Tourist Office, 178 Piccadilly, London, W1V 0AL ☎ (071 493 3171) in the form of brochures, maps, etc.

British Consul

The office and telephone number of the British consul on the mainland coast is:
24 avenue du Prado, 13006 Marseille. ☎ 91 53 43 32.
There is no consul in La Corse; contact Marseille.

Post offices

The *Bureau de Poste* usually labelled *PTT* (*or La Poste*) has been marked as such on the various plans. The hours of opening which vary from place to place are displayed outside the building. In addition to the normal telegraphic facilities they often have cabins which work because they have not been vandalised as have the coin boxes outside. There are now many call boxes using cards bought from the PTT. The *poste restante* service works well and it is possible to have correspondence redirected to another town as you sail along the coast, but careful planning is necessary as this service will only hold mail for two weeks and after this time it will be returned to the sender. The postal service to and from Britain varies from amazingly fast to very slow for reasons that are not apparent.

Health

The three main health hazards encountered in the Mediterranean are sunburn, heat stroke (or heat exhaustion) and stomach upsets, all of which can be guarded against. The sun, which is more powerful than at higher altitudes can produce sunburn with a very short exposure especially if coupled with the effects of wind and salt spray, in addition the reflection of the sun off the water will increase the rate of burning. Despite the heat, clothing should be worn and the skin only exposed for very limited periods at first until a tan has been acquired.

Heat exhaustion and in more severe cases heat stroke is caused by the loss of salt from the system through perspiration and in a hot climate such as this it is essential to increase the daily intake of salt by adding more to dishes when cooking than is usual so that all the crew remain fit, alternatively salt tablets should be taken. Stomach and bowel disorders can be occasioned by contaminated food or water, or food that has gone bad and this can only be guarded against by normal commonsense hygiene. Another cause of this trouble is the highly spiced foods liberally cooked and served with olive oil which if taken in quantity may be too much for systems used to more simple fare.

Medical

Excellent medical services exist along this stretch of the French coast but the services of doctors, hospitals, etc. have to be paid for and their fees are very high. It is therefore advisable to take out an insurance policy to cover medical and associated expenses or get National Health *Certificate E111* from your local Department of Health and Social Security, or from the DHSS, Overseas Branch, Newcastle upon Tyne, NE98 1YX before leaving.

Bathing

As might be expected bathing in the Mediterranean is excellent, the water warms up in May and remains warm well into the autumn. When bathing from rocks great care must be exercised in keeping a lookout for sea urchins, the spines of which if touched penetrate the skin and break off below the surface, being very difficult to remove and very painful. There are several different types of jellyfish to be found, some of which can sting if touched.

Other sports

Good facilities exist along the greater part of the coast for those who want to fish, shoot, ride, ski, fly, etc. and details can usually be obtained from the nearest information bureau of the *Syndicat d'Initiative*.

Communications

The communications to the south of France are excellent by both air and rail. There are frequent regular air services to Marseille and Nice, also the charter airlines run services to Perpignan, Montpellier, Nîmes, Toulon, Hyères, Cannes, Calvi, Ajaccio, Solenzara, Bastia and sometimes to other minor airfields. There are direct rail connections between Paris and all the major ports along the coast and some services from London go direct to Marseille and major coastal towns as far as Italy. Comprehensive bus services run from the major towns to the smallest harbours along the coast.

It is therefore very simple to change crews while cruising on this coast. There are both sea and ferry and air services from the mainland to Corsica.

Emergency messages

In a great emergency a close relative can have a message broadcast in France. The relative must phone the BBC News Room on ☎ 071 580 4468 Extension 4136. The BBC will contact Paris and the message will be broadcast in French on France Inter on 164 kHz (1829m) at 0200, 0445 (0345 Sundays), 0550, 0755 (0845 Sundays), 1157 and 1950.

Routes to the Mediterranean

United Kingdom to the Mediterranean

General

There are three main routes to the Mediterranean from the UK.
- The sea route around Spain and Portugal and through the Strait of Gibraltar. This route is obligatory to the larger yachts which draw too much water for the canals but has an advantage as it is possible to visit very pleasant harbours on the way out and see some interesting countries, although it entails a major sea voyage.
- The canal route via Paris and Lyon by one or more of the many different canal systems from several English Channel to several Mediterranean harbours. This route has the shortest sea crossing and passes through some beautiful scenery, but it is in total a lengthy journey as the canals are not direct. The dangerous lower reaches of the River Rhône are now canalised and present no difficulty.
- By sea to the Gironde estuary and by the Canal du Midi* to several Mediterranean ports. The shortest route and certainly the most beautiful though it entails a longish sea voyage down the Biscay coast, however there are many attractive harbours to visit on this route.

It is quite impossible to describe in detail the above routes in a book of this nature but the following notes may assist.

Selection of the route

The selection of the actual route to be used should be made after careful consideration of the following factors:
- Time available bearing in mind the speed of the vessel, speed limits and that canals are only open by day, allow 30 minutes per lock.
- Draught, height, beam and length of vessel and will it be small enough for the canal.
- Strength and capabilities of the crew. A strong crew is desirable for a sea voyage and is also required in the canals if in a hurry.
- The wish to see other harbours and countries on the way out.
- If it is practical or desirable to remove and stow the mast on deck and to restep it on arrival in the Mediterranean.
- The comparative number of locks and the comparative distances.

Sources of information

For those who may wish to make use of the canals detailed information may be obtained from:
- The French Government Tourist Office, 178 Piccadilly, London WIV 0AL, which also provides free of charge several useful brochures and maps. It also has for sale guides and maps produced by the Touring Club de France which are worth having.

*Closed due to lack of water and repairs (1990)

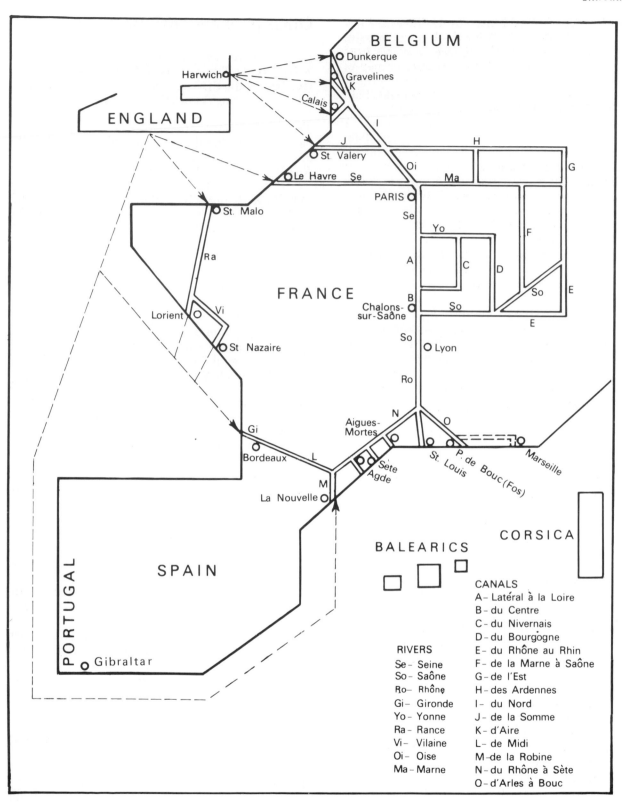

Routes to the Mediterranean

- *Inland Waterways of France* by D. Edwards-May (Imray, Laurie, Norie & Wilson). A comprehensive guide to all of the canals of France, available from most yachting bookshops. Also, separate, a map of the same title.
- *Cruising French Waterways*. Hugh McKnight. Published by Stanford Maritime.
- *Cartes et Guide Vagnon de Navigation Fluviale*. A set of 9 atlases covering the through routes. Published in France with English translations (obtainable from Imray, Laurie, Norie & Wilson).
- *Navicarte. Carte-Guide Fluviale*. A set of 15 atlases covering the navigable waterways. Published by Editions Cartographiques Maritimes, 7 Quai Gabriel Péri, 94340 Joinville-Le-Port, France ☎ (1) 48 85 77 00 Fax (1) 48 85 20 21.
- The Michelin series of maps and guides make a useful adjunct to the above books, they can be obtained from most large bookshops.
- There are a number of books of varying quality that provide background information on the canals and France which can be studied at large bookshops. Prospective purchasers should realise that there are on the market a number of catch penny books which are in fact almost useless.

Imray, Laurie, Norie & Wilson Ltd will provide assistance in obtaining publications.

Bibliography   See also page 38

Navigational

Admiralty publications. Published by the Hydrographer of the Navy
Sailing Directions No. 46, Mediterranean Pilot Vol. II and supplements, South Coast of France, Corsica and South-west Coast of Italy. Inclined to be out of date and caters for large warships and commercial vessels over 1000 tons.
List of Lights, Vol. E, Mediterranean, Black and Red Seas.
List of Radio Signals
Vol. I Part I, Coast Radio Stations.
Vol. 2 Radio Direction Finding Stations, Radiobeacons, Coast Radar Stations and Radar Beacons.
Vol. 3 Radio Weather Messages Services.
Vol. 4 Meteorological Observation Stations.
Vol. 5 Radio Time Signals, Radio Navigational Warnings and Position Fixing Systems.
Vol. 6 Part I, Operations, Pilot Services and Traffic Management.

French Navy Publications. Published by Service Hydrographique de la Marine
Instructions Nautiques Series 'D' Vol.II, Mer Méditerranée, Côtes de France *Fascicule No. 2 des Corrections*. Covers the same area as this book and is the same as the Admiralty pilot but includes information for yachtsmen. It has a separate volume with harbour plans and photographs of the coast.

Other publications

Foreign Port Information Folio. Mediterranean France by the Royal Cruising Club, available only to members of the RCC and the Cruising Club of America. The Cruising Association holds a copy.

Sea of Seas by H. Scott (Van Nostrand). A half guide half story covering the West Mediterranean, very out of date and now out of print, but a delightful book to read.

Votre Livre de Bord. Bloc Marin. Distributed by Imray, Laurie Norie & Wilson Ltd. A kind of Reed's Almanac with excellent plans and many advertisements, published yearly.

Guides Pratiques des Ports. Jacques Anglès. (Guides Pen Diuck) Similar but not as complete as *Votre Livre de Bord*.

Annuaire de Nautisme (Les Editions de Chabassol). A yearly publication which provides names, addresses and phone numbers of all firms and persons connected with yachting for every French port.

Portulans – Nos 507/8 de Port de Bouc à Cap d'Agde and *503 de Toulon à Cavalaire*. Detailed guides with excellent photographs and charts covering small sections of the French coast.

Pilot Côtier No. 3 Fenwick Alain Rondeau (Praxys Diffusion). A series of small guides in French with many photographs. Nos 1, 2 and 3 cover the South of France and La Corse.

Background

The South of France by Archibald Lyall (Collins). Interesting details of the area.

By Way of the Golden Isles by Anthony Rushworth Lund (Chapman and Hall). A pleasing description of a voyage.

Les Guides Michelin, Provence and Côte d'Azur, excellent background information.

Yachtsman's Eight Language Dictionary by Barbara Webb (Adlard Coles). Technical dictionary.

West of the Rhône by Freda White (Faber). A readable guide to Languedoc-Roussillon and the Massif Central.

PART II
La Corse

Introduction to La Corse

General description

The island of La Corse (Corsica) lies 100M off the coast of the French Riviera and from 50 to 120M off the Italian coast. To the N of the island is the Gulf of Genoa and the Ligurian Sea, to the E are the Tuscan Islands and the Tyrrhenian Sea, to the S lies the island of Sardinia which is only 7M away across Les Bouches de Bonifacio while to the W lies the Islas Baleares 220M away. The island of La Corse is therefore ideally located for the mainland yachtsman who wishes to take an offshore cruise to a 'foreign' land.

The island itself is 100M long and 45M wide at its maximum but its coastline is over 600M long due to the large number of indentations and projections making it longer than the French coast that lies between the Spanish and Italian frontiers.

Many illustrious writers have tried to describe this indescribable island in a short phrase, and to paraphrase some of these efforts, from a yachtsman's point of view, the island could be described as 'a scented granite mountain surrounded by anchorages' but any such short description does little justice to what is the most superb cruising area in the W Mediterranean and, what is very important, it has not suffered badly in the hands of the developers.

The island is sparsely populated and there are hundreds of square miles of deserted countryside. The few roads that are established tend to follow the easy routes in the valleys or along the coast and those tracks that penetrate the mountains are extremely tortuous and preclude any fast driving.

Except for the bare rocky mountainous peaks and some small areas of cultivation, the whole island is covered with the *maquis*, a scrub of mixed shrubs and trees, many of which are aromatic, resulting in a wonderfully perfumed air at all times which, with an offshore wind, can be smelt some twenty miles out to sea. It is almost impossible and could be dangerous to leave any road or track and to wander off into the undergrowth as within a few yards all sense of direction may be lost.

Layout of the pilotage

The first pages are concerned with background information data, safety, approach routes, details of La Corse and the Corsicans, documentation, etc.

Next there is a planning guide to assist the navigator's planning, consisting of a list of harbours, anchorages, headlands with distances between harbours. The directions of the winds and seas that can enter harbours and anchorages are also given.

The pilotage section which starts at Bastia continues in an anticlockwise direction around the island with the harbours, anchorages, promontories etc. in geographical order. Also included in the pilotage are general descriptions of the four differing types of coast.

Section A – Bastia to St Florent
Section B – St Florent to Ajaccio
Section C – Ajaccio to Porto Vecchio
Section D – Porto Vecchio to Bastia

Duplicate names

There are many examples in La Corse where features usually miles apart but sometimes close together have the same name e.g. Rosso, Mortella, Feno, etc., make sure you have identified the correct one when navigating.

Spelling of place names

The older French charts and books use the French spelling e.g. Cap de la Morsetta, however new editions have adopted some Corsican spelling e.g. Capo di a Morsetta. Either spelling has been used in this book and where there could be some confusion both have been used. Note that Punta and Pointe are the same thing and that 'O' in French becomes 'U' in Corsican. In addition local variations may be encountered.

Old charts

Old charts contain a large amount of inshore detail which has been excluded from new editions. This is particularly true of the French charts of this area; try to obtain old editions if possible. See page 37.

Beaches

Descriptions of the beaches at anchorages have been given e.g. rocky, stone, shingle, sand, etc. but it should be noted that after heavy rain storms the finer

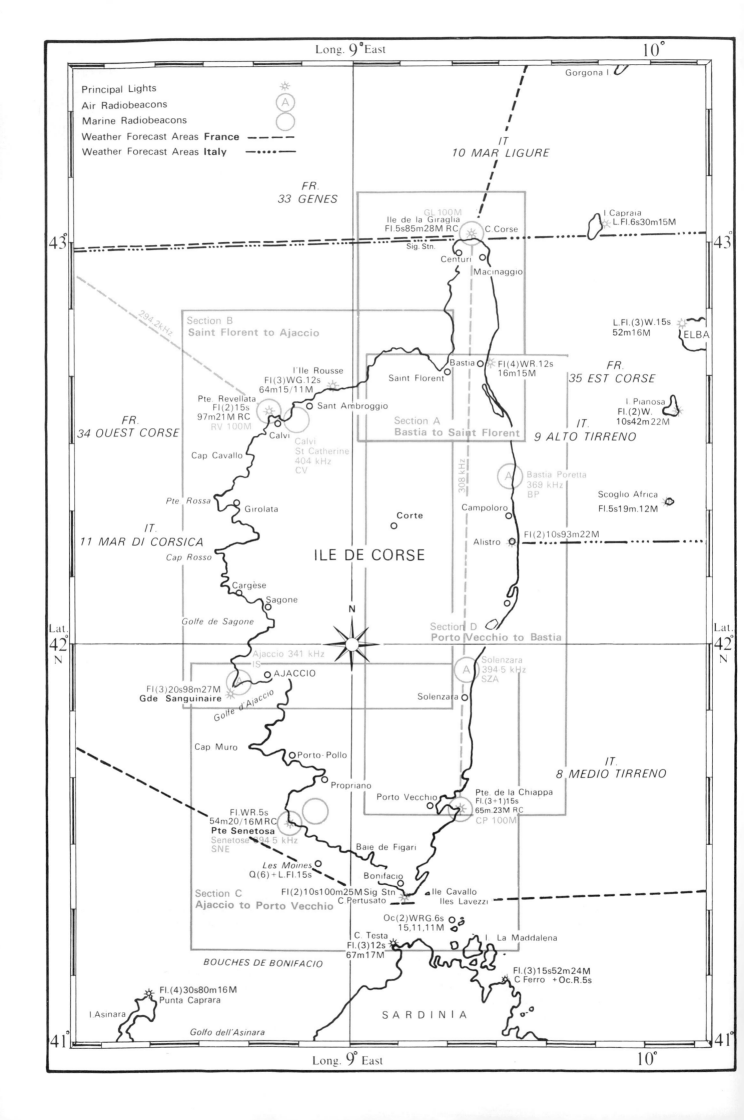

material, like sand, can be washed out to sea only to be restored after a series of gales. A good example of this is at Anse de Fuime Santu near St Florent, where a large beach was completely washed away after a cloud burst.

Small anchorages – See also page 19

Details of some small and very small anchorages have been given for expert navigators who like to anchor in a 'duck pond' and those who like to take striking pictures of their yacht at anchor.

Passages

Many useful passages have been detailed for use by experienced navigators and a few very narrow and exciting ones have been included for the 'entertainment' of the crew.

Rocky shapes

It is worthwhile following the coast close in, especially the W coast, for the amusement of the crew in spotting the many faces, figures, animals and inanimate objects sculptured by nature in the rocks. Some have been described in this pilot book to help in identification of a place.

Photography

The vast majority of photographs were taken out of season, when there were only a few yachts cruising around the island and many anchorages were deserted.

Naturism

It must be expected to find nudists on any of the secluded beaches around La Corse or on parts of any of the large beaches. The authorities seem to adopt a policy of noninterference with nudism provided it is not practised on crowded town beaches, perhaps causing offence to others. The nudist beaches usually have a mixture of people some with and some without clothing.

Known centres of nudism are:
North Anse de Faggiola, Anse de Porajola, Anse de Corbara (near Ile Rousse)
East Tropica, Corsicana, Riva Bella (which are between Morani Plage and Tavignano River), Baie de Bona Matina, Anse de Chiappino
South Tonnara (near Cap de Feno)

Warnings

Winds and seas – See also page 10

NW *mistral (maestrale)* This sometimes reaches La Corse and blows with considerable force. Normally some 12–24 hours warning on the radio can be expected prior to the arrival of this wind. Because of the fetch, the seas on the Corsican coasts are much more severe than those near the S French coast. Due

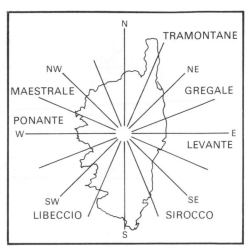

Local winds

to a fanning out effect, the *mistral* blows from a SW direction over the W side of La Corse as far as Pointe de Senetosa and also through the Bouches de Bonifacio. This wind can be recognised from the more usual W–SW *libeccio* because it is much colder and generally drier, but both *mistral* and *libeccio* winds are dangerous because of the combined effect of heavy seas they produce and the lack of good shelter on the coasts onto which they blow. A *libeccio* often precedes a *mistral* by about 6 hours.

N–NW *tramontane* This is a similar type of wind to the *mistral* but not so fierce. It blows from the Alps and across the N of Italy reaching the E and NE coasts of La Corse. The swell created by the *tramontane* sometimes arrives before the wind itself.

Raggiature This is a most dangerous wind consisting of violent gusts which blow down a valley without warning. These are particularly severe at Porto Vecchio, Bastia and along the E side of the Cap Corse peninsula. If the wind is blowing offshore the possibility of a *raggiature* should be considered when selecting any anchorage.

Brise de Mer, the sea breeze, will be encountered in calm weather especially on the E coast. It blows towards the land, commencing around 0800 to 0900 every morning reaching a maximum between 1300 and 1400 hours and then dies away each evening around 1700.

Brise de Terre, which blows off the land, starts at 1900 and reaches its maximum around 0700 in the morning dying away with the sunrise.

When rounding the major headlands a change in the direction and strength of the wind may be experienced. On occasions this change of direction may be over 90°.

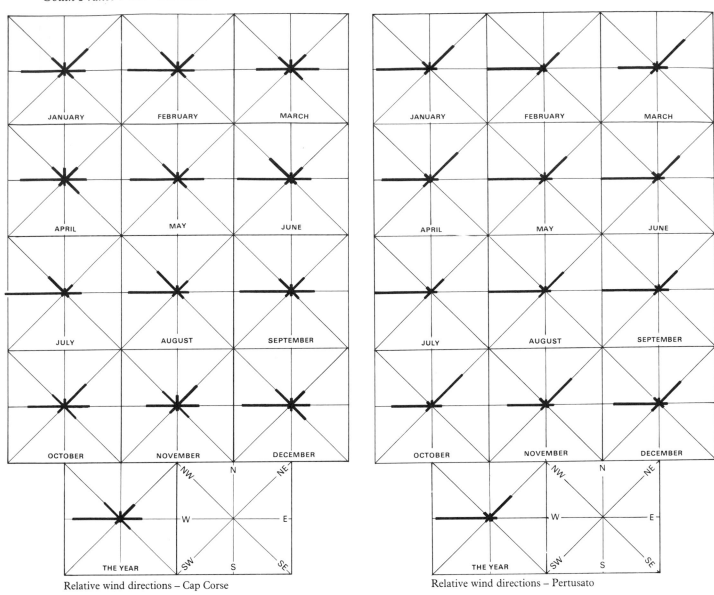

Relative wind directions – Cap Corse   Relative wind directions – Pertusato

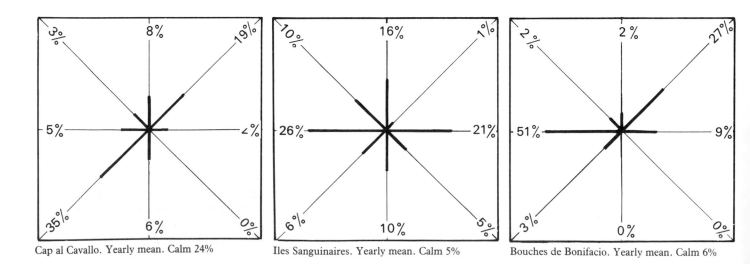

Cap al Cavallo. Yearly mean. Calm 24%   Iles Sanguinaires. Yearly mean. Calm 5%   Bouches de Bonifacio. Yearly mean. Calm 6%

Restricted areas

Nature reserves These have been established near the following places:
Bastia
St Florent
Ile Rousse
Calvi
Ile de Gargalu
Porto Piana
Propriano
Bonifacio
Iles Cavallo-Lavezzi
Porto Vecchio

Details are given in the section dealing with the harbour concerned. In addition there are plans to make the whole of the Bouches de Bonifacio a restricted area.

No anchoring, fishing or subaqua diving is permitted in these areas. The boundaries are shown on the plans of the areas concerned. See chart.

Underwater cables Anchorage or fishing is not permitted in the following areas, see plans of areas concerned.
S of Bastia
N of St Florent
W of Ile Rousse
S of Bonifacio
N and S of Iles Lavezzi

Offshore oil terminals Anchorage or fishing is forbidden near the following places:
S of Bastia
Near Bastia-Poretta airfield
Near Solenzara airfield
Locations are shown on plan concerned

Underwater and air training areas The following underwater training area must not be entered:
E of Ajaccio harbour near Pointe d'Aspretto. If a blue flag or light is displayed from Point d'Aspretto seaplane exercises may take place. See plans concerned.

Fire fighting planes

The French use large flying boats in their efforts to fight forest fires and to save the houses from destruction. These Canadair planes scoop water up into body tanks while taxiing at high speed along the surface of the sea, they then climb away and drop the water on the fire. There are usually two or three planes engaged in fighting a fire but there may at times be six, seven or even twelve.

The first plane to arrive will fly down the pick-up area at low level and it is most important that all yachts should leave the area of the flight path as quickly as possible and stay well clear of this pick-up area.

In Corsica the usual areas used by these planes are as follows:
Golfe de St Florent
Golfe de Calvi

Golfe de Girolata
Golfe de Porto
Golfe de Sagone
Golfe de la Lisca
Golfe d'Ajaccio
Golfe de Valinco
Golfe de Figari
Golfe de Ventilegne
Golfe de Sta Manza (Golfe de Sant'Amanza)
Golfe de Porto Vecchio

If necessary and especially on the E coast the planes may use the open seas. Warning is also given in the relevant parts of this pilot.

Offlying dangers

Virtually every headland has offlying dangers in the form of small islets, half covered rocks or shallow submerged rocks. These dangers can usually be observed by reason of breaking water or change of colour but on very calm days and at night extra care must be exercised and a careful study of the chart is essential. These dangers also exist around the offshore islands.

Magnetic anomalies

Magnetic deviations of up to 5° exist between Porto Vecchio and Campoloro on the E coast and compass errors should be expected when sailing in this area.

Anchorages

One of the main features of this island is the large number of pleasant anchorages to be found. These should only be used in settled weather and then only by day. If it is necessary to remain at anchor overnight, it is advised to make preparations in advance so that the anchorage can be left with the minimum delay should a dangerous situation develop. Many of the anchorages described in this pilot have areas of dangerous rocks and foul ground near them and care must be taken to avoid these. This presents no difficulty as due to the clarity of the water any obstructions can be seen with ease especially if the lookout is high up and is wearing polarised glasses.

Time of year

During the summer months and especially July and August harbours and popular anchorages become very overcrowded due to the large number of charter yachts based in La Corse and nearby harbours and the large number of private yachts that visit the island during the high season. Readers are strongly advised to visit the island at other times of the year if possible.

Navigational aids

Lights, beacons and buoys are few in number. There are many unmarked headlands, rocks and offlying dangers to be found around this island. The standard of navigation aids is below that of mainland France. See also page 33.

Data

Charts – See pages 5–8
The area charts for this coast are as follows:
Admiralty *1985, 1992, 1999*
France 7025
ECM Navicarte 1006, 1007, 1008 and Routier R3
(see pages 5–8.)

Tides – See also page 13
Because the range of the spring tide is only 0·15m
(6ins) tidal effects can be disregarded for any practical purpose.

Currents

With the exception of the currents that flow in the
Bouches de Bonifacio, usually E-going and of up to 2
knots, there are no permanent currents around La
Corse. However during and after prolonged winds a
surface current of up to 2 knots may be experienced
flowing in the same direction as the wind, but this
direction may be modified by any obstructions.

Sea levels

The sea levels, especially at the heads of gulfs and
bays, tend to increase when onshore winds blow with
any strength for more than a day. The larger and
deeper the gulf the greater will be the increase up to
as much as 0·5m (1·5ft). Conversely offshore winds
tend to lower the levels but not by the same amount.
As is normal elsewhere, the sea levels are higher
when the barometric pressure is low and vice versa.

Radio – See also page 13

Marine radiobeacons

West Corsica group 294·2 kHz
Pointe Revellata RV (· — ·/· · · —) 100M every 6 minutes
Seq. 3, 4
La Garoupe GO (— — ·/— — —) 100M every 6 minutes Seq.
5, 6

East Corsica group 308 kHz
Ile de la Giraglia GL (— — ·/· — · ·) 60M every 6 minutes Seq
1, 2
Pointe de la Chiappa CP (— · — ·/· — — ·) 100M every 4
minutes

Air radiobeacons

Ajaccio, Campo del'Oro IS (· ·/· · ·) 341 kHz 50M 41°54′N
8°36′·9E
Ajaccio CT (— · — ·/— ·) 387·5 kHz 41°47′·42N 8°43′·29E
Ajaccio RO (· — ·/— — —) 365 kHz 41°56′·95N 8°49′·10E
Calvi, St Catherine CV (— · — ·/· · · —) 404 kHz 42°34′·7N
8°48′·5E
Solenzara SZA (· · ·/— — ·/— ·) 349·5 kHz 80M 41°55′·9N
9°23′·8E. Bearings may be unreliable 080° to 120°
Bastia, Poretta BP (— · · ·/· — — ·) 369 kHz 50M 42°25′·7N
9°32′·2E
Pointe de Senetosa SNE (· · ·/— ·/· ·) 394·5 kHz 15M
41°33′·5N 8°47′·90E

Coast radio stations – See also page 14
The following VHF stations are remotely controlled from
Marseille or Grasse:
Ajaccio Transmits Ch 16, 24. Receives Ch 16, 24. Con-
tinuous
Bastia Transmits Ch 16, 65. Receives Ch 65.
(0630–2200[1]).★
Porto Vecchio Transmits Ch 05, 16, 25. Receives Ch 05,
25. (0630–2200[1])★

Weather forecasts – See also page 14
Forecasts and storm warnings in French
This island has three French forecast areas: No. 33 Golfe
de Gênes to N; No. 34 Ouest Corse to W and No. 35 Est
Corse to E.
   The best forecasts are from Grasse (TKM) and Monte
Carlo-Monaco, though the latter cannot always be received
on the S coast of the island.
Grasse (TKM) 2649, 3722 kHz at 0733, 1233, 1645. VHF
Ch 02 on receipt. Storm warnings on receipt and every
even H+33.
Radio Monte Carlo 218 and 1466 kHz (0800 and 1900)
Storm warnings on receipt.
Monaco (3AC and 3AF) 4363·6, 6509·5, 8728·2 0803,
1303, 1715 and 0715, 1715. VHF Ch 22, 23 at 0803, 1303,
1715 and 0600–2200. Continuous.
Cross Med Corse VHF Ch 09 0745, 1745 local time.
Radio Riviera 104·1, 106·5 MHz at 0730, 1930. In Eng-
lish[1]. Coastal waters between St Tropez and Italian fron-
tier.

Forecasts and storm warnings in Italian
This island has four Italian forecasts areas: To the N is No.
10 Mar Ligure; to the W is No. 11 Mar di Corsica; to the E
is No. 9 Alto Tirreno and to the SE is No. 8 Medio Tirreno.
Porto Cervo VHF Ch 26 in Italian and English at 0150,
0750, 1350 and 1950. Storm warnings in Italian and English at H+15. Areas 8, 11, 12.
Porto Torres 1806 kHz and Ch 26. In Italian and English
at 0150, 0750, 1350 and 1950. Storm warnings in Italian
and English on 1806 kHz at 0433, 0833, 1433, 1833 and
2333 and on VHF at H+15. Areas 8, 11, 12.
Genova (ICB) 2642, 2722 kHz and Ch 25, 26, 27. In
Italian and English at 0135, 0735, 1335 and 1935. Storm
warnings in Italian and English on 2642, 2722 kHz at
0333, 0833, 1233, 1633 and 2033 and on VHF H+15.
Areas 9, 10, 11.
Livorno 2591 kHz and Ch 26, 84. In Italian and English at
0135, 0735, 1335 and 1935. Storm warnings in Italian
and English on 2591 kHz at 0433, 0933, 1533, 1833 and
2333 and on VHF at H+15. Areas 8, 9, 10.
Civitavecchia 1888 kHz and Ch 27 (Monte Argentario). In
Italian and English at 0135, 0735, 1335 and 1935. Storm
warnings in Italian and English on 1888 kHz at 0433,
0833, 1233, 1633 and 2033 and on VHF at H+15. Areas
7, 8, 9.
Roma (IAR) Ch 25. In Italian and English at 0135, 0735,
1335 and 1935. Storm warnings in Italian and English at
H+15. Areas 8, 9, 10.

★One hour earlier during DST

Telephone
Meteorological forecasts in French can be obtained from
the following:
Ajaccio Automatic prerecorded forecast ☎ 95 21 32 71.
Airport Meteorological Office ☎ 95 21 05 81.

Calvi Airport Meteorological Office ☎ 95 65 91 11 extension 135.

Bastia Airport Meteorological Office ☎ 95 31 08 80.

Major lights – See also page 15

Bastia, Jetée du Dragon head Fl(4)WR.12s16m15/12M Grey tower. 193°-W-328°-R-342°-W-040°.

Cap Corse, Ile de la Giraglia Fl.W.5s85m28M White tower, black top. 057°-vis-314°. RC Signal station.

Cap Sagro Fl(3)W.12s10M White tower, green top.

Ile Rousse Fl(3)WG.12s64m15/11M White square tower and house. Shore-G-079°-W-234°-G-shore.

Pointe Revellata Fl(2)W.10s97m21M White square tower, black top and corners. Obscured bearing less than 060°. RC.

Ajaccio. Citadelle Fl(2)WR.10s19m20/16M White tower, red top. 045°-R-057° over Ecueil de la Guardiola, obscured when bearing 057°, 057°-W-045°.

Iles Sanguinaires, Grande Sanguinaire Fl(3)W.15s98m 27M White square tower black top and white house. Signal station.

Pointe de Senetosa Fl.WR.5s54m20/16M Two white towers, black tops, white house between. 328°-W-306°-R-328°.

Cap de Feno DirFl(4)W.15s21m21M White square tower, black top. 109·4°-intens-111·4°. Fl(4)WR.15s23m7/4M from same structure. 270°-W-150°-R-270°.

Cap Pertusato Fl(2)W.10s100m25M White square tower, black top. Vis 239°-obscd-133°.

Ile Lavezzi Oc(2)WRG.6s27m15-11M Square tower, red band and white house. 053°-W-111°-G-237°-W-278°-G-334°-W-346°-R-053°. Partially obscured 138°-218°.

Pointe de la Chiappa Fl(3+1)W.15s65m24M White square tower, red lantern. 198°-vis-027°. RC

Alistro Fl(2)W.10s93m22M Grey 8-sided tower, red house, black lantern.

Harbours of refuge

The following harbours of refuge can be entered under storm conditions although in some cases with difficulty:

Bastia Use the commercial Port St Nicolas if gale from NE–E.

Calvi Secure in the yacht harbour if gale is from SW–W–NW.

Ajaccio Be prepared for uncomfortable swell if gale is from E–SE.

Bonifacio Heavy gusts of wind from gales E–W.

Porto-Vecchio Swell enters harbour with gales from NE and there are difficult seas outside the harbour.

Approach from the mainland

The approach to this island from the mainland can be dangerous due to the fierce and unpredictable *mistral* and *tramontane* winds, the seas that these winds raise, and the lack of safe harbours which can be entered under storm conditions on arrival in La Corse. It is important to obtain good meteorological information before leaving the shelter of the mainland coast and to keep a constant radio listening watch for any storm warnings. It is also advisable to maintain a good average speed towards a safe harbour. All of the safe harbours in La Corse have good long range lights and radiobeacons nearby which should assist navigation to the correct part of the coast, but bearings on lights and from radiobeacons should be taken carefully at frequent intervals because it is almost impossible to make an accurate landfall by visual means due to of the lack of features that can be positively identified when out at sea under conditions of poor visibility. A yacht arriving on the Corsican coast under onshore storm conditions may find itself in serious difficulties if it cannot immediately enter a safe harbour.

Routes from the French mainland coast

Approach to the NW of La Corse is usually made from a harbour on the coast between Hyères and Menton with the intention of reaching the safe harbours of Calvi or Ajaccio, a distance of between 100M to 130M. Should the weather still be favourable in the closer approach a diversion to Saint Florent, Ile Rousse, Girolata or Propriano might be considered though these harbours do not have such good navigational aids.

Routes from the Italian mainland coast

The Italian coast around the Golfe di Genova forms an arc of a circle 80M from Cap Corse and yachts can make either Calvi or Bastia their destination. Harbours between Livorno and Roma lie between 50 to 120M from La Corse but if intermediate stops are made at Elba or the Tuscan islands these distances are much reduced. In fair weather the harbours of Campoloro and Macinaggio may be used as alternatives.

Routes from Sardinia

The distances in this case are very short being only 9M from Porto Lango-Sardo to Bonifacio and 50M from Porto Torres to the same harbour. Bonifacio and Porto Vecchio are the safe harbours that should be used when crossing from Sardinia to La Corse.

Return voyage

When planning the return voyage consideration should be given to the 'fanning out' effect of the *mistral* which tends to blow from a SW direction near the NW side of La Corse and if caught out in this wind it may be necessary to make a landfall near the French-Italian frontier before working towards the W to reach the yacht's home port. In a similar way yachts making for harbours in the Golfo di Genova and caught out in a *tramontane* may have to make their landfall further to the SE and then work up the coast to N.

Customs See also page 22

If arriving in La Corse from any country other than France, it is essential to put into a major harbour where customs officers are stationed. Fly the signal flag Q (Yellow) or a red over white light if night-time and to clear customs in the normal way.

Visits

Details of local places of interest are given in the sections dealing with the harbours concerned. There are however a large number of other interesting things to see further inland which can be visited by bus, train or taxi. At all harbours there are garages where cars and motorcycles may be hired and this method of seeing the island is highly recommended.

La Corse and the Corsican

La Corse has a number of organisations fighting for the independence of the island from France and their slogans will be seen everywhere. It is also a popular base for smuggling and evidence of this may be encountered. To a large extent Corsicans mete out their own punishments for misdemeanours committed without recourse to the police. They have a long tradition of banditry, vendettas and toughness and the best advice that can be given to a visitor who sees something out of the ordinary is to keep clear and do not get involved.

The Corsican will be found to be a delightful person once his natural reserve has been evaporated, he is then your friend for life who will do everything in his power for you.

All over the island and on many boats the Tête de Maure (Moor's Head) flag will be seen flying. This flag was originally used by the Aragonese during the Crusades. It was adopted by Pascal Paoli in 1762 and used by his patriots when trying to expel the Genoese from La Corse. This flag has been used ever since as the national flag of La Corse. There is no objection to visiting yachts flying this flag below the French tricolour as a courtesy ensign in the same manner as the flags of Brittany and Normandy are sometimes flown.

Sport

Facilities for sports exist and details can be obtained from the office of the local Syndicat d'Initiative regarding walking, climbing, camping, skiing, riding, shooting, fishing (both river and sea), sub-aqua diving, water skiing, tennis, motor racing and other activities.

Food and drink   See also page 24

In addition to the normal range of foods and drink which are similar to those obtainable in mainland France, La Corse has some special dishes of her own. These have a unique flavour because they are often made from animals who have fed from the berries and chestnuts that are to be found in the *maquis*. Ham and sausages made from chestnut-fed pigs and smoked over aromatic shrubs; woodcock, partridge, pigeon and blackbird fed on the berries of the wild shrubs are special to La Corse. Wild boar with a wine and chestnut sauce is another out of the ordinary dish. Chestnut flour is used to make fritters and pancakes of many varieties. Cheeses from sheep

and goat milk are specialities of the island. Needless to say sea food is plentiful and of good quality; sea urchins, an acquired taste, are a popular local dish.

La Corse produces its own wines which are of good quality and come from vineyards around Calvi, Ajaccio, Sartène, Bastia and Cap Corse. There are two liqueurs one *myrte* made from the arbutus berry from the *maquis*, the other *cedratine* made from lemons.

History

It is impossible in this work to give anything but a bare outline of the long and complex history of La Corse but there are two books that cover the subject in detail, *History of Corsica* by Paul Arighi, 1966, and *The Tragic History of the Corsicans* by Dom J.B.Gai, 1951.

Around 3000 BC the first known megalithic inhabitants of the island left a series of *dolmens* and *menhirs* in the SW and by 1600 BC these early people were building *statue-menhirs* representing men with daggers and swords which were probably funerary monuments. Another early group the Torreens became established in the SE about 2000 BC and left a series of tower-like buildings, rounded and domed. This latter civilisation expanded over the south of the island clashing with the earlier group at Filitosa and driving them to settlements in the N of the island. The Torreens vanished about 1200 BC and may have moved to Sardinia.

The Phoenicians were probably the next to establish themselves on the island though little evidence remains of them. The foundation of Alalia (Aleria) in 560 BC by the Phoenicians and Greeks from Asia Minor, was an event of importance as they remained here despite the invasions and occupations by the Etruscans and Carthaginians between 278 and 259 BC.

When the Romans conquered the island in 259 BC, they colonised it and established several towns including Mariana.

In 450 AD the Vandals followed by the Ostrogoths devastated La Corse but the latter were driven out by the Byzantines in 552 AD who in their turn were succeeded by the Lombards and the Saracens.

In 1077, the Pope assigned the administration of La Corse to the Pisans but from 1133 Genoa disputed this control and Pisa did not eventually gain full possession until 1284.

In 1296 La Corse was assigned to Aragon by a later Pope, because of its state of anarchy, but the unrest continued until 1420 when a strong force of Aragonese captured the island. Troubles still prevailed however and the island was later left in charge of a commercial concern, the Bank of St George, by the Genoese. In 1553 the French captured it but gave it back again to the Genoese in 1559 who then remained in complete control until 1729. It was during this period that the majority of watch towers, forts, churches and bridges were built although a few churches date from earlier periods.

The first Corsican rebellion broke out in 1729, but it was not until Pascal Paoli organised the indepen-

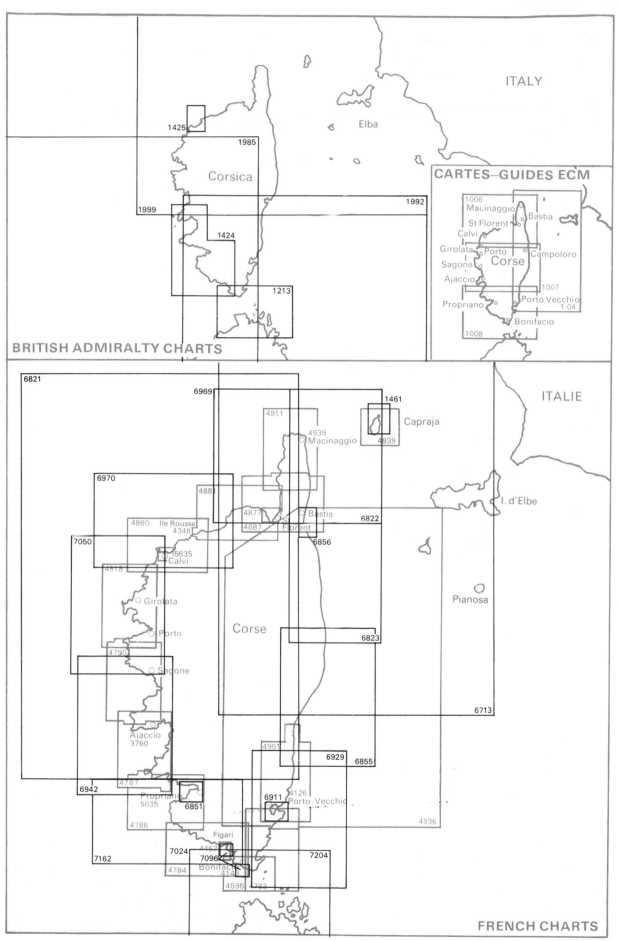

ITALY

Elba

Corsica

1425

1985

1999

1424

1992

1213

CARTES—GUIDES ECM

1006
Macinaggio
Bastia
St Florent
Calvi
Girolata
Porto
Campoloro
Corse
Sagone
Ajaccio
1007
Porto Vecchio
Propriano
1 04
1008
Bonifacio

BRITISH ADMIRALTY CHARTS

6821

6969

4911

1461

4939
Macinaggio

4939

Capraja

ITALIE

6970

488

4877

Bastia

6822

4860
Ile Rousse
4348

4087
S
Florent

6856

I. d'Elbe

7050

5635
Calvi

4818

Girolata

Pianosa

Porto

Corse

6823

4790

Sagone

6713

Ajaccio
3760

4951

6929

6855

6942

4787

Propriano
5635

6851

6911

4126
Porto-Vecchio

4786

4936

7162

4784

7024

4457

7096
Bonifacio
4146

Figari

7204

4595

783

FRENCH CHARTS

Charts for Corsica. Obsolete French charts are shown grey.

dent state in 1755 that events started to move. Genoa sold her rights of La Corse to France in 1768 and the latter once again occupied the island. Paoli was defeated and fled to England but returned again after the French revolution in 1790 and in 1792 declared La Corse independent of France, appealing to Britain for protection. The British were thus in occupation from 1794 to 1796 when for the third time the French reoccupied the island and it became a part of France. The Germans and Italians held the island during the last war, the Corsicans being responsible for liberating themselves in 1943.

Tourism, which commenced before the last war, is on the increase and the depopulation of the island has been halted. Currently considerable efforts are being made to improve its economic state.

Bibliography – La Corse

In addition to those books listed in Part I page 28, the following titles are concerned especially with the island of La Corse:

Navigational

Petits Ports de Corse by Jean Merrien (Denoel) 1960 (in French). Outline descriptions of many of the harbours and anchorages. Out of print.

The Tyrrhenian Sea by H.M. Denham (Murray). Out of print. Details of many harbours and anchorages including those in Sardinia, the Italian coast and islands offshore, with plans, histories and some details of facilities. A pleasant book to read.

Guide Nautique de la Corse by La Fédération Corse des Ports de Plaisance (colour) in French. An official outline description of the harbours and their facilities with excellent coloured aerial photos.

Pilot Côtiers Fenwick No. 3 Alain Rondeau, Editions du Pen Duick.

Reed's Mediterranean Navigator. Useful tables and data published annually.

Votre Livre de Bord – Méditerranée Bloc Marin. A useful French almanac. Available in UK from Imray, Laurie, Norie & Wilson Ltd.

Background

The Granite Island by Dorothy Carrington (Longman).

This Corsica by Dorothy Carrington (Hammond).

Unknown Corsica by G. Pillement (Johnson) which describes, in outline, the country, places of interest and towns and villages.

Corsica by Ian Thomson (David and Charles).

Les Guides Seuil No. 20, Corse (in French). A useful guide to the towns, villages and places of interest in Corsica.

Regions of France No. 24, Corsica. Issued gratis by the French Tourist Office giving general information.

Corsica Today by Jean Hureau (Editions j.a.). Interesting guide with good photos.

Green Guide Michelin – Corse. Useful detail but not up to the usual standard.

Mediterranean Island Hopping. Diana Facanos and Michael Pauls. Only 63 pages on Corsica but containing a lot of data.

Planning guide

Ports harbours, anchorages, headlands, islands, landings, passages and special features.

Note This guide is listed in an anticlockwise direction from Ports de Bastia. There are many other fair-weather anchorages to be found which are not listed below. Additional anchorages are detailed in the sections dealing with the various harbours and ports.

Distances	Headlands and features		Ports, anchorages and landings	Open to winds from
	Pointe Grisgione	**3·1**	**Ports de Bastia** 1–2–2 page 45	NE
		3·2	**Port Toga** 1–2–2 page 50	NE
		⚓	*Marine de Miomo*	NE–E–SE
	Pointe de la Vasina			
		⚓	*Marine de la Vasina*	NE–E–SE
		⚓	*Marine de Erbalunga*	NE–E–SE
	Cap Sagro	⚓	*Port de Erbalunga*	E
		⚓	*Erbalunga N*	NE–E–SE
		⚓	*Marine de Sisco*	NE–E–SE
16M	Ancien Convent de Ste Catalina			
		⚓	*Marine de Pietracorbara*	NE–E–SE
	Punta di Ghiunchi			
		⚓	*Marine de Portocciolo*	NE–E–SE
		⚓	*Anse de Portocciolo*	NE–E–SE
		⚓	*Marine de Luri (Santa Severa)*	NE–E–SE
		⚓	*Port de Luri*	E–SE
		⚓	*Anse de Alessandro*	NE–E–SE
		⚓	*Marine de Meria*	E–SE
		+	*Macinaggio S*	NE–E SE
		3·3	**Port de Macinaggio** 2–3–3 page 57	NE
		⚓	*Baie de Macinaggio*	NE–E–SE
	Pointe de la Coscia			
		⚓	*Baie de Tamarone*	NE–E–SE
		⚓	*Iles Finocchiarola S*	E–SE
	Iles Finocchiarola and passages			
	Punta de Santa Maria	⚓	*Rade de Santa Maria*	NW–N–NE–E
	Punta Vecchia	⚓	*Punta Vecchia SE*	NW–N–NE–E
		⚓	*Punta Vecchia NW*	NW–N–NE–E
11M		⚓	*Baie de Capandola*	N–NE–E
	Pointe d'Agnello			
		⚓	*Pointe d'Agnello NW*	N–NE
		⚓	*Marine de Barcaggio*	NW–N–NE
	Ile de la Giraglia	⚓	*Marine de Tollare*	NW–N–NE
		⚓	*Anse de l'Arinella*	NW–N–NE
	Cap Corse			
	Cap Grosso			
	Pointe Corno di Becco			
	Cap Bianco			
		3·4	**Port de Centuri** 1–4–4 page 66	W–NW–N
		⚓	*Baie de Centuri*	W–NW–N
	Ile de Capense			
		⚓	*Marine de Morsiglia N*	SW–W–NW
		⚓	*Marine de Morsiglia S*	SW–W–NW
17M	Pointe d'Aliso			
		⚓	*Anse d'Aliso (Golfu Alisu)*	SW–W–NW
	Pino Landing			
	Pointe Minervio	⚓	*Marine de Giottani*	SW–W–NW
	Canari (Pointe de Scala) landing			
	Pointe de Scala (Punta di a Scala)			
	Pointe de Canelle (Punta di Canelle)			

Coastal feature	⚓ Anchorage	Winds
Marine de Canelle landing		
Albo asbestos mine and works		
	⚓ *Marine d'Albo*	SW–W–NW–N
	⚓ *Marine de Nonza*	SW–W–NW–N
	⚓ *Marine de Negro (Marine di Negru)*	SW–W–NW–N
	⚓ *Marine de Farinole*	SW–W–NW–N
	⚓ *Punta di Saeta N (Albino)*	SW–W–NW–N
Punta di Saeta		
Pointe Vecchiaja (Vecchiaia)		
Punta di Cani		
	⚓ *Les Marines de Soleil*	SW–W–NW–N

3·5 Port de Saint Florent 2–2–3 page 76

Coastal feature	⚓ Anchorage	Winds
	⚓ *Rade de Fornali*	NE–E–SE
Pointe de Fornali	*Punta di Cepo S*	N–NE–E–SE
	⚓ *Anse de Fornali*	N–NE–E–SE
Punta di Cepo		
	⚓ *Anse de Valdolese*	N–NE–E
	⚓ *Anse de Fiume Santu*	N–NE–E
	⚓ *Baie de la Mortella*	N–NE–E–SE
Pointe de la Mortella		
Pointe Cavallata		
	⚓ *Plage du Loto E*	NW–N–NE
	⚓ *Plage du Loto W*	N–NE–E
Pointe de Curza (Perallo)	⚓ *Plage de Saleccia*	
	(Anse de Faggiola)	NW–N–NE
Pointe de Mignole (di Mignola) (Santolino)		
	⚓ *Pointe Genibareta E*	NW–N–NE
Pointe Genibareta		
	⚓ *Pointe Genibareta W*	NW–N–NE
Pointe Mortella	⚓ *Anse de Malfalco*	NW–N
Pointe de l'Arinetta	⚓ *Marine d'Alga*	W–NW–N–NE
Pointe de Solche (Punta di Solche)		
Pointe de l'Alciolo	⚓ *Anse de Orlando*	NW–N–NE
(Punta di l'Acciolu)	⚓ *Anse de Porajola (Periola)*	SW–W–NW–N
Pointe d'Arco	⚓ *Anse de Lozari*	W–NW–N–NE
Pointe de Lozari		
Pointe Saleccia		

3·6 Port de L'Ile Rousse 3–3–3 page 87   NE–E

Coastal feature	⚓ Anchorage	Winds
Passage between Le Grand Ile Rousse and Ile de Bruccio		
	⚓ *Anse de Corbara*	W–NW–N–NE
	⚓ *Anse de la Galère*	NW–N–NE
Pointe Vallitone	⚓ *Marine de Davia*	SW–W–NW
Pointe de Varcale	⚓ *Anse d'Algajola*	W–NW–N
	⚓ *Port d'Algajola*	N–NE
Pointe St Damiano (Punta San Damiano)		
Danger de l'Algajola		
	⚓ *Anse de Sant'Ambrogio*	N–NE

3·7 Port de Sant'Ambrogio 3–3–3 page 94

Coastal feature	⚓ Anchorage	Winds
	⚓ *Cala Stella*	NW–N–NE
Punta Spano (Pointe d'Espano)		
Iles de Spano		
	⚓ *Baie Algajola (Algajo)*	SW–W–NW–N
	⚓ *Portu Algajola (Algajo)*	W–NW–N
	⚓ *Portu a Diaghia*	W–NW
Punta Caldanu (Carchincu)		
	⚓ *Portu Ricciaiu*	S–SW–W
	⚓ *Golfe de Calvi*	NW–N–NE

3·8 Port de Calvi 1–1–3 page 99   NE

Coastal feature	⚓ Anchorage	Winds
Punta San Francesco		
	⚓ *Golfe de la Revellata*	N–NE
Punta di l'Oscelluccia		
	⚓ *Anse de l'Oscelluccia*	N–NE–E
	Station de Recherches Océanographique	E–SE
Pointe de la Revellata	Passage Ile de la Revellata	
(Punta de la Revellata)		
Pointe Rossa (Punta Rossa)	⚓ *Anse Margonaia*	SW–W–NW
Pointe Bianca		
	⚓ *Porto Vecchio*	S–SW–W
	⚓ *Anse Recisa*	S–SW–W–NW

Scale markers (left margin): 20M, 4M, 5M

	⚓	*Port Agro*	S–SW–W–NW
Pointe Caprara	⚓	*Pointe Caprara S*	SW–W–NW
	⚓	*Baie de Nichiareto*	W–NW
Pointe Cantaleli	⚓	*Anse d'Alusi*	NW–N–NE
Cap Cavallo			
Cap de la Morsetta			
(Capo Mursetta)			
Ile de la Morsetta and passage			
	⚓	*Baie de Crovani*	SW–W–NW
	⚓	*Baie de Martino*	W–NW–N
Pointe Ciuttone	⚓	*Golfe de Galéria N*	W–NW–N
	⚓	*Golfe de Galéria S*	W–NW–N
Pointe Stollo		Les Scoglietti and passage	
Punta Rossa	⚓	*Punta Rossa S*	SW–W–NW
Pointe Bianca (Punta Bianca)	⚓	*Anse d'Elpa Nera (de la Foata)*	SW–W–NW
Pointe de Validori	⚓	*Baie de Focolara*	W–NW–N
Pointe Scandola		Ilot Pori and passage	
	⚓	*Anse Pori*	W–NW–N
Pointe Nera			
		Baie d'Elbo	NW–N–NE
	⚓	*Marine d'Elbo*	NW–N–NE
Pointe Palazzo			
Ilot Palazzo and passage			
Ile di Gargalu (Cargolo) and passage			
	⚓	*Baie di Solana*	S–SW–W
		'Dog Leg' Passage	
	⚓	*Anse de Gattoja (Gattaghia)*	S–SW–W
Pointe Rossa (Punta Muchillina)			
Pointe Scandola			
	⚓	*Cala Moretta*	E–SE–S
	⚓	*Cala Vecchi*	E–SE–S
	⚓	*Girolata W*	S–SW
	3·9	**Port de Girolata** 1–2–4 page 113	S–SW
	⚓	*Anse de Tuara*	S–SW–W
		Golfe de Porto	SW–W–NW
Cap Senino (Osani)			
Pointe Scopa (Punta a Scoppa)	⚓	*Anse Lignaggia*	SE–S–SW–W
	⚓	*Anse Gradelle W*	SE–S–SW
	⚓	*Anse Gradelle E (Pilatri or Caspio)*	S–SW–W
	⚓	*Golfe di Miserinu*	S–SW–W
	⚓	*Golfe de u Pastricciola*	S–SW–W
Pointe Bianca	⚓	*Marine de Bussagna (Bussoghio)*	S–SW–W
	⚓	*Porto*	SW–W–NW
	⚓	*Porto Marina*	SW–W–NW
	⚓	*Anse de la Castagna (Porto)*	N–NE
	⚓	*Anse de Ficajola E*	NW–N–NE
Pointe Ficajola	⚓	*Pointe Ficajola W*	W–NW–N
Pointe Piana	⚓	*Pointe Piana W*	W–NW–N
Ilot Vardiola			
	⚓	*Pointe Vardiola E*	NW–N–NE
Pointe Vardiola			
	⚓	*Pointe Vardiola W*	W–NW–N
Cap Rosso (Cap Rossu)	⚓	*Cap Rosso N*	NW–N–NE
Cap Rosso Passage			
	⚓	*Cala Genovese*	S–SW–W
	⚓	*Anse de Polo (Palu) NW*	S–SW
	⚓	*Anse de Polo (Palu) E*	S–SW–W
Punta i Tuselli	⚓	*Porta â Leccia*	SW–W–NW
(Punta a i Tuselli)			
Pointe d'Orchino	⚓	*Anse d'Arone*	S–SW–W
(Punta d'Orchino)	⚓	*Golfe de Topiti (Orchino)*	W–NW–N
	⚓	*Baie de Chioni*	SW–W–NW
Pointe d'Omignia	⚓	*Baie de Pero (Golfe de Peru)*	S–SW–W
Pointe de Cargèse			
(Punta di u Puntiglione)			
	3·10	**Port de Cargèse** 3–3–3 page 126	SE–S
	⚓	*Baie de Cargèse*	SE–S–SW–W
Pointe Molendino (Punta di Molendinu)			
Rocher Marifaja (Morifeja)			
	⚓	*Pointe des Moines N*	S–SW–W
Pointe des Moines			
	⚓	*Plage de Ménasina (Marina de Monaccia)*	SE–S–SW–W
Pointe Puntiglione			
Pointe de la Batterie			

22M

15M

5M

	Coastal features		Anchorage	Wind
		3·11	**Port de Sagone** 3–3–3 page 130	SE–S
		⚓	*Baie de Sagone*	SE–S–SW
	Pointe St Joseph			
	Récif de St Joseph and passage	⚓	*Plage de Liamone*	S–SW–W
	Pointe Locca	⚓	*Baie de Liscia*	SW–W–NW
	Pointe Palmentojo			
	Iles de Pointe Palmentojo and passage			
		⚓	*Anse d'Ancone*	SW–W–NW
	Pointe Paliagi			
	Récif de Paliagi and passage			
	Pointe Pelusella			
		⚓	*Port Provençale*	SW–W–NW
	Ile Piètra Piombata and passage			
	Cap de Feno			
		⚓	*Anse de Fico N and S*	S–SW–W
21M	Ecueil de Fico			
	Ile la Botte			
		⚓	*Anse de Minaccia N and S*	S–SW–W
		⚓	*Anse d'Alta*	SW–W–NW
		⚓	*Anse de la Parata W*	SW–W–NW
	Iles Sanguinaires			
	Passages des Sanguinaires			
		⚓	*La Grande Sanguinaire*	E–E–SE–S
	Pointe de la Corba			
		⚓	*Anse de la Parata E*	E–SE–S
	Pointe Scudo			
		⚓	*Pointe Scudo E*	E–SE–S–SW
	Rocher La Botte			
	Rocher La Guardiola			
		⚓	*Anse Maestrello (Maestrellu)*	E–SE–S–SW
	Rocher Citadelle			
		3·12	**Ports d' Ajaccio** 2–1–4 page 142	
	Pointe d'Aspretto			
		⚓	*Pointe d'Aspretto E*	SE–S–SW
		⚓	*Pointe Porticcio NE*	W–NW–N
	Pointe de Porticcio			
	Ecueil d'Orbera			
		⚓	*Pointe de Porticcio SE*	SW–W–NW
		⚓	*Plage d'Agosta*	SW–W–NW
		⚓	*Anse Ste Barbe*	W–NW–N
	Pointe de Sette Nave			
		⚓	*Anse Medea*	S–SW
19M	La Campanina beacon			
		⚓	*Anse Ottioni*	SW–W–NW
		⚓	*Port de Chiavari*	W–NW–N
		⚓	*Ile Piana E*	NW–N–NE
		⚓	*Ile Piana SW*	SW–W–NW
		⚓	*Anse de Portigliolo*	W–NW–N
		⚓	*Pointe de la Castagna NE*	NW–N–NE
	Pointe de la Castagna	⚓	*Pointe de la Castagna SE*	S–SW–W
	Carapono radio TV mast			
		⚓	*Anse de Cacao (Cacau)*	N–NE–E
	Pointe Guardiola and passage			
	Cap Muro (Capu di Muru)	⚓	*Cap Muro SE*	E–SE–S–SW
		⚓	*Anse des Deux Rochers*	SE–S–SW
		⚓	*Anse d'Orzo*	S–SW–W
	Cap Nero	⚓	*Baie de Copabia (Cupabia)*	S–SW–W
		⚓	*Pointe de Porto Pollo W*	S–SW–W
	Pointe de Porto Pollo			
		3·13	**Port de Porto Pollo** 3–2–4 page 156	E–SE–S
5M		⚓	*Orimeto Plage*	SE–S–SW
		⚓	*Plage de Campitellu*	S–SW–W
	Pointe d'Agliu	⚓	*Plage de Baracci*	W–NW
		3·14	**Port de Propriano** 3–3–3 page 158	W–NW
	Cap Laurosu			
		⚓	*Plage de Laurosu (Tavaria)*	SW–W–NW–N
		⚓	*Portigliolo*	W–NW–N
		⚓	*Campo Moro*	NW–N–NE
	Pointe de Campo Moro			

	⚓	*Anse d'Agulia*	W–NW
Pointe d'Eccica (Essica)		Ile d'Eccica reef and passages	
	⚓	*Anse de Ferro*	S–SW–W
	⚓	*Anse d'Arana*	S–SW–W
	⚓	*Calanque de la Concha*	SW–W–NW
Pointe de Senetosa (Sénétose) and Pointe d'Aquila			
	⚓	*Pointe d'Aquila E*	SE–S–SW
	⚓	*Anse de Tivella*	SE–S–SW–W
	⚓	*Cala Longa*	S–SW–W
	⚓	*Anse Bercajo*	SE–S–SW
	⚓	*Anse de Tromba*	S–SW–W
	⚓	*Port de Tizzano*	S–SW
	⚓	*Baie de l'Avena*	SW–W–NW
Pointe Latoniccia (Cap de Zivia) Ilot Latoniccia and passage			
	⚓	*Anse de Brieche*	E–SE–S–SW
	⚓	*Golfe de Mortoli*	SE–S–SW–W
Pointe Mortoli	⚓	*Golfe de Roccapina*	SE–S–SW–W
Pointe de Roccapina			
	⚓	*Anse de Roccapina*	SE–S–SW
		Ecueil des Moines (Islets and reefs and passage)	
	⚓	*Anse delli Balconi*	S–SW–W
	⚓	*Anse du Prêtre*	NS–SW–W
	⚓	*Anse du Prêtre*	NES–SW–W
Pointe de Fornello			
Ecueils d'Olmeto and Le Prêtre and passages			
	⚓	*Anse Fornello*	SE–S–SW
	⚓	*Anse d'Arbitro (Anse d'Albitru)*	S–SW
	⚓	*Iles Bruzzi*	SW–W
Iles Bruzzi			
	⚓	*Anse de Capinero (Anse de Chevanu)*	SE–S–SW
Pointe de Figari			
	3·15	**Port de Baie de Figari** 2–3–5 page 173	SE–S–SW
Pointe de Ventilegne	⚓	*Anse de Piscio Cane*	S–SW
	⚓	*Golfe de Ventilegne*	SW–W
	⚓	*Iles de la Tonnara*	NW–N
	⚓	*Port de Stagnolo*	SW–W–NW
	⚓	*Anse Grande*	S–SW
Cap de Feno	⚓	*Anse de Paragnano*	S–SW
	⚓	*Iles et Anse de Fazzuolo (Fazziolu)*	S–SW
	3·16	**Port de Bonifacio** 1–2–2 page 179	S–SW
Cap Pertusato		Ile St Antoine and passage	
Pte Sprono – (Punta di Sperono)		Le Prêtre Beacon	
	⚓	*Pointe Sprono W*	S–SW–W
	⚓	*Anse Piantarella*	NE–E–SE–S
	⚓	*Ile Piana NE*	NE–E–SE–S–SW
		Landing Ile Piana	NW
	⚓	*Cala Longa*	E–SE–S
	3·17	**Les Bouches de Bonifacio** page 186	
	3·18	**Iles Lavezzi** 1–3–5 page 190	
	3·19	**Ile Cavallo** 2–4–3 page 194	
Pointe Cappiciolo (Punta di u Cappiciolu)	⚓	*Golfe de Santa Manza (Sant'Amanza)*	NE–E
	⚓	*Anse de Balistro*	NE–E–SE
	⚓	*Pointe de Rondinara S*	SE–S–SW
Pointe de Rondinara			
	⚓	*Port de Rondinara*	NE–E–SE
Pointe de Sponsaglia			
	⚓	*Golfe de Port Nuovo*	N–NE–E
	⚓	*Golfe de Santa Giulia*	NE–E–SE
Ile du Toro			
	⚓	*Pointe d'Aciajo (Capu d'Acciaju) W*	E–SE–S
	⚓	*Anse de la Folaca (Folacca)*	NE–E–SE
	⚓	*Plage de Palombaggia (Anse d'Acciajo)*	NE–E–SE–S–SW
Pointe Cerbicale (Caja Cavallu) Iles Cerbicales			
	⚓	*Anse de Carataggio (Piccovaggio)*	NE–E–SE–S
	⚓	*Baie de Bona Matina*	E–SE–S

Distances (left margin): 26M, 6M, 6M, 20M

Pointe de la Chiappa		
Roches de Chiappino and beacon		
	3·20 Port de Porto Vecchio 2–2–3 page 203	NE
	Roches de Pecorella and beacon	
Pointe d'Araso (Punta d'Arasu)		
Pointe Capicciola	⚓ *Pointe Capicciola W*	E–SE–S
	Ile de Pinarellu	
	⚓ *Anse de Cola*	E–SE–S
	⚓ *Golfe de Pinarellu*	NE–E–SE–S
	⚓ *Pointe de Fautéa SW*	E–SE–S
Ile et Pointe de Fautéa	⚓ *Anse de Fautea*	NE–E–SE
	⚓ *Anse de Tarco (Tarcu)*	NE–E–SE
	⚓ *Anse de Favone*	N–NE–E
	⚓ *Anse de Tanone*	NE–E–SE
	⚓ *Anse de Cannella*	NE–E–SE
	⚓ *Marine de Cala d'Oro*	NE–E–SE
	⚓ *Marine de Manichino (Marine de Manichinu)*	NE–E–SE
	3·21 Port de Solenzara 2–2–2 page 214	E–SE
La Rivière Solenzara		
Aérodrome de Solenzara		
Offshore fuel terminal–Solenzara		
Foce di u Fium Orbu (mouth of the river Fium Orbu) and wreck		
Etang d'Urbino		
Foce de Tavignano Fleuve (mouth of river Tavignano)		
Port Etang de Diane		
Champ de Tir de Diane (firing range)		
Phare d'Alistro (lighthouse)		
	3·22 Port de Campoloro 3–2–3 page 220	NE–E
Résidence des Iles, Dome and Aero RC beacon		
Foce di Fium Altu (mouth of river Fium Altu)		
Foce di Ciavattone (mouth of river Le Golu and L'Olmi)		
'Lucciana Offshore' fuel terminal-Aérodrome de Bastia-Poretta		
Punta di Arcu		
	⚓ *Punta di Arcu N*	N–NE–E–SE
Offshore fuel terminal-Bastia		
	⚓ *Anse de Porto Vecchio*	NE–S–SE–S
	3·1 Ports de Bastia 1–2–2 page 45	NE

19M

31M

22M

Pilotage
Section A – Bastia to St Florent

The coast

This section is probably unique in that it is in effect a peninsula 20M long by only 5M wide lying in a N–S direction with a high mountain range as its backbone reaching to 1305m (4280ft) at its highest point. There are several natural harbours and many anchorages in the bays and creeks around the peninsula. The coast is of steep rocky cliffs sloping sharply up to the mountains behind. At the heads of the many bays and estuaries lie beaches, most of which are of stone and sand. The coast is steep-to and except for the Ile Finocchiarola, and a shallow area just to NW of it and the large Ile de la Giraglia, there are no off-lying dangers. In general the W side is more rugged than the E and the slope of the hills much steeper.

A *corniche*-type road follows the coast around the peninsula and there are several roads that cross the mountains. There are no towns and only a few small villages in this area and between these villages the country is almost deserted.

Particular attention should be paid to the dangers of the SW *lebeccio* which causes heavy gusts of wind to sweep down the valleys even when strong onshore winds are blowing.

Winds from an E *levante* direction bring in heavy seas and they make all anchorages dangerous. Entrance to ports and harbours become difficult.

3·1 Ports de Bastia
20200 Haute Corse

Vieux Port
Position 42°41'·73N 9°27'·28E
Minimum depth   in the entrance 10m (33ft)
                                 in the harbour 7·1 to 1m (23 to 3ft)
Width of the entrance 85m (279ft)
Number of berths 250 (1991)
Maximum length overall 25m (82ft)

Port St Nicolas
Position 42°41'·82N 9°27'·40N
Minimum depth   in the entrance 25m (82ft)
                                 in the harbour 12 to 4m (39 to 13·1ft)
Width of the entrance 400m (1312ft)
Number of berths None
Maximum length overall Unlimited

Port Toga
Position 42°42'·54N 9°27'·48E
Minimum depth   in the entrance 6m (20ft)
                                 in the harbour 6 to 2m (20 to 6·6ft)
Width of the entrance 50m (164ft)
Number of berths 411
Maximum length overall 25m (82ft)

Population 50,622
Rating 1–2–2

General

Bastia has three ports, the delightful picturesque old fishing harbour, the Vieux Port at the S end of the town which has good facilities but only limited space for yachts and becomes very crowded in the season. The commercial and ferry harbour, Port St Nicolas which is in the centre and should only be used by yachts with prior permission or in the event of an emergency. The modern yacht harbour Port Toga, with 411 berths, is at the N of the town and will have all facilities★. The attractive old town surrounds the port in the true Mediterranean style. Approach and entrance are easy and protection is offered once inside though heavy swell from the NE–E makes the port very uncomfortable and sometimes untenable. The town, which is the largest in La Corse, has very smart and excellent shops which can supply most requirements. Port Saint Nicolas, the commercial port to N and the airfield to S provide excellent communications for the exchange of crews. A road tunnel passes under the harbour.

Note
★In 1990 the harbour had been completed but the *Bureau de Port* was blown up and it has not opened for use since.

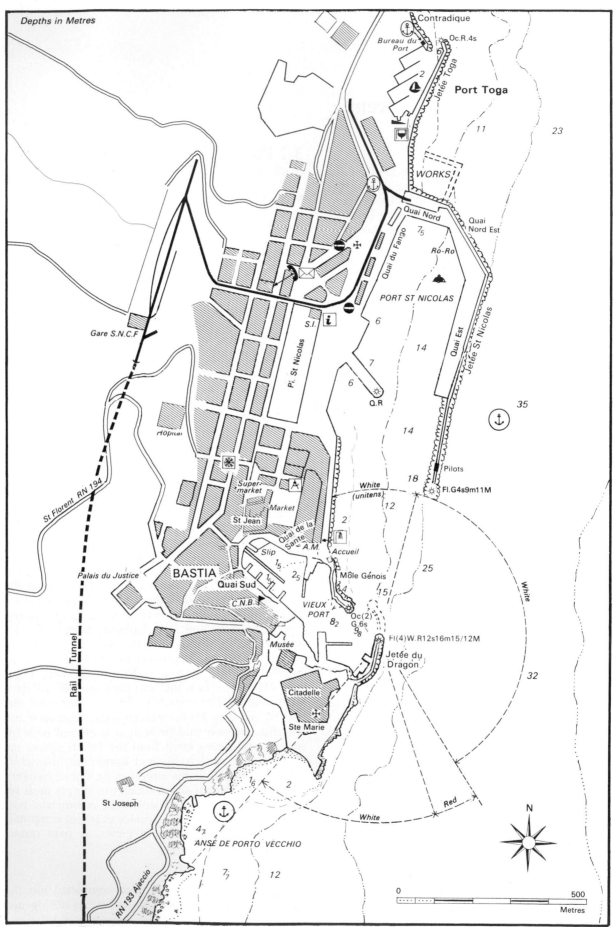

Depths in Metres

Contradique

Bureau du Port

Oc.R.4s

Port Toga

Jetée Toga

11

23

WORKS

Quai Nord

Quai Nord Est

7,5

Ro-Ro

PORT ST NICOLAS

Quai du Fango

Quai Est

Jetée St Nicolas

6

14

7

6

S.I.

Pl. St Nicolas

Q.R

14

35

Gare S.N.C.F

18

Pilots

Fl.G4s9m11M

Hôpital

White
(unitens)

12

2

St Florent RN 194

Super-
market

Market

St Jean

Quai de la
Sante

A.M.

Accueil

25

Palais du Justice

Slip

1,5

2,5

Môle Génois

15

White

BASTIA

Quai Sud

1,7

3,4

C.N.B.

VIEUX
PORT

Oc(2)
G.6s

8,2

9,8

Fl(4)W.R12s16m15/12M

32

Rail   Tunnel

Musée

Jetée du
Dragon

Citadelle

Ste Marie

1,6

2

St Joseph

Red

4,7

White

N

ANSE DE PORTO VECCHIO

RN 193 Ajaccio

7,7

12

0   500

Metres

Bastia and Port Toga

Data

Charts
Admiralty *1425, 1999*
French *6822, 6823, 6856*
ECM *1006*

Magnetic variation
0°05′W (1990) decreasing by 7′ each year.

Air radiobeacon
Bastia/Poretta (42°25′·7N 9°32′·2E) BP(····/····) 369 kHz 50M. Continuous.

Port radio
VHF Channel 16 and 9 (French). Pilots (☎ 31 07 15)

Weather forecasts
Posted at the *Bureau de Port* in Vieux Port daily or ☎ 95 36 04 96 for a recorded forecast (French).

Speed limit
4 knots.

Lights
Jetée du Dragon head Fl(4)WR.12s16m15/12M Grey tower, red lantern. 040°-W-130°-W (intens)-136°-W-328°-R-342°-W-040°.
Môle Génois head Oc(2)G.6s13m8M Light grey tower, dark green top. 045°-vis-135°.
Jetée Saint Nicolas head Fl.G.4s9m11M White tower, dark green band and lantern.
Car ferry berth head QR.2m7M White tower, red top. 167°-vis-077°.
TV tower Pigno 2·45M to west F.Rs.

Warning
If there is a strong gale from NE–E it may be necessary to seek shelter in the Port Saint Nicolas due to the swell. Heavy gusts of wind can also be experienced when the wind is blowing from the SW *libeccio* direction. If an anchor has to be used in the Vieux Port it is essential to use an anchor tripping line because the bottom is foul. Pay attention to rocks at the foot of quays. Commercial craft and ferries have right of way in the area and must not be obstructed.

Restricted areas
An area to N of Bastia between the Tour de Miomo and Port Toga extending 1·5M seawards is a nature reserve. Fishing, sub-aqua diving and anchoring is forbidden within this area. See plan page 52.

Approach by day
From S The coast is low flat and sandy with only a few recognisable features. The building with a large white dome and some other large buildings near the mouth of the Fiume Alto where there are some training walls, can be identified as can the *Lucciana* E cardinal light buoy BYB ♦ topmark (VQ(3)5s) which is located outside a series of mooring buoys at the oil pipe terminal for the airport. There are some black painted tanks on shore here. The houses of Bastia

Bastia. Approach looking SW

will be seen from afar and in the closer approach the walled Citadelle which has a tall square church tower rising above the buildings. The harbour is just to N of this Citadelle. The red and white TV tower on Pigno (961m) 2·5M to W of Bastia (F.Rs) is conspicuous as are the ferries if in harbour.
From N From Macinaggio to S the coast is of rocky cliffs with many small indentations and bays mostly with sandy beaches. The following may be recognised:
The breakwater at Luri, the village of Porticciolo which has two small breakwaters, Sisco village which has a training wall at the mouth of a river and a statue ¼M to N standing on the cliff by a convent. The tower and village of Erbalunga with a small harbour is unmistakable. The TV tower (see above) is also conspicuous from this direction.
The houses of Bastia will be seen from afar and in the closer approach the Jetée St Nicolas will be seen usually with ferry ships behind it.

Approach by night
The following lights allow a night approach though in the close approach only the lights from Bastia will be seen:
Cap Corse. Ile de Giraglia Fl.W.5s85m28M White tower, black top, 057°-vis-314°. RC signal station.
Macinaggio. Jetée Est head Oc(2)WR.6s10m12/9M White tower, red top, 120°-R-218°-W-331°-R-000°-R (unintens)-120°.
Radio tower F.Rs, 2·45M to west of Bastia.
Alistro Fl(2)W.10s93m22M Grey 8-sided tower, red house, black lantern.

Anchorage in the approach
A deep anchorage in 30m sand and mud off the Jetée St Nicolas and shallow anchorages in the Anse de Porto Vecchio 300m to SSW of the Citadelle in 5m sand.

Bastia. Vieux Port looking W (1990)

Head of Jetée du Dragon   *Head of Môle Génois*

Bastia. Entrance to Vieux Port looking SW

Entrance

By day Approach the entrance on a W–SW course and enter between the head of Jetée du Dragon to port and the head of the Môle Génois to starboard. Do not obstruct commercial vessels entering and leaving Port St Nicolas which lies to the N of the Vieux Port.

By night Approach Fl(4)WR.12s on a W–SW course in the white sector. Leave it 20m to port and then Oc(2)G.6s 20m to starboard. The many lights along the shore are confusing at night.

Berths

Secure stern-to the inner side of the Môle Génois with bow-to mooring buoy. The seaward end has rocky feet. If there is no space here, secure stern-to the Jetée du Dragon with anchor and tripline from the bow in good weather only. Note that the rocky feet of this jetty extends some distance under water. If both of these berths are full then a berth can sometimes be found in the Port Saint Nicolas on the E or NE side. Check with the *Bureau de Port* that commercial vessels will not want to use this berth. Anchorage is not permitted near harbour works. If the E *libeccio* is blowing try to get a berth as near the root of the Môle Génois as possible.

Formalities

Report on arrival to the *Bureau de Port* ☎ 95 31 31 10 if secured in the Vieux Port, open in summer 0800–1200 and 1600–2000, in winter 0800–1200 and 1400–1800, or to the *Bureau de Port de Commerce* 0800–2000 if in Saint Nicolas. The *Affaires Maritimes* ☎ 95 31 67 08 and 95 31 62 24 is located on the N side of the Vieux Port and customs ☎ 95 31 07 31 to NW of Port Saint Nicolas.

Bureau de Port   *Port St Nicolas*   *Jetée du Dragon*

Bastia. Vieux Port looking NE

Bastia. Port St Nicolas looking SW

Charges

There are harbour charges.

Facilities

Slip There is a slip at the NW end of the Vieux Port.
Slipway A 40-tonne slipway is at the NW corner of the Vieux Port.
Crane A 5-tonne mobile crane available.
Fuel Diesel (*gasoil*) is only delivered by bowser lorry.
Water Water points on the Môle Génois.
Ice Available in season also from Bar Pigalle.
Electricity Points for 220V and 380V AC on Môle Génois.
Provisions Many shops of all types including supermarkets and an excellent daily market near the Vieux Port.
Garbage A few drums for rubbish on the quay.
Chandlery A shop to the N of the harbour and others in the town and on its outskirts.
Repairs Repairs to hull and engines possible, also electricians and electronic experts.

Laundrettes Several in the town.
Post office The PTT is located to the W of Port Saint Nicolas.
Hotels Three ***, seven **, six * hotels and eight unclassified.
Restaurants Very many restaurants to suit all tastes also many café/bars.
Yacht club The Club Nautique Bastias (CNB) (☎ 95 31 27 18) is a dinghy club and has its clubhouse on the NW side of the harbour in a shed.
Showers In the *Bureau de Port* open 0800–2000 hours, there are 7 WCs and 4 showers.
Information office The Syndicat d'Initiative (☎ 95 31 81 34 and 95 31 99 89) has an office at the E side of Place St Nicolas to the N of this port.
Lifeboat An all weather and an inshore rescue craft kept here.
Medical Hospital, doctors and dentists.
Visits The Citadelle and the many old churches in the town are worth visiting as is the Ethnographic and Sea Museum; details from the information bureau.
Beaches Rather poor beaches to N and S of the harbour.

Communications Bus and rail services. Air services from the airport 14M to S and from Paris, Marseille and Nice. Ferry service to Marseille, Nice, Genoa, Livorno and Sardinia. Hydrofoil to Elba and Italy.

Festivals 19th March, 24th June, 9th September. Religious procession.

Future development

Plans exist for the reconstruction of the Vieux Port to provide 200 to 300 extra berths but they are still to be implemented (1990).

History

The old fishing village of Cardo was established here from time immemorial but fame did not reach it until 1380 when the Genoese, Leonelle Lomellino, built a *donjoh* on the promontory overlooking the harbour. A fortress in Italian is *bastia* or *bastiglia* hence the new name for the village. The Genoese soon installed governors who, by 1480, had erected the Citadelle walls. Between 1570 and 1801, Bastia was the seat of the Bishops of Mariana and Accia who subsequently moved to Ajaccio.

For a long time Bastia was the capital of the island and as such the town and surrounding countryside prospered.

In 1794 Napoleon Bonaparte fleeing his enemies, embarked for France from this port to commence his historic career. In the same year the British, after two attacks, finally captured the town, but in 1796 Nelson, on orders from London, evacuated the British forces to Elba.

During the second world war, in 1942 the Italian troops landed here but after the Italian capitulation they joined the Corsican Resistance and in 1943 helped to liberate the town from the Germans.

In more recent times the surrounding countryside has become deserted and poverty-stricken whilst Bastia has remained relatively prosperous by virtue of her commerce and, latterly, the tourist trade.

3·2 Port Toga

Position 42°42'·54N 9°27'·48E
Minimum depth   in the entrance 6m (20ft)
                        in the harbour 6 to 2m (20 to 6·6ft)
Width of the entrance 50m (164ft)
Number of berths 411
Maximum length overall 25m (82ft)
Population 50,622
Rating 1–2–2

General

It would appear that this new yacht harbour will remain closed until the various legal matters have been solved. The harbourmaster's office is being rebuilt.

Data, Warnings, Approach See 3·1 Ports de Bastia page 45.

Lights
Port Toga, digue head Oc.R.4s10m5M

Entrance by day

From N Follow the coast at 200m and in the close approach the harbour mouth will open up. Enter between a squat light tower, red top to port and a building (ruins) to starboard.

From S Pass the entrance to the Vieux Port and the Port St Nicolas then follow the Jetée St Nicolas at 100m continuing outside its extension, the Jetée Toga. Round its head at 20m leaving it to port and into the harbour.

Head of Jetée du Toga   Ruins of Bureau de Port

Bastia. Port Toga entrance looking SW

Approach by night

Not advised because at the moment there are no harbour lights.

Berths

Secure alongside the inner side of the *contradigue* or in a vacant berth.

Formalities

Report to the *Bureau de Port* (☎ 95 31 51 37) with the ships papers. Customs and *Affaires Maritimes* to be established.

Bastia. Port Toga looking SW

Charges

Harbour charges will be made.

Facilities

See also page 49.
Slip At S corner of the harbour.
Travel-lift dock At S corner of the harbour. Lift to be provided.
Crane Mobile crane of 20 tonnes.
Fuel Pumps to be provided.
Water Taps on all pontoons and quays.
Electricity Points for 220v AC and 380v AC.
Provisions Many shops less than ½M away.
Ice From local bars.
Garbage Rubbish sacks at roots of pontoons.

Future development

Many facilities which are planned have still to be installed when the harbour is opened.

Pointe Grisgione

A very inconspicuous point which only shows when coasting close inshore. The point slopes up to 279m inland. Rocks inshore. Coast road.

⌁ **Marine de Miomo**

An anchorage open to NE–E–SE with two stony beaches, conspicuous tower and road bridge over river. A *** hotel and one unclassified, cafés, restaurants, and some shops. Deep valley behind the village. Anchor in 3m shingle, avoid rocks near the tower.

Pointe de la Vasina

Small point sloping up to 132m with low rocky cliffs at foot. Coast road.

⌁ **Marine de la Vasina**

A smallish anchorage open to NE–E–SE with shingle beach. A conspicuous church tower with statue on top behind a small village. A deep valley runs inland. Anchor in 3m shingle.

⌁ **Marine de Erbalunga**

A pleasant anchorage just to S of the most attractive little harbour of Erbalunga. Open to NE–E–SE. Some inshore rocks, small rocky beach. Anchor in 3 to 4m shingle and sand. Supplies from the small village.

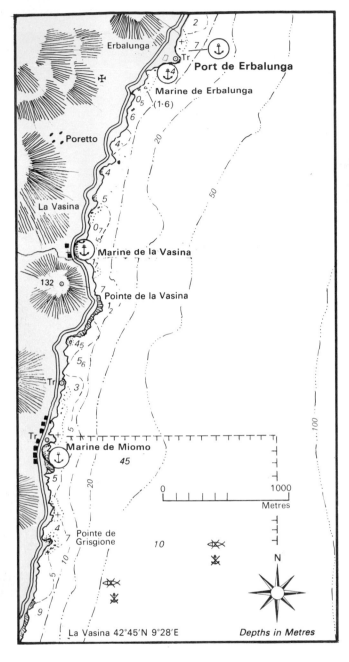

La Vasina 42°45′N 9°28′E

Depths in Metres

Port de Erbalunga

A beautiful little harbour for small fishing boats and dinghies drawing less than 1·5m. 23 berths for local boats. Open to E. A useful landing place for yachts' tenders. A shingle hard and concrete slip at W end of the harbour. Cafés and restaurants, an unclassified hotel, some shops and an engineer. The ruined tower at the entrance can be seen from afar.

Ruined to

⚓ Marine de Erbalunga looking NW

⚓ Erbalunga N

Similar to the anchorage S of the Port de Erbalunga except that there are two offshore rocks, to avoid them anchor in 6m shingle, sand and weed and locate the rocks by dinghy. Shingle beach. Open to NE–E–SE.

Ruined tower

⚓ Erbalunga N looking SW

Tower

⚓ Marine de Miomo looking SW

Cap Sagro

A headland with conspicuous signal station on top, rocky cliffs and coast road at bottom. Light: Fl(3)W.12s10M.

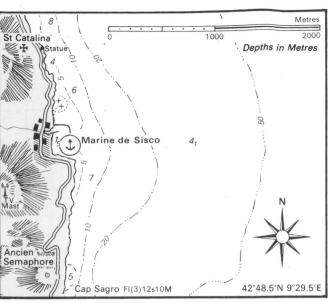

Marine de Sisco

⚓ Cap Sagro signal station and light tower looking SW

⚓ Marine de Sisco

A wide open bay with a wide deep valley, a few houses around it and a small boat harbour at the mouth of the river for craft drawing less than 1m. Anchor off the harbour in 3m sand. The bay is open to NE–E–SE and entrance to the harbour is not possible in strong E winds. There is a slip and hard in the harbour, a 3-tonne crane, water point, petrol pump and the Club Nautique de Sisco (CNS) (☎ 95 35 21 09) which has showers at the clubhouse. A motor mechanic, a garage, some shops, an un-classified hotel and a beach of shingle. Conspicuous TV tower to S.

Ancien Convent de Ste Catalina

Has a statue close to the rocky cliffs with a large church behind it, which has a tower like a clover leaf.

⚓ Marine de Sisco

River mouth

⚓ Marine de Sisco

53

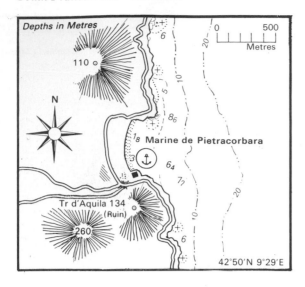

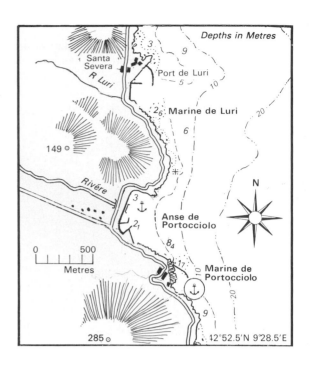

⚓ **Marine de Pietracorbara**

A wide bay with the road running behind the sand and stone beach and a few houses scattered around. One * hotel and a restaurant in the small village. Anchor near the moorings at the S side of the bay in 3m sand and shingle. Open to NE–E–SE. The village has a small jetty where landing is possible. A few dinghies are kept in the river mouth in the S side of the bay. The river has a training wall. A ruined square fort Tour d'Aquila on top of a peaked hill (134m) to S of this area is conspicuous.

⚓ **Marine de Portocciolo**

A very small fishing harbour and anchorage open to NE–E–SE with a T-shaped breakwater. Anchor off in 4m stone and sand. Village has a *** hotel, small shingle beach at head of cove with the coast road behind.

Rivière

⚓ Marine de Pietracorbara looking SW–W–NW

Punta di Ghiunchi

A small headland rising up to 214m with rocky cliffs and coast road at the bottom. The tower Losse lies ½M to N close to the coast.

Harbour

⚓ Marine de Portocciolo looking W. Note. Dredger in the harbour

⚓ **Anse de Portocciolo**

A large bay open to NE–E–SE with a small harbour for a few boats drawing less than 1·5m in the S corner where there is the mouth of a river. Anchor in 3m sand. Sandy beaches, conspicuous church and tower inland on a hill.

54

Harbour entrance

⚓ Anse de Portocciolo looking W

Harbour

⚓ Anse de Portocciolo

⚓ Port de Luri looking SW

⚓ Marine de Luri (Santa Severa)

A wide bay open to NE–E–SE with a sand stone and shingle beach and a conspicuous road bridge at its SW corner. Some housing development on the N side. The small village has cafés, a garage and some shops. A small harbour in the N corner of the bay (see below). Anchor in 3m sand.

Port de Luri

A harbour built for a limited number of small yachts and boats. With depths of 2 to 3m on the E side and shallow on the W side open to E–SE. The entrance is on the SW side, secure and report to the harbour officer for allocation of a berth. Fuel station on road nearby and mechanic. Slip on NW side of the harbour.

⚓ Anse de Alessandro

A wide bay open to NE–E–SE with the coast road running behind it, otherwise virtually deserted. A narrow stone and shingle beach. Some rocks off the centre and N parts of the beach. Anchor in 3m sand in the S half with care.

⚓ Marine de Meria

A small bay open to E–SE. Conspicuous tower on the N side of the bay. Coast road with some houses and a shop. Deep valley behind an old windmill just to N and village ½M inland. Anchor in 3 to 4m sand and rock.

Harbour entrance

⚓ Marine de Luri (Santa Severa) looking SW–W

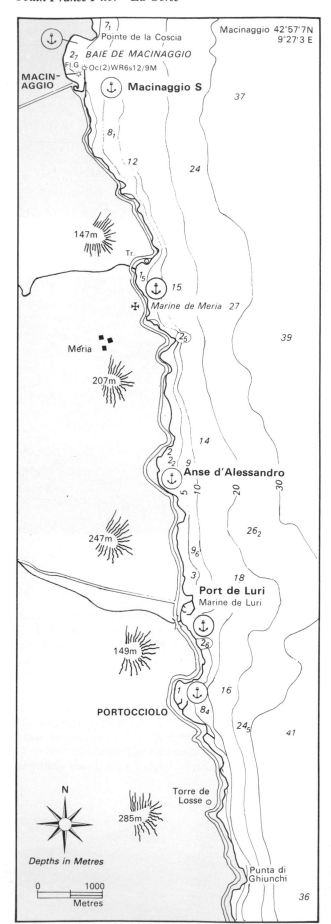

Macinaggio 42°57'7N
9°27'3 E

⚓ Marine de Meria looking SW

⚓ Macinaggio S

An open anchorage exposed to NE–E–SE. Anchor in 9m sand and weed 1000m to E of Macinaggio harbour or 200m E of the root of the breakwater in 2m sand.

Pointe de la ●

⚓ Baie de Macinaggio and Pointe de la Coscia looking W–NW

3·3 Port de Macinaggio

20248 Haute Corse

Position 42°57'·73N 9°27'·32E
Minimum depth in the entrance 3m (9·8ft)
in the harbour 3 to 1m (9·8 to 3·3ft)
Width of the entrance 35m (115ft)
Number of berths 500
Population 300 (approx)
Rating 2–3–3

General

This modern yacht harbour is based on an old fishing
harbour and it has managed to maintain much of the
attractiveness of the original. The surrounding area is
beautiful and the small village pleasant in an un-
sophisticated way but shows signs of tourist development. Approach and entry are easy but would be
hazardous in heavy seas from NE–E. Protection
within is good though a heavy swell from the NE–E
makes it uncomfortable. Facilities fair and everyday
requirements can be met. The harbour becomes very
crowded in the summer.

Data

Charts

Admiralty *1425,1999*
French *6822, 6850*
ECM *1006*

Magnetic variation

0°05'W (1990) decreasing by 7' each year.

Weather forecast

Posted twice a day at the *Bureau de Port*.

Speed limit

3 knots.

Port radio

VHF Ch 9 (French)

Lights

Jetée Est head Oc(2)WR.6s10m12/9M White tower, red
top. 120°-R-218°-W-331°-R-000°-R (unintens)-120°.
Epi Nord head Fl.G.2s4m2M. White tower, green top.

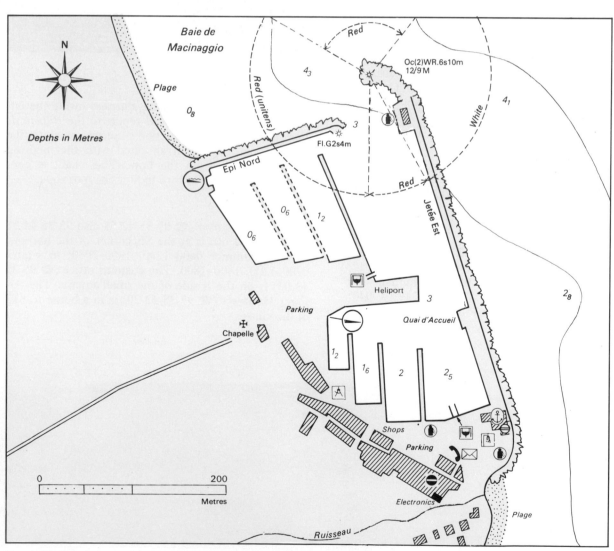

Port de Macinaggio

Buoy

E cardinal BYB light buoy topmark ⧫ Q(3)5s7M located ½M to NW of Iles Finocchiarola.

Warning

Heavy swell from the NE–E will break near the entrance and make it dangerous to enter. Heavy gusts of wind from SW sometimes occur. Depths in the harbour may be different to the plan due to periodic dredging.

Approach by day

From S From Bastia the coastline is broken by many small bays but it lacks any conspicuous landmarks. The houses, tower and small harbour at Erbalunga, the villages of Sisco and Portocciolo, both of which have training walls at the mouths of their rivers, and the small harbour at Luri may be identified. In the closer approach the village of Macinaggio will be seen but not until the bay opens up. A conspicuous radar and TV tower and dome are located 3M to W on the skyline.

From N Round Cap Corse either inside or outside the Ile de la Giraglia which is conspicuous and has a lighthouse and signal station on its top. Follow the coast round and in bad weather give it a 1·5M berth to avoid the Banc de Santa Maria (9·5m). Pass outside the light buoy listed above and round the Iles Finocchiarola which extend ½M from the coast and has a tower on the top of the outer island. The passes between it and the coast are only suitable for boats drawing less than 1m (3·3ft) in calm weather after careful reconnaissance in a dinghy. The houses of Macinaggio will be seen from here.

Approach by night

Using the following lights, the approach to the area may be made:

Cap Corse. Ile de Giraglia Fl.W.5s85m28M White tower, black top. 057°-vis-314°. RC, Signal station.

Saint Toricella radar tower F.R.

Bastia. Jetée du Dragon Fl(4)WR.12s16m15/12M Grey tower, red lantern. 040°-W(unintens)-130°-W-136°-W(unintens)-193°-W-328°-R-342°-W-040°.

Isola Capraia LFl.W.6s30m15M White square tower and house.

Entrance

By day Approach the head of the Jetée Est which has a conspicuous white light tower, red top, on a course between NW and SW and round it leaving it 20m to port onto a S course.

By night Approach Oc(2)WR.6s on course between NW and SW in the white sector. Divert in the close approach towards N into the red sector and round the light at 20m leaving it to port and onto a S course. Leave Fl.G.2s 20m to starboard.

Tower (old mill)

Macinaggio. Entrance looking S

Berths

On arrival secure to the *quai d'accueil* inside the entrance on the port hand and report to the *Bureau de Port* for berthing instructions. Secure stern-to the pontoon or quay berth allocated with the mooring chain (*pendillo*) from the bow. This chain is connected to the pontoon by a lighter chain or rope.

Formalities

The *Bureau de Port* (☎ 95 35 42 57 also 95 35 44 95 and 95 35 44 60) is at the SE corner of the harbour open in summer 0600–1200, 1300–2030, in winter 0700–1200, 1400–1800. The customs office (☎ 95 35 43 03) is on the S side of the small square. The *Affaires Maritimes* (☎ 95 35 43 20) is in a house to SW of the village.

Tower (old mill)   *Entrance*

Macinaggio. Approach looking SW

Macinaggio looking W

Bureau de Port

Macinaggio looking N–NE

Charges

There are harbour charges.

Facilities

Slip A slip in the NW corner of the harbour, 1·5m of water.

Travel-lift A travel-lift of 15 tonnes is available.

Fuel Petrol and diesel (*gasoil*) from pumps on the E side of the harbour just inside the harbour to port (☎ 95 35 43 94) and also from the service station on the S side of the harbour. Open summer 0600–2000, winter 0700–1900.

Water Water points on the pontoons and quays.

Electricity Outlets for 220v AC on the pontoons and quays.

Provisions Several shops in the village can supply all normal everyday requirements, a supermarket and more shops to W of the church.

Ice Ice is available in the season from two village shops.

Garbage Rubbish containers on the pontoons and quays.

Chandlery A shop in the village.

Repairs A mechanic is available in the season and there is a small yard. Electronic repairs possible.

Post office A small PTT to S side of the harbour.

Hotels Four unclassified hotels.

Restaurants Many restaurants in addition to the hotels, also many café/bars.

Showers Available at the *Bureau de Port*, 12 WCs and 12 showers.

Lifeboat A lifeboat is kept here.

Information office At *Bureau de Port* (☎ 95 35 42 57)

Visits The Archaeological Museum in the village and the old Chapelle Saint Marc may be visited. Rogliano 1.5M away is a village dating from Roman times and has many interesting ruins. Contact M. Lucien Saldani.

Beach A fine beach to N of the harbour.

Communications A bus service once a day.

Bureau de Port   Tower (old mill)

Macinaggio looking S–SW

Future development
Improvements are planned to the facilities including more pontoons. Some berths may be leased on a 10–35 year basis (a very rare situation).

History
The bay has been used as a small fishing shelter and landing place since Roman times and probably was in use many years before though no evidence of this has yet been found. The history of the harbour is however naturally connected with that of the village Rogliano (from the Roman *Ragus Aurelianus*) which it served. The area was ruled by the de Mare family whose Château-Fort San Colombano, built in the 12th century, was razed in 1553 by the Genoese. In 1571 a fleet of local ships joined the force that defeated the Turks at Lepanto and in 1767 Pascal Paoli's army embarked here to invade Capraja.

In 1790 Pascal Paoli returning from his exile in England landed at Macinaggio and is reported to have said '*O ma Patrie, je t'ai quitté enslave, je te retrouve libre.*'

In 1792 Napoleon Bonaparte, whilst fleeing from his enemies, left here for Bastia from whence he sailed to France to commence his historic career.

The only other event of consequence in past years was in 1869 when the ship carrying the Empress Eugenie on her way to open the Suez Canal encountered a SW *libeccio* gale and put in here for shelter. The new yacht harbour was commenced in 1971. This harbour is sometimes referred to as the 'right eye of Corsica' for obvious reasons.

⚓ Baie de Macinaggio
A wide bay with the Port of Macinaggio at the S end and the conspicuous Pointe de Coscia at the other. A long sandy beach stretches along the coast with gently sloping ground behind. Open to NE–E–SE. Anchor in 3m sand.

Pointe de la Coscia
A conspicuous pyramid-shaped point (60m) with a TV tower and the round stone base of an old windmill on top. The point is steep-to.

⚓ Pointe de la Coscia looking W

⚓ Baie de Tamarone
Another wide bay open to NE–E–SE with a long sandy beach and an open valley behind. There are rocks lying 100m offshore at either end. A long, low white house (farm) inland and a track to the beach but otherwise deserted. Anchor in 4 to 5m sand in the NW corner.

⚓ Iles Finocchiarola S
A semi open anchorage in a bay to S of the Iles Finocchiarola open to E–SE. A sandy beach with a track inland surrounded by deserted low rolling hills. Anchor in 3 to 5m sand in NW corner.

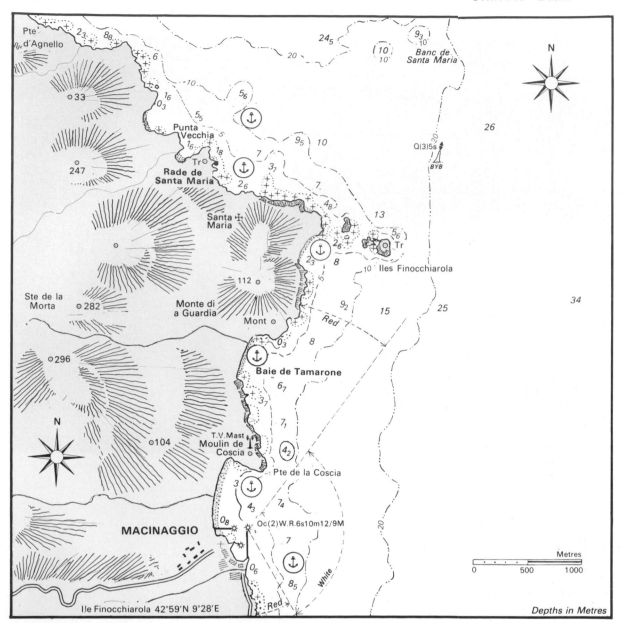

Ile Finocchiarola 42°59'N 9°28'E

Depths in Metres

Farm

⚓ Baie de Tamarone looking W

Iles Finocchiarola and passages

There are three rocky islands with some islets and rocky heads extending 700m offshore. These islands are a nature reserve and landings not permitted. The outer island (27m) is the largest and has a conspicuous ruined tower and small hut. The middle island (12m) is separated from the outer island by a narrow gap partially blocked by two rocks and a wreck of a small coaster. The inner island (5m) is of irregular shape and has many rocks to SE–S–SW including a small islet, there are also rocks along the Corsican coast.

The outer and inner passages can only be used by small dinghies drawing less than 1m with care and in calm conditions. The centre passage has a minimum depth of 1.5m and can be used in calm conditions after a preliminary reconnaissance in a dinghy.

Tower   Anchorage

⚓ Iles Finocchiarola looking W

⚓ Iles Finocchiarola S looking NW

⚓ Iles Finocchiarola looking S

⚓ **Rade de Santa Maria**

A wide open bay with a conspicuous ruined tower on its NW point and Chapelle Ste Maria standing inland. Open to NW–N–NE–E. Several shingle beaches with rocks between. Track to beach otherwise deserted. Anchor in 4m rock and sand in the centre of the bay, paying attention to offlying rocks to SE. Another anchorage is available in 10m sand and weed 350m NNE of the tower.

Punta de Santa Maria

A low flat rocky point sloping up inland, a conspicuous tower stands on the SE spur.

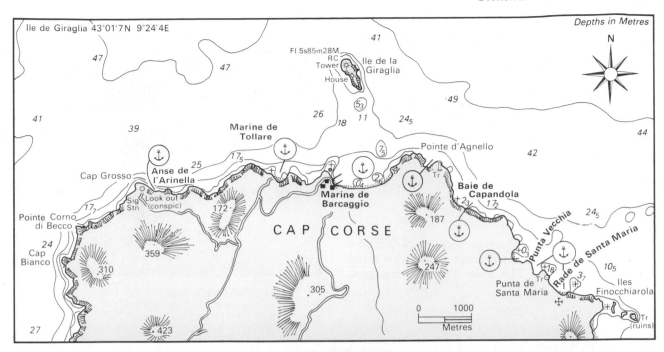

⚓ Rade Santa Maria looking SE

⚓ Punta Vecchia SE

Two small sandy beaches with a large rocky promontory between them, anchor off either beach in 3m sand open to NW–N–NE–E. A track ashore, deserted.

Punta Vecchia

A low rocky-cliffed point with shingle beaches either side.

⚓ Punta Vecchia NW

A bay open to NW–N–NE–E with an isolated 0·6m deep rock in the centre. Deserted shingle beach. Approach the head of the bay with care avoiding the rock mentioned above which usually has breaking seas over it. Anchor in 3m rock and stone.

⚓ Punta Vecchia

63

Baie de Capandola

A large bay open to N–NE–E with rocky cliffs and rocks close inshore. Anchor in 3m sand near middle of the bay, hilly inland, deserted.

Pointe d'Agnello

A conspicuous promontory of green-grey rocks in two parts, it has a ruined tower on its NE point. The land behind the point is round and high (141m). Rocky dangers extend 100m towards NE. The point is split into two parts by a narrow creek. The NW part of the promontory is lower with whitish coloured cliffs.

⚓ Pointe d'Agnello NW

An attractive small anchorage open to N–NE and deserted, it has three small coves with rocky sides. Anchor in 4m sand. The Tour d'Agnello is a good landmark.

Tower

⚓ Pointe d'Agnello NW looking SW

Tower   *Entrance to* ⚓

Pointe d'Agnello looking SE–E

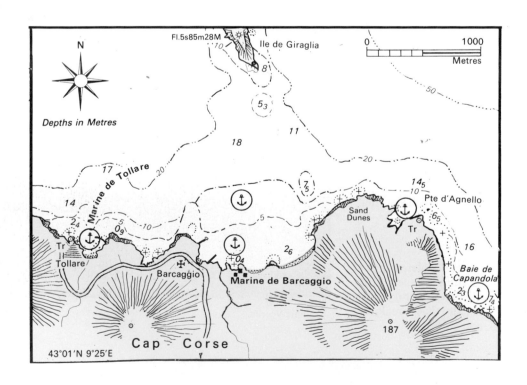

⚓ Marine de Barcaggio looking S

⚓ Marine de Barcaggio

A large bay open to NW–N–NE with a small harbour for fishing boats and dinghies in the W corner where there is a small fishing village with church, shop and road inland. A long sand and shingle beach divided by a group of rocks often used by nudists. Anchor in 3m sand to N of the harbour. A deep water (16m) anchorage is available 300m to N of the village in sand and weed.

Ile de la Giraglia

1M to N of Barcaggio lies the Ile de la Giraglia which is 1200m long, 300m wide and 65m high with whitish rocky cliffs. There is an old square stone fort at the NW end of the island with a white lighthouse tower black top (22m) alongside (Fl.W.5s85m28M) a low flat white house is near the centre of the island. There are landings on the NE side of the island where there is a small hut and a road cut out of the rock.

Marine de Tollare

A narrow V-shaped bay open to NW–N–NE with a sand and shingle beach at its head. On its W side is a small fishing village which has a shallow harbour for fishing boats and dinghies. A very conspicuous tower stands at the head of the E breakwater. Anchor in 3m sand and rock near the centre of the beach. A shop and café also a road inland. A deep water anchorage lies 350m to N of the tower in 15m sand and weed.

⚓ Marine de Tollare looking SE

Harbour entrance

⚓ Marine de Tollare looking S

Ile de la Giraglia looking NE

Cap Corse

This is the general term for the whole of the N section of Haute-Corse and it covers the coast from Iles Finocchiarola to Cap Bianco including the Ile de la Giraglia.

Cap Corse looking NE showing Cap Bianco (white rocks) to Pointe d'Agnello (white low cliffs) and Ile de la Giraglia

⚓ Anse de l'Arinella

A small V-shaped bay with a stony beach at its head. High sloping hills surround it. Open to NW–N–NE. Anchor in 3m rock near its head. Deserted.

Cap Grosso

A pointed headland with a conspicuous signal station on its top. Steep cliffs and one small rock close into the point otherwise steep-to. The land slopes up to 364m inland.

Pointe Corno di Becco

A similar headland to the above sloping more steeply up to 300m. This point has a beak-like profile and it is steep-to.

Cap Bianco

A black rocky-cliffed headland with one close inshore rock otherwise steep-to.

Cap Bianco (white rock), Pointe Corno di Becco (beak), Cap Grosso (signal station) and Ile de de la Giraglia looking SW

3·4 Port de Centuri

20238 Haute Corse

Position 42°58'·70N 9°20'·98E
Minimum depth in the entrance 4m (13ft)
in the harbour 4 to 1m (13 to 3·3ft)
Width of the entrance 30m (98ft)
Maximum length overall 7m (22ft) (approx)
Number of berths 170 but only 10 for yachts
Population 275
Rating 1–4–4

General

A most beautiful old fishing harbour and village but very small and really only suitable for small shallow draught yachts and dinghies. Care is needed in the approach and entrance which are impossible in strong winds from N–NW–W–SW. Protection is only possible in the shallow inner harbour. Facilities are limited and the area can become very crowded in the season.

Data

Charts

Admiralty *1999*
French *6969, 6850*
ECM *1006*

Magnetic variation

0°05'W (1990) decreasing by 7' each year.

Beacons

A R pole beacon cylinder topmark is located 50m to N of the jetty and marks an isolated rock.

Weather forecasts

Pre-recorded forecast (French) (☎ 95 65 01 35).

Warning

A rocky shallow (0·4m) lies 200m to NNW of the tip of Ile de Capense and is unmarked. The head of the jetty has been washed away and there is foul ground at its foot. The harbour is slowly silting up.

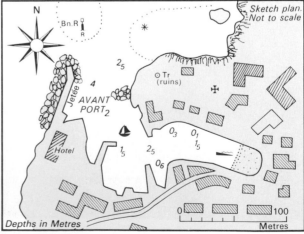

Port de Centuri

Entrance

Centuri. Approach looking E–SE

Approach by day

From N Round Cap Corse either inside or outside the Ile de la Giraglia which has a conspicuous lighthouse and signal station on its summit. Follow the coast around the high steep-to headlands of Cap Grosso, Pointe Corno di Becco and Cap Bianco. The Baie de Centuri will open up and the pyramid-shaped Ile Capense will be seen. A conspicuous radar dome and tower lies 1¾M inland. In the closer approach the houses of the village will be seen. A low dark tower and a large house stand behind the entrance.

From S Follow the high broken coast from Saint Florent to N, the village of Nonza on a saddle, the white cliffs and factory at Albo are easily recognised. The headlands of Pointe de Canelle and Minerbio show up if coasting close in. The Ile de Capense will be seen in the closer approach. Round this island outside the shallow patch that lies 200m to NNW and approach the group of houses that lie ESE. The entrance lies by a dark squat tower and a large house.

Approach by night

Due to the lack of suitable navigational lights and offlying dangers a night approach and entrance are not advised.

Anchorage in the approach

There is no secure anchorage nearby, the bottom is rock and weed. However in fair and settled weather it is possible to anchor between the Ile de Capense and the entrance to the harbour in 5m rock and weed, poor holding. A more secure deep water anchorage in 19m shell and weed is 500m to N of the island. Both anchorages should be vacated should the weather deteriorate. Alternative anchorages lie to SE of the Ile de Capense in the Marine de Morsiglia, 2m rock and weed.

Entrance

By day Approach the head of the jetty at slow speed with care on an ESE course and round it at 15m leaving a R beacon to port. Enter the Avant Port in mid-channel.

Beacon   Tower   *Jetée*

Centuri. Close approach and entrance

Beacon   Tower

Centuri. Entrance

Berths

Unless drawing less than 1m secure the stern-to a suitable bollard ashore in the Avant Port with an anchor from the bow or vice-versa. Leave a route for fishing craft to enter and leave the harbour. It may be necessary to leave crew in board to slip securing lines as and when necessary to allow fishing craft to pass. At night an anchor light will be necessary. Should the weather deteriorate this Avant Port must be left and shelter found elsewhere. Smaller craft will be able to find a berth in the inner harbour with stern-to the quay and anchor from the bow but be careful not to occupy a berth belonging to a fisherman still at sea.

Formalities

The *capitaine du port* will visit yachts. *Mairie* (☎ 95 35 66 06).

Charges

There are harbour charges.

Facilities

Hard and slip The head of the harbour consists of a shallow sandy hard with a concrete slip alongside.
Fuel Petrol and diesel *(gasoil)* pumps at the S side of Avant Port.
Water Available by arrangement. Contact official.
Provisions Several small shops provide everyday requirements.
Post office Small PTT.
Hotels One ★ hotel and two unclassified.
Restaurants Several and some café/bars.
Medical Doctor available.
Visits Beautiful coastal walks. The *village perche* of Cannelle on the hill ½M inland is very old and worth visiting.
Beaches Some small beaches to S.

Future development

Plans to dredge the harbour exist.

History

This harbour was built as a private venture in the 18th century to help the local fishermen to catch *langoustes* and anchovies. There was then deep water right into the inner harbour. This fishing industry was successful but in recent years the tourist industry has been taking over.

Centuri. Inside harbour looking E

⚓ Baie de Centuri

A large bay open to W–NW–N with Port de Centuri in the SE corner and the Ile de Capense in the SW corner. Anchor in S part in 5m rock and sand, the holding is not good. A deep water anchorage lies 500m to N of the island in 16m shell and weed, this mooring is rather exposed and the holding is only fair.

Ile de Capense

An island 300m by 200m which is 43m high. It has foul ground to E and to NW extending to 200m. A dangerous unmarked rock covered 0·4m lies 200m N from the island.

Centuri

Ile de C

⚓ Baie de Centuri looking SE

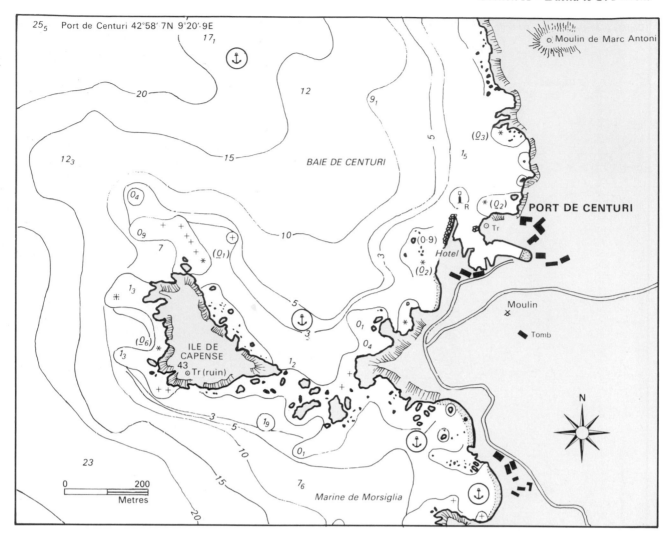

25_5 Port de Centuri 42°58'·7N 9°20'·9E

BAIE DE CENTURI

PORT DE CENTURI

Hotel

ILE DE CAPENSE
43
◦ Tr (ruin)

Moulin

• Tomb

N

0   200
Metres

Marine de Morsiglia

Ile de Capense   *Centuri*

⚓ **Marine de Morsiglia N**

A fair weather anchorage off a stony beach in a small
bay, offlying rocks, open to SW–W–NW. It lies
about 200m to N of the village of Mute. Anchor with
care in 3m rock and weed near to the centre of the
bay between a group of four islets and a single islet.
Road ashore.

Marine de Morsiglia S

A more open bay than that described above with the
rocks confined to the sides, open to the SW–W–NW.
A small group of houses ashore behind a stony beach
and a road. Anchor in 3m rock, stone and weed near
the centre of the bay.

⚓ Marine de Morsiglia looking NE

69

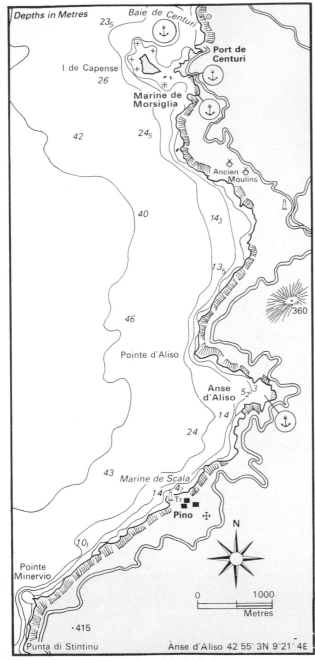

Pointe d'Aliso

A steep-to rocky-cliffed point sloping up steeply to 404m. The coast road follows the contours around the point.

⚓ Anse d'Aliso (Golfu Alisu)

A deep bay surrounded by low rocky cliffs with a sandy beach at its head above which is the coast road. Open to SW–W–NW. Anchor in the middle of the bay in 6m sand. There are rocky patches further in. The bay is deserted except for the traffic on the road and a lone house on the N side of the bay.

⚓ Anse d'Aliso looking E

Pino landing

A small fishing hamlet around a small creek where fishing boats and dinghies can be hauled ashore over a shingle beach. A small quay with 1m alongside. Road to the coast road and on to Pino village which is worth visiting. A conspicuous ruined tower stands just to the S of the hamlet.

⚓ Marine de Morsiglia S looking E

Pino landing looking E

Pointe Minervio

A conspicuous tree covered headland sheer-to with rocky cliffs and coast road above. The land slopes up to 418m in a pyramid shape. Rocks extend 100m from the cliff 1000m to N of the point.

Marine de Giottani

A deep bay with white rocky cliffs and a rocky beach at its head where there is also a small fishing boat and dinghy harbour with two slips and a tower on the hill behind it. The bay is open to SW–W–NW. Anchor near the centre of the bay in 6m sand. A few houses and a restaurant stand behind the beach while the coast road runs further inland. There is a conspicuous church with a tall steeple up the valley behind, and a village further inland.

⚓ Marine de Giottani looking E

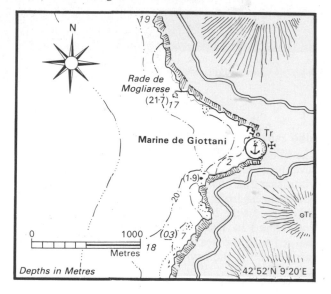

Canari landing

A small hamlet with a narrow slip where small fishing boats and dinghies can be hauled ashore. Track to coast road above. Use with care due to many rocks in the close approach. Dangers extend 350m seaward from Pointe de Scala.

Canari (Pointe de Scala) landing looking E

Pointe de Scala (Punta di a Scala)

A not very conspicuous point with land behind sloping up to Mount Cucearo (935m) 1½M inland. Rocky dangers extend 350m from the low-cliffed point. The coast road is above.

Pointe de Scala looking S

Pointe de Canelle (Punta di Canelle)

A more conspicuous point of whitish rock with a
218m hill just behind it. It then slopes up to 935m. A
few rocks up to 100m from the rocky cliffs. A wind-
ing coast road and some houses.

Marine de Canelle landing looking E

Pointe de Canelle looking S

Marine de Canelle landing

A very small creek 600m to S of the Pointe de
Canelle. There is a small breakwater, quay (1m) a
slip and a stony beach where small fishing boats and
dinghies are hauled ashore, several fisherman's
houses and a restaurant on the road to the coast road.
Anchor off in 6m rock in good conditions.

Albo asbestos mine and works

The hills above the Roches d'Albo and Punta Bianca
have been extensively mined for asbestos and the
white scar that has been left on the sloping hillside
can be seen from afar. In the closer approach the
huge processing buildings will be seen. The works
were closed in 1965 but the debris which was dis-
charged into the sea is still washing along the coast
partially filling the bays and indentations.

⚓ Marine d'Albo

A wide bay partially filled by the grey debris from
the asbestos works. The NW side has a few rocks
close inshore, a small village and restaurant stands
behind the beach of grey stones and a conspicuous
tower marks the S side of the bay. The coast road
loops behind the head of the beach. Anchor in 4m
sand and stone in the middle of the bay open
SW–W–NW–N.

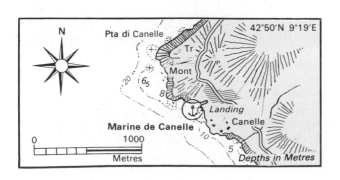

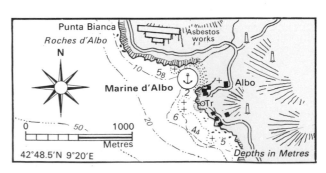

⌁ Marine de Albo looking E.

⌁ **Marine de Nonza**

An attractive anchorage below an old village with conspicuous square tower and a white belfry all on a very steep rocky hill (162m). Unfortunately the old anchorage tucked away in the corner has silted up with the grey stones from the asbestos works and the only anchorage possible is off this grey beach in 4m rock open to SW–W–NW–N. Depths shallow very quickly near the shore. Tracks and steps to village on main coast road above.

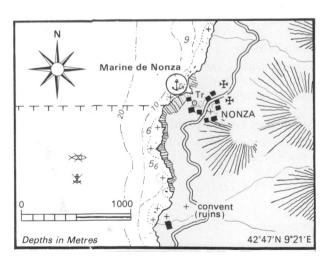

⌁ Marine de Negro (Negru) looking E

⌁ **Marine de Negro (Marine de Negru)**

A small bay at the foot of a deep valley, a stony beach with a tower on its N side, some houses, a road to the coast road behind a conspicuous road bridge across the valley. A small rock off the S side of the beach, anchor off the centre of the beach in 4m stone and weed. Open to SW–W–NW–N.

⌁ Marine de Negro (Negru) looking SE

73

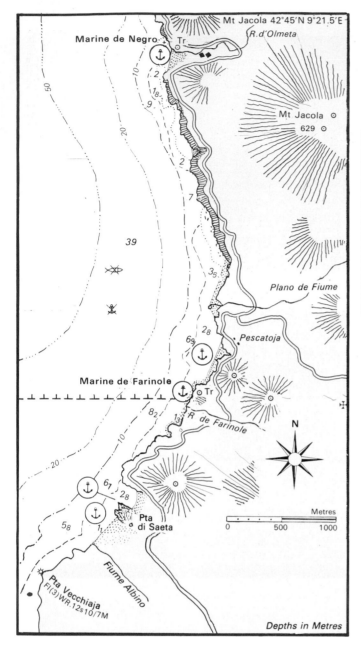

⌁ Marine de Farinole looking SE

⌁ Marine de Farinole

An open anchorage off the coast in 3m sand and rock open to SW–W–NW–N. A long sand and stone beach with a tower on a hillock near the centre. Some houses with main coast road behind, beach restaurant. Cable comes ashore near the tower.

⌁ Punta di Saeta N (Albino)

Two long deserted sandy beaches with a large white rock dividing them, flat ground behind. A vineyard, two farm houses and a pyramid shaped tree covered hill, behind which lies the coast road. Anchor in 3m sand off the beach open to SW–W–NW–N. Cable comes ashore at S end of the S beach. Keep clear of this area.

Punta di Saeta

A rocky-cliffed point 1000m to N of Pointe Vecchiaja. Whitish cliffs, wooded and a small islet close inshore, otherwise steep-to.

Pointe Vecchiaja (Vecchiaia)

A low sloping prominent headland, tree covered with a track running N–S. The point has a whitish rock cliff with a small lighthouse tower (5m) white, red top (Fl(3)WR.12s35m10/7M). The point is steep-to.

Punta di Saeta

⌁ Punta di Saeta (Albino) N looking SE

Punta di Saeta

⚓ Punta di Saeta (Albino) N looking E

Pointe Vecchiaja looking SE

Punta di Cani

A low inconspicuous point with flat land behind, rocks extend 200m offshore.

⚓ Les Marines de Soleil

An open anchorage in 3m sand 200m to SW of the *Blockhaus* situated on the coast ¾M to SSW of Punta di Cani. Sound carefully because there are shallows to N. A large holiday camp on shore near the coast road. This anchorage is open to SW–W–NW–N.

Section B – St Florent to Ajaccio

The coast

The coast between Saint Florent and Ajaccio is the most impressive of the whole island. It is extremely rugged, mountainous and in places of awe-inspiring beauty, but it is a dangerous coast in bad weather and there are very few safe harbours of refuge. With the exception of the towns of Calvi, Ile Rousse and half a dozen coastal villages the land is virtually deserted. There is a very tortuous coastal road running along the foot of mountains that reach up to peaks 2710m (8891ft) high and these lie only 22M inland.

This section though only some 80M in distance around the out-lying headlands has in point of fact a very much longer coastline because of its broken nature.

In the NW, the wide and deep Golfe de Saint Florent gives way to a 16M stretch along the Désert des Agriates, an uninhabited section of bare rock and scrub with many deserted anchorages. The next stretch which includes the harbours of Ile Rousse, Sant'Ambrogio and Calvi is backed by a fertile region, La Balagne, and is relatively well populated. From Calvi to S as far as Cargèse the coast is wildly mountainous with deep steep-sided bays and gulfs some of which offer anchorages; Girolata is the only anchorage with any pretence of security. The incredible red-rocked Golfe de Porto, though a dangerous place, is well worth a visit in order to see the fantastic mountains that surround it.

From Cargèse to Ajaccio the coast is spectacular though still impressive consisting of the very wide and deep Golfe de Sagone, the NE side of which is populated to a limited extent but the SE side and the coast as far as the Iles Sanguinaires is again virtually deserted. From the extraordinary chain of islands, Iles Sanguinaires, the coast becomes more and more populated as Ajaccio is approached.

Yachts coming from France usually arrive on this section of the coast and it offers a most impressive if dangerous introduction to La Corse.

3·5 Port de Saint Florent

20217 Haute Corse

Position 42°38'·50N 8°17'·89E
Minimum depth   in the entrance 3m (9·8ft)
　　　　　　　　 in the harbour 3 to 2m (9·8 to 6·6ft)
　　　　　　　　 in the Rivière Aliso 1·5m (4·9ft)
Clearance river bridge 2·5m (8·2ft)
Width of the entrance 30m (98ft)
Number of berths 500, plus 100 in the river
Population 805
Rating 2–2–3

General

This fishing and yacht harbour is situated at the head of the wide Golfe de Saint Florent at the edge of a flat delta of the Rivière Aliso with high ranges of mountains in the background. Approach and entrance are easy but in heavy weather from NW could become difficult and perhaps dangerous. There is good shelter once inside the harbour though heavy gusts of wind off the mountains can be experienced from an E–SE direction. The old and attractive town has a number of shops which can provide everyday requirements. The town and harbour are very crowded in the season.

Data

Charts

Admiralty *1999*
French *6850, 6969*
ECM *1006*

Magnetic variation

0°05'W (1990) decreasing by 7' each year.

Weather forecasts

Posted at *Bureau de Port* twice each day. Recorded forecast (French) (☎ 95 65 01 35 and 95 36 04 96).

Port radio

VHF Ch 9 (French)

Lights

Ecueil de la Tignosu Fl.R.2s6m2M Red tower with name in white.
Jetée Nord head Oc(2)WR.6s6m9/6M White column red top. 116°-R-227°-W-116° Red sector covers the dangers to NW–N of the harbour.
Contra Jetée Sud head Fl.G.2s4m2M. White tower, dark green top.

Beacons

A red beacon tower (Fl.R.2s6m2M) marks the Ecueil de la Tignosu, a rocky patch 0·1m deep.

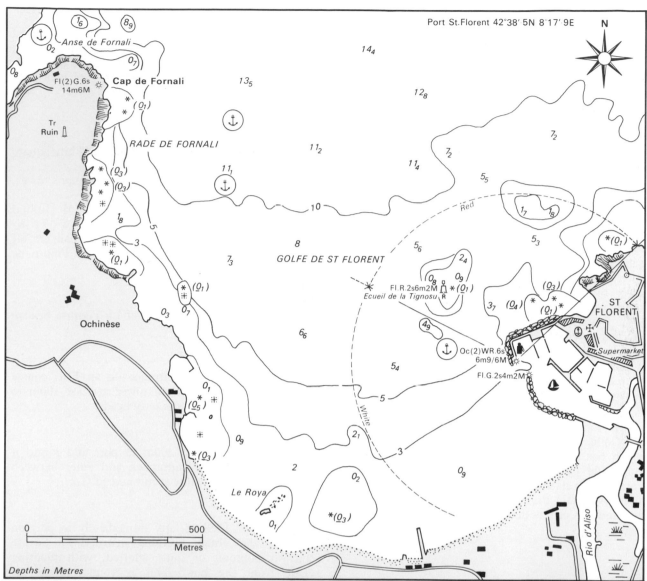

Port St.Florent 42°38′·5N 8°17′·9E

N

Anse de Fornali

8_9

1_6

0_2

0_8

Cap de Fornali

Fl(2)G.6s
14m6M

0_7

(Q_1)

Tr
Ruin

RADE DE FORNALI

(Q_3)

(Q_3)

1_8

3

(Q_1)

(Q_1)

Ochinèse

0_3

0_7

14_4

13_5

12_8

11_2

11_1

10

8

7_3

6_6

11_4

7_2

7_2

5_5

GOLFE DE ST FLORENT

Red

1_7

1_8

5_3

5_6

2_4

0_8

0_9

(Q_1)

Fl.R.2s6m2M
Ecueil de la Tignosu   R

4_9

5_4

5_3

3_7

(Q_4)

(Q_3)

(Q_1)

(Q_1)

ST
FLORENT

Supermarket

Oc(2)WR.6s
6m9/6M

Fl.G.2s4m2M

0_1

(Q_5)

(Q_3)

0_9

5

White

2_1

3

5_4

5

2

0_2

0_9

Le Roya

0_1

(Q_3)

Rio d'Aliso

0   500
Metres

Depths in Metres

Golfe de St Florent

St Florent looking SE. Ecueil de Tignosu beacon in foreground

Warning

The shores of the Golfe de Saint Florent are fronted by shallow banks and rocky patches. Two isolated rocky patches lie near the entrance of the harbour: the Ecueil de la Tignosu, 0·1m deep, some 500m to NW of the entrance and another rocky patch, 1·7m deep, some 600m to N of the entrance. The area S of the harbour entrance shallows quickly.

Important

Fire fighting flying boats may use the Golfe de St Florent to pick up water. See page 33.

Approach by day

From N Follow the rocky, mountainous and broken coast southwards. The white cliffs and disused quarry and asbestos factory at Marine d'Albo, the town of Nonza perched on a steep rocky hill and the lower rounded Pointe Vecchiaja with a very small lighthouse will all be easily identified. The town of Saint Florent will be seen in the closer approach. Proceed down the centre of the Golfe on a S course leaving the beacon tower La Tignosu 200m to port. When this beacon is in line with Saint Florent church tower, course may be altered towards the harbour entrance.

From W Follow the broken rocky coast with white sandy beaches of the Désert des Agriates around into the Golfe de Saint Florent. Pointe de la Mortella which has a disused signal station and lighthouse, Pointe de Cepo which has an old fort and Cap Fornali with its small lighthouse are all easily recognised. Maintain the centre of the golfe in a S direction and proceed as detailed in the approach from N above.

Restricted area

A nature reserve where fishing, subaqua diving and anchoring are forbidden lies to the N of this harbour, it stretches from the tower de Farinole to the tower de Nonza and extends 2M seawards. (See plan page 73.)

Approach by night

Use the following lights:

Pointe de la Mortella Oc.G.4s43m9M White square tower, green top.

Cap Fornali Fl(2)G.6s14m6M White square tower, green top and corners.

Pointe Vecchiaja Fl(3)WR.12s35m10/7M Round white tower, red top. Shore-R-035°-W-174°-R-shore. *Note* The R sector covers the dangers off this harbour and the coast as far as Pointe de Canelle.

Anchorage in the approach

Anchor in 5m sand 400m to S of La Tignosu beacon tower.

Entrance

By day Approach the entrance on an ESE course leaving La Tignosu beacon tower at least 100m to port and enter between the jetty heads.

Approach by night

Leave Fl.R.2s at least 200m to port and round it onto an ESE course, approach and enter between Oc(2)WR.6s in the white sector and Fl.G.2s.

Berths

Secure to the fuelling jetty immediately to port on entering and obtain berthing instructions. Secure stern-to pontoon or quay allotted, with mooring chain from the bow. This is connected to the pontoon or quay by a light pick-up chain.

Fort   Church spire   Ecueil de la Tignosu beacon (entrance beyond)

St Florent. Approach looking SE

Church   La Tignosu beacon   Entrance

St Florent. Approach looking SE

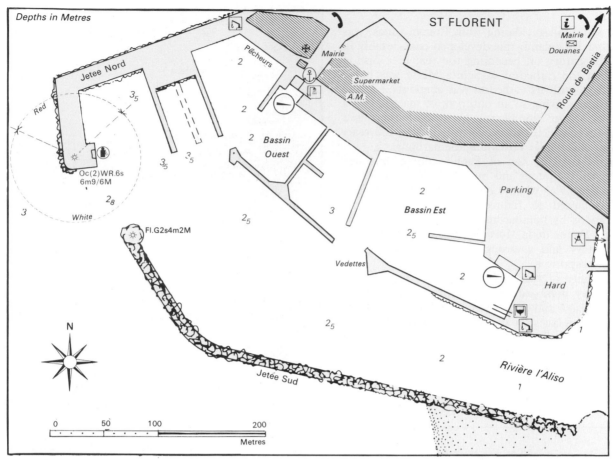

Port de St Florent

Prohibited anchorage
Anchoring is not permitted inside the harbour.

Formalities
On arrival report to the *Bureau de Port* ☎ 95 37 00 79 open 0800–2100 summer, 0900–1200 and 1400–1700 in winter, located on the NE side of the harbour above the lifeboat house. The offices of *Affaires Maritimes* (☎ 95 37 00 51) and customs (☎ 95 37 00 02) are at the *Mairie* to NE of the town.

Charges
There are harbour charges.

Facilities
Slips There are two slips, one on the NE side and the other on the E side of the harbour.
Crane Mobile cranes of 15 and 12 tonnes are available.
Travel-lift Travel-lift of 20 tonnes at E end of the harbour.
Fuel Petrol and diesel (*gasoil*) available from pumps at the head of the Jetée Ouest (☎ 95 37 00 53). Summer 0900–1200 and 1400–1900. Diesel (*gasoil*) is also delivered by tanker lorry. Contact the garage in the town.
Water Water points on the quays and pontoons.
Electricity Points for 220v AC supply on the quays and pontoons.
Provisions Many shops and supermarkets in the town can supply all normal requirements.

Ice In season ice can be obtained from Spar supermarket, small ice is available from the bars.
Garbage Rubbish bins on the quays.
Chandlery Ship chandlers' shop on the E side of the harbour.
Repairs Repairs to hull, engines and radio equipment are possible.
Post office The PTT is located on the NE side of the town at the *Mairie* on the road to Bastia.
Hotels One ***, six ** and one * hotel.
Restaurants A large number of restaurants and café/bars.
Yacht club Centre de Voile, a small dinghy club and a large sailing school.
Showers Available at the *Bureau de Port*. 4 WCs (more being built), 12 showers.
Lifeboat A small motor lifeboat is kept here. *Vedette* 2nd class.
Medical Doctors and dentist available.
Information office At *Mairie* (☎ 95 37 06 04).
Visits The 12th century Pisan Cathedral at Nebbio which was abandoned in the 16th century and is still virtually intact is only 1M away to ESE. The key is kept at the Hotel d'Europe. This is an outstanding example of a Romanesque building. A dinghy trip up the river is also possible.
Beaches A fine beach lies to the SW of the harbour across a footbridge over the Rivière l'Aliso.
Communications Bus service.

Future development
Extra facilities and more pontoons to be established.

History

The original village, dating from Roman times, was at Nebbio 1M inland; this developed considerably in the 12th century on becoming the seat of a bishop and when the cathedral of Sainte Marie was built. The village with its cathedral was abandoned in the 16th century owing to an outbreak of malaria and a new town, Saint Florent, was built beside the round Genoese fort which had been erected some 100 years earlier on a low hill overlooking the harbour.

General Gentile, one of Paoli's companions was born in Saint Florent and buried in the cathedral at Nebbio. In 1794 when Lord Hood and the British fleet attempted to reduce the town and nearby fortifications by bombardment, the defenders of the tower on Pointe de la Mortella, now in ruins, refused to surrender and a strong shore party had to be landed to capture it.

The ability of these Genoese towers and forts to resist heavy bombardment so impressed the British that the design and details were sent back to England and used as a basis for the Martello towers that were subsequently built on the south coast of England as a defence against the threatened attack of the Corsican, Napoleon Bonaparte.

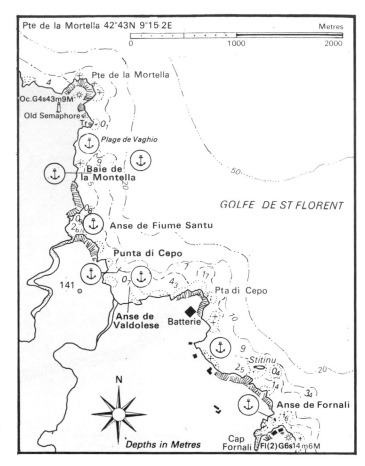

⚓ Rade de Fornali

Deep water anchorages in 12m sand 500m to SE of the light on Pointe de Fornali and 500m to ESE. Open to NE–E–SE.

Pointe de Fornali

An easily recognised headland with an old square fort on the top of the hill behind the point and a white square lighthouse on the point with green top and corners, white house alongside (Fl(2)G.6s14m6M).

⚓ Anse de Fornali

An old harbour once used by large sailing vessels, over the years it has silted up, old guns are embedded along the coast for mooring and warping purposes. A private landing stage and house stand on the S side of the Anse. Sound carefully 1·6m shallow patch is located in the mouth of the Anse and a lone rock is in mid-channel further in. Anchor N of the landing stage in 2m sand and mud open to N–NE–E–SE. Road on SE coast.

Punta di Cepo

A prominent headland with rocks extending 100m. An old fortified battery on the top of the hill behind. Road around the point.

Lighthouse   Fort

⚓ Anse de Fornali looking SW

⚓ Punta di Cepo

Anchorage off rocky coast, several rocky patches to N and S. Anchor in 3m sand and weed open N–NE–E–SE.

⚓ Anse de Valdolese

A shallow bay at the mouth of a river with hills at either side. The anchorage which is open N–NE–E is located 200m NNE of the river mouth, sound carefully. Road on S side. Sandy beach (Plage de Vaghio), deserted.

⚓ Anse de Fiume Santu looking SW

⚓ Anse de Fiume Santu looking SW

⚓ Baie de la Mortella (tower) looking SW

Pointe de la Mortella

A very prominent point with a lighthouse on a higher hill behind. A coast road. Rocky dangers extend 200m. A conspicuous ruined tower stands on a small point 300m to S. This is the famous tower that Lord Hood's force failed to destroy in the 1794. See Port de St Florent history page 80.

⚓ **Anse de Fiume Santu**

A good anchorage open to N–NE–E in 3m sand in a bay at the mouth of a river which once had a large sand and shingle beach to NW of its mouth. One hut and track on both sides of the bay, deserted. The beach was swept away after a cloud burst in the hills behind (1989).

⚓ **Baie de la Mortella**

A deep anchorage in 25m sand lies halfway between Punta de la Mortella and Anse de Fiume Santu 600m offshore. A shallow anchorage in 6m sand lies inshore 200m off the coast which is fronted by, rocky dangers extending 100m. These anchorages are open to N–NE–E–SE.

Pointe de la Mortella lighthouse and signal station looking SE

81

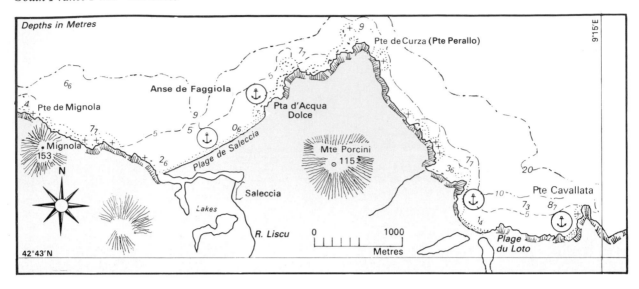

Pointe Cavallata

A narrow pointed headland sloping up inland and then falling away, sheer-to with a small anchorage on its W side.

⚓ Plage du Loto E looking S

⚓ Plage du Loto E

An attractive small anchorage open to NW–N–NE. Enter sounding carefully. Anchor in 2m sand. White sandy beach, small river behind, deserted.

Cap Cavallata   Anchorage

Plage du Loto E

⚓ Plage du Loto W looking S

⚓ Plage du Loto W

A wide white sandy bay open to N–NE–E. Anchor in 3m sand off sandy beach. Low ground with lagoons behind beach. Deserted, wreck at W end of bay.

Pointe de Curza (Perallo)

A prominent headland of whitish rock sloping up to 115m with a stony pyramid on top. Rocky offliers extend 200m.

Pointe de la Curza looking E

⚓ Plage de Salaccia (Anse de Faggiola) looking S

⚓ Plage de Saleccia (Anse de Faggiola)
A very large bay backed by a long white sandy beach. Anchor in 3m sand off the beach, open to NW–N–NE. Sand dunes and track along back of the beach. Deserted. River at SW end of beach.

Pointe de Mignole (di Mignola) (Santolino)
A low wide headland with offlying rocks extending 100m. A hill (153m) lies ½M inland and has a black pyramid on its top.

⚓ Pointe de Genibareta E
A small deep bay with a white sandy beach at its head and a lone rock. Several deserted wood houses either side of the bay. Anchor in 3m sand, open to NW–N–NE. Track running inland. High sand dunes to W. Deserted.

Pointe Genibareta
A small headland not very prominent, with large sand dunes and rocks extending 200m offshore.

⚓ Pointe de Genibareta W
A bay with a white sand beach and sand dunes to E. Four old wood houses to W, a dry river bed and a track inland. Anchor in 3m sand open to NW–N–NE. Deserted.

⚓ Pointe Genibareta W looking SE

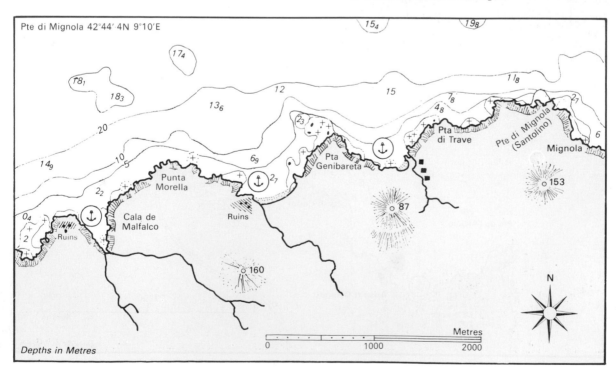

⚓ Pointe Genibareta E looking SE

Pointe Mortella

Not a very prominent headland which has rocky dangers out to 100m. Inland it slopes up to 51m. (Do not muddle with Pointe de la Mortella on W side of Golfe de Saint Florent.)

⚓ Anse de Malfalco

An attractive narrow *calanque*-type anchorage with hills around it and low cliffs with some close inshore rocks. Sound carefully while approaching due to shallows. Anchor and moor with 2nd anchor in 3m sand inside the entrance, open to NW–N. Small white sand and shingle beach at head. Ruined house to SW. Tracks along coast and inland. Deserted.

⚓ Anse de Malfalco looking SE

Pointe de l'Arinetta

A small point with rocks extending 100m, a small hill (81m) stands behind.

⚓ Marine d'Alga

A wide open bay with rocky sides and several rocks extending up to 100m from the sides. Enter with care on a SE course towards the small white sand and shingle beach where there is the mouth of a river. Anchor in 3m sand off the beach, open to W–NW–N–NE. Deserted.

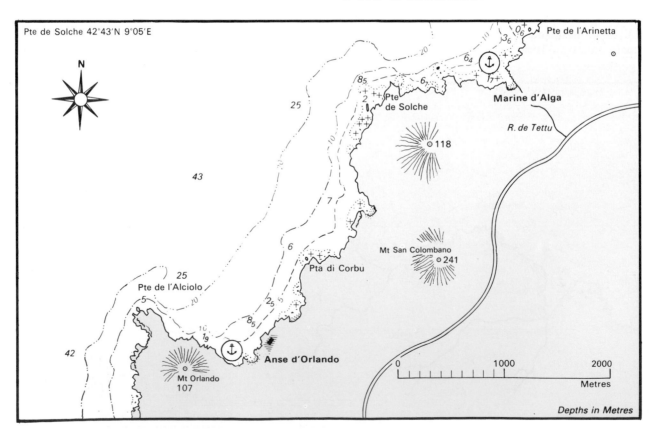

⚓ Marine d'Alga looking SE

⚓ Anse de Orlando looking SE

Pointe de Solche (Punta di Solche)

A large headland sloping up to 118m and 241m further inland it is low near its point. Rocky dangers extend 300m off its point.

⚓ Anse de Orlando

A small white sand and shingle beach in the centre of a wide bay with Mont Orlando (107m) towering over it. The sides of the bay are rocky. Enter on a S course and anchor off the beach in 3m sand, open to NW–N–NE. Track inland. Deserted.

Pointe de l'Alciolo (Punta di l'Acciolu)

A conspicuous headland with a narrow jutting rocky point, sheer-to. The W side resembles a beak. Mont Orlando (107m) stands behind this point.

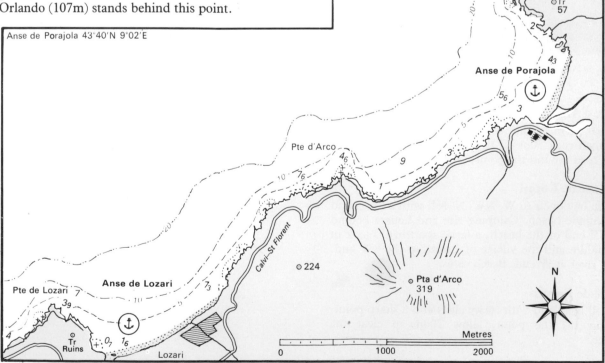

⚓ **Anse de Porajola (Periola)**

A wide bay open to SW–W–NW–N with a long white sandy beach with dunes behind, it has a river mouth at the S end. Some houses and a café on the road that is above the river. There is a tower 500m to N of the N end of the beach. Anchor in 3m sand off the beach.

⚓ Anse de Lozari looking SE

Anse de Porajola looking E

Pointe Saleccia

A small headland with a tower on its point the coast road and railway behind.

⚓ Anse de Porajola looking E

Pointe d'Arco

A small point at the foot of Summit d'Arco (319m) one small rock 50m off the point otherwise steep-to. Coast road around the point.

⚓ **Anse de Lozari**

A wide bay open to W–NW–N–NE with a long sand and shingle beach. Camping site and houses behind the NE end of the beach, a large apartment block in the middle and the village of Lozari at the SW end. Small river at W end. Beach cafés.

Pointe de Lozari

A small headland with rocky cliffs and a sharp point. Shallow off the point, allow 200m to clear the danger.

3·6 Port de l'Ile Rousse
20220 Haute Corse

Position 42°38'·50N 8°56'·45E
Minimum depth in the entrance 14m (46ft)
in the harbour 10 to 1m (33 to 3·3ft)
Bridge depth 1·5m, clearance 2m (6·6ft)
Width of the entrance 350m (1148ft)
Number of berths 10+
Population 3881
Rating 3–3–3

General

This harbour consists of two large rocky islands of a red/orange colour, which have been joined to the mainland by a causeway leaving two small islets unattached. A jetty protects an L-shaped quay and anchorage. Approach and entrance are easy but only limited protection is available because the harbour is open to winds and swell from N to E and also to strong winds from W to SW which blow across the causeway. Only a small number of berths are available for yachts because most of the jetties and quays are reserved for commercial and fishing craft. There is also a small fishing harbour which is normally full up. The town, which is old, is most attractive, it lies about ½M to S of the harbour. Here all normal requirements may be purchased from a good range of shops.

Data

Charts

Admiralty *1992*
French *6970, 6980*
ECM *1006*

Magnetic variation

0°35'W (1990) decreasing by 7' each year.

Lights

L'Ile Rousse, La Pietra Fl(3)WG.12s64m15/11M White square tower and house, green top. Shore-G-079°-W-234°-G-shore covering Danger de l'Algajola.

Jetée head Iso.G.4s12m5M White tower, dark green top. The light is partly obscured by Ile de la Pietra between about 80°-140°.

Port de Pêche Oc.R.4s2m11M Red structure.

Weather forecasts

Recorded forecasts (French) (☎ 96 36 04 96) (☎ 95 21 32 71) and (☎ 95 21 05 81).

Warning

Should the warning of a NW or E wind be received, this harbour must be vacated at once and shelter obtained at the ports of Saint Florent, Calvi or with

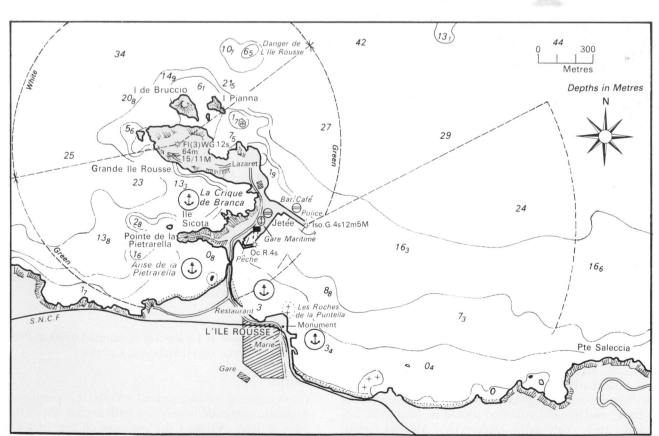

Port de l'Ile Rousse

Jetée   Passage

L'Ile Rousse looking SE. Showing passage between Grande Ile Rousse and Ile de Bruccio

caution in the anchorage to the W of the harbour. If caught out, some shelter may be obtained in the lee of the jetty as near to the root as draught will allow always providing a commercial ship or ferry is not due in. This is primarily a commercial harbour and the approach and manoeuvring area in front of the quay and jetty must not be obstructed. Commercial ships and ferries have right of way.

Restricted area

A nature reserve where fishing, subaqua diving and anchoring is forbidden stretches for 2M to N of Le Grande Ile Rousse and is 1M wide. (See plan page 87).

Approach by day

From E From the Golfe de Saint Florent the coast of the Désert des Agriates consists of very broken low rocky cliffs and small bays with white sandy beaches backed by deserted hills and mountains. This area ends at the wide deep Anse de Porajola where there is a long white sandy beach. The conspicuous Ile Rousse is easily recognised from afar. In the closer approach the town and the jetée will be observed.

From W The mass of holiday residences around the harbour of Sant'Ambrogio and the small village of Algajoa situated upon a low hill with an old fort and a small harbour will be easily identified. The Pointe Vallitone must be given a ¼M berth due to offlying rocky patches and attention should be paid to an isolated rocky patch, the Danger de l'Algajola (0·8m) deep, which lies ½M off the coast, and is marked by

a BR metal post with two balls topmark* which is sometimes difficult to see. Ile Rousse is easy to recognise from afar as it projects some distance from the mainland. Round the islands at 300m to avoid danger or if experienced use the Passage between Isola la Pietra and Insula del Bruccio (see page 90.)

*Note. The two balls were missing (1990) and only a rusty black post remained.

Approach by night

Use the following lights:

Pointe de la Mortella Oc.G.4s43m9M. White square tower, green top.

Pointe Revellata Fl(2)W.10s97m21M. White square tower, black top and corners.

Sant'Ambrogio Fl.G.2s7m2M. White post, green top, name in white.

Note The green sector of Ile Rousse covers the Danger de l'Algajola.

Signal station

The Sémaphore at Ile Rousse is manned 0700 to 1900 and replaces the signal station at Cavallo.

Berths

If not required for commercial vessels, it is permitted to secure alongside or stern-to with anchor ahead the jetée or quay. Contact the *capitaine du port* first for permission.

Town landing

Ile Rousse looking W–NW

Moorings

Yachts can often use the large warping buoy as a mooring with an anchor to hold the yacht away from it. There are some private moorings to S.

Anchorage

Anchor in some 6m sand 200m to the SW of the warping buoy or to the NE of the town some 300m from the shore. Alternative anchorage in La Crique de Branca or in the Anse de la Pietrarella (Sicota).

Prohibited anchorage

Do not anchor N of a line E–W through the warping buoy as this area is required by commercial vessels manoeuvring.

Bridge

A bridge which permits small craft to pass under the causeway lies 100m S of the fishing harbour, it leads into the Anse de la Pietrarella, there is 1·5m of water and 2m height above water level.

Landing place

A small quay and jetty are located at the N end of the town where small craft can secure in fair weather and dinghies can land. Less than 1m of water alongside.

Formalities

The *capitaine du port* is also the lighthouse keeper, his office is in the Gare Maritime (☎ 95 60 00 68). Contact him or his staff on arrival if wishing to use the jetty or quay. *Affaires Maritimes* office is on the jetée (☎ 95 60 05 59). The customs office is in the town at the *Mairie* (☎ 95 60 00 78).

Jetée   *Gare Maritime*

L'Ile Rousse looking E–SE–S

L'Ile Rousse. Port des Pêcheurs looking SW

Charges

Harbour charges may be raised.

Facilities

Slip A slip with 2m water lies at the S end of the quay in the fishing harbour.

Fuel From garages in the town. Arrangements can be made for fuel to be delivered by lorry.

Water One water point near the root of the jetty or from the café/bar.

Provisions Many shops in the town and an excellent market.

Ice From the café/bar.

Garbage One rubbish container on the quay.

Chandlery A chandlery shop on the way into the town and another in town.

Repairs Repairs to hull and engines can be carried out. Electronic engineer.

Laundrette A laundrette in the town by Allée de Charles de Gaulle.

Post office The PTT on outside of the town on the road S to Montello.

Hotels One ***, two **, one * and five unclassified and many more in the area.

Restaurants Many restaurants and café/bars in the town and near the harbour.

Information office The Syndicat d'Initiative is located at SE side of Place de Paoli (☎ 95 60 04 35). In summer season at the *Mairie*.

Medical Doctors and dentist.

Visits There is a pleasant view of the coast from the top of Ile de la Pietra, L'Ile Rousse. In the hills to the S of the town will be found a series of interesting old villages.

Beaches A long beach lies to the SE of the harbour.

Communications Bus and rail services. Ferry service to Toulon, Nice and Marseille.

Future development

Plans have existed for more than 12 years to improve this harbour and create a separate harbour for yachts with 250 berths. A plebiscite is to be held in 1989 on this project.

History

Originally a Roman settlement and fishing village, l'Ile Rousse expanded considerably when Pascal Paoli created a commercial centre here in 1758, because the towns and villages of Algajola, Calvi and Ajaccio remained faithful to Genoa and would not let his 'patriots' land. Later it further developed as a ferry terminal as its harbour could accommodate large vessels. With the improvement of the facilities of Calvi, this ferry traffic is now decreasing.

PASSAGE BETWEEN LE GRANDE ILE ROUSSE AND ILE DE BRUCCIO

A passage exists between Iles Bruccio and Grande Ile Rousse 50m wide, 250m long and 2·5 deep which can be used by an experienced navigator in good weather. It is spectacular because the red rocky sides are high and steep and the water is a dark blue colour.

Approach

From W There is no problem because depths are in excess of 18m and the entrance wide, enter on an ESE course and cross the mouth of the Crique de Fontanacci close in.

Ile de Bruccio   *Grande Ile Rousse*

Passage between le Grande Ile Rousse and Ile de Bruccio. Approach from W

From E Care is necessary from this direction, keep near the Grande Ile Rousse to avoid small isolated rock 120m to N of the point at the E side of the Crique de Fontanacci. Enter on a WNW course. Depths vary from 18 to 2·5m.

Grande Ile Rousse   *Ile de Bruccio*

Passage between Grande Ile Rousse and Ile de Bruccio. Approach from E.

Passage The actual passage is 8·5 to 18m deep and is steep-to, the only problem a 2·5m rock lying in the approach from the E side.

⚓ Anse de Corbara

A wide bay with two whitish sandy beaches divided by a tree covered rocky point which has offlying rocks. Two cables come ashore in the centre of the

Anse de Corbara looking SE

⚓ Anse de Corbara looking SE

W beach. Some houses and beach cafés ashore, sand dunes at the NE end, railway behind the beach. Anchor in 3m sand open to W–NW–N–NE.

⚓ Anse de la Galère

A *calanque*-type bay 1000m to W of the tower on Pointe Vallitone, it has a small white sand beach, deserted. Anchor in 3m sand open to NW–N–NE. Railway inland and track. Note: A similar bay between this anchorage and Pointe Vallitone has many rocky dangers and should not be used.

Pointe Vallitone

A prominent point with offlying dangers extending to 300m to NW and N. It is low and has a tower near the point, houses have been built over this area.

⚓ Marine de Davia

Two similar small *calanque*-type bays divided by a rocky outcrop both surrounded by houses with a road ashore and a railway line inland. Both bays have white sandy beaches with a number of rocks close inshore and small sand dunes. Anchor in 3m sand open to SW–W–NW.

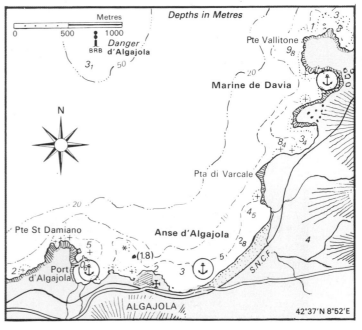

Pointe de Varcale

A wide low point not conspicuous, low cliffs and railway behind.

Pointe Vallitone looking NE

⚓ Marine de Davia looking E

⚓ **Anse d'Algajola**

A wide bay with a long white sand beach. Pointe de Varcale is at the N end of this beach and the town of Algajola which has a conspicuous church tower and fortress is on a point at the SW end. There are sand dunes behind the beach, a railway line and a road. A number of apartment blocks and houses have been built and several beach cafés. Anchor in 3m sand off the beach open to W–NW–N. Everyday supplies obtainable from the town where there is a mechanic and chandlers.

⚓ Anse d'Algajola looking S

Jetée

⚓ Port d'Algajola looking S

⚓ Port d'Algajola

A small harbour for fishing boats and dinghies. There is 6m in the entrance and 3m in the centre of the harbour but the sides are very shallow. On the NW side is a slip and a small jetty, a road leading to the main road lies behind the jetty. The area is surrounded by a housing estate and the railway passes behind. A small islet (1·8m) lies 300m to NW of the town. Anchor in 3m sand and rock just inside the harbour, open to N–NE.

⚓ Port d'Algajola looking SW

Pointe St Damiano (Punta San Damiano)

A small point to W of the Port de Algajola which slopes gently inland and is covered by a housing estate. This point is virtually steep-to.

Danger de l'Algajola

A shallow group of rocks submerged and awash, minimum depth 0·8m lies 3000m to NW of Point St Damiano. A beacon consisting of a BR iron pole with two balls topmark located at the centre of this shoal which extends about 200m around it. The balls were missing and the pole was rusty and black in 1989 and it was very difficult to see. A 1500m passage exists between this danger and the shore. The lighthouse on L'Ile Rousse on Pointe Vallitone on 68° leads through this passage. The white sector of this lighthouse leads outside this danger and the green covers it. In rough weather the seas break over the shallows.

⚓ Anse de Sant'Ambrogio

A wide bay surrounded by housing estates, which has a harbour on the W side. It has a white sandy beach at its head. Anchor off the beach in 3m sand open to N–NE. Craft drawing 1·5m or less can use a small bay to N of the harbour which is only open to NE. Everyday facilities are available at the Port de Sant'Ambrogio.

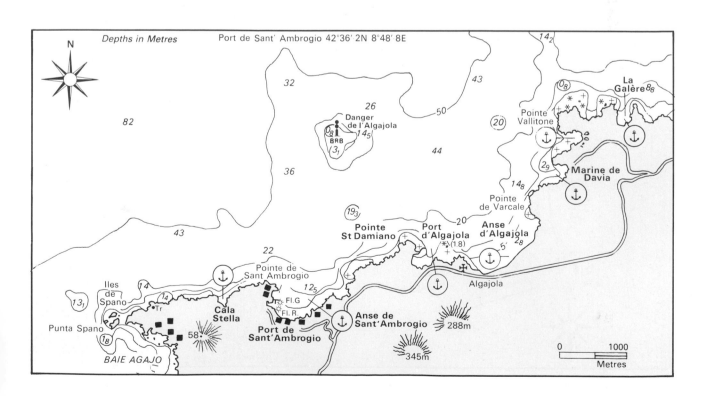

93

3·7 Port de Sant'Ambrogio

20260 Haute Corse

Position 42°36'·26N 8°48'·79E
Minimum depth   in the entrance 2·6m (8·5ft)
                  in the harbour 1 to 2·5m (3·3 to 8·2ft)
Width of the entrance 25m (82ft)
Maximum length overall 20m (66ft)
Number of berths 150
Population 200 (approx)
Rating 3–3–3

General

A modern yacht harbour which is a part of a large holiday housing complex, it becomes very crowded in season. Approach and entrance are not difficult in good weather but the entrance lies in shallow water close to the beach and so is dangerous in heavy weather from the NE *tramontane*. The shelter inside the harbour is good though some swell enters with strong NE–E *tramontane* winds. In season, adequate supplies of provisions are available from shops beside the harbour but out of season the nearest shops are at Algajola over 1M away. Very crowded in season. The entrance tends to silt up during storms.

Data

Charts

Admiralty *1999*
French *6970, 6980*
ECM *1006*

Magnetic variation

0°35'W (1990) decreasing by 7' each year.

Weather forecasts

Posted each day in season at the *Bureau de Port*. Recorded forecast (☎ 95 65 01 35) and (☎ 95 36 04 96) (French).

Speed limit

3 knots.

Lights

Jetée NE head Fl.G.2s7m2M. White column, green top.
Jetée SW head Fl.R.2s7m2M. White column, red top.

Beacons

A beacon, BR topmark 2 balls vertical* is located on a rocky patch 0·8m (2·5ft) deep. This beacon marks the Danger de l'Algajola which is situated ¾M to NNW of this harbour.

Note *The two balls were missing 1989 and only a rusty black pole remains.

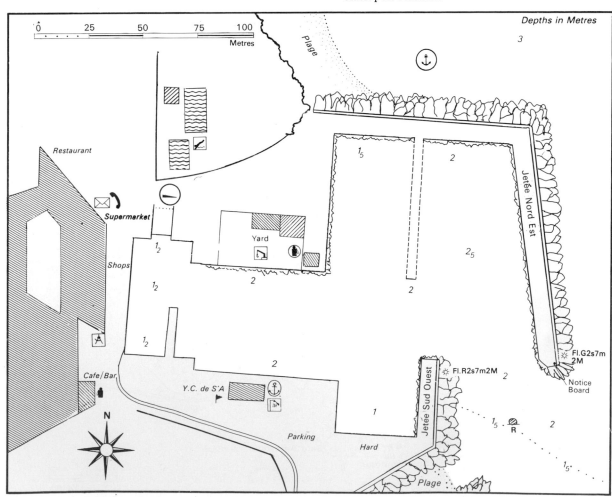

Port de Sant'Ambrogio

Cala Stella

Sant'Ambrogio looking S

Buoys

Small R buoy(s) mark the shallow port side of the entrance channel.

Warning

The entrance to this harbour lies close to the beach and it is necessary to turn parallel to the swell when entering. Entrance should never be attempted in heavy on-shore weather. The beacon which marks the rocky patch the Danger de l'Algajola is not always easy to observe and this should be allowed for when approaching this harbour. Harbour lights are not very bright and difficult to see against the many lights on shore. The entrance silts up and is periodically dredged. Depths in the channel are shown on a notice board at the head of the Jetée Nord Est. Some quays have extended rocky feet, this includes the fuel quay.

Approach by day

From E From the easily recognised Ile Rousse with its lighthouse on the reddish-orange coloured rocky Le Grande Ile Rousse, Ile de la Pietra, the coast is low and rocky with a mountainous background. The village of Algajola on a low hill can be identified and the holiday housing estates around Sant'Ambrogio will be seen from afar. Underwater rocky shoals extend some ¼M off Pointe Vallitone and the Danger de l'Algajola lies ¾M off this harbour. In the closer approach the rocky harbour breakwaters will be seen and the small light towers at the entrance.

From W Cross the deep wide Golfe de Calvi from the very conspicuous lighthouse on Pointe Revellata towards the lower Pointe d'Espano which has a shallow rocky patch on its W side extending some ¼M. Beyond this point ¼M inland lies Le Rocher Eléphant, a group of light grey rocks which have the shape of an elephant. This harbour and the holiday housing estate do not fully appear until Pointe de Sant'Ambrogio has been rounded. Do not round this point too close in before approaching the harbour on a S course.

Approach by night

Approach with care using the following lights:

Ile Rousse Fl(3)WG.12s64m15/11M White square tower and house, green top. Shore-G-079°-W-234°-G-234°-shore. *Note* The green sector covers the Danger de l'Algajola.

Pointe Revellata Fl(2)W.10s97m21M. White square tower, black top and corners.

Anchorage in the approach

Anchor in 3 to 8m sand in the bay some 300m to E of this harbour or N of it. It is a popular summer anchorage.

Entrance

By day Approach the harbour entrance on a course between S and SW. Round the head of the Jetée SW at 10m onto a N course close to this head and leaving a small red buoy(s) marking shallows on the port hand well to port.

Bureau de Port   Fuel

Sant'Ambrogio. Entrance looking W–NW–N from the head of
Jetée NE

Sant'Ambrogio harbour

By night Approach Fl.G.2s on a SW course and
round it leaving it 10m to starboard and then Fl.R.2s
some 25m to port. Note that in the approach the
position of these lights appear not as normal but
reversed. It is recommended that a first visit should
be made by day.

Berth

Secure near the fuelling berth and await berthing instructions. Then secure stern-to the quay or pontoon
with bow-to mooring that has a pick-up line
(*pendillo*) attached to the quay or pontoon.

Prohibited anchorages

Anchoring is not permitted in this harbour.

Formalities

The temporary *Bureau de Port* located on the N side
of the harbour (☎ 95 60 70 88). It is open 0800–2000
hours. Report there on arrival. The new *Bureau de
Port* is on the S side of the harbour. Customs (☎ 95
65 00 78).

Charges

There are harbour charges.

Facilities

Slip There is a slip in the SW corner of this harbour.
There is only 1·2m of water.
Hard A hard standing for yachts at S side of the harbour.
Crane A 15-tonne mobile crane is available.
Fuel Pumps for diesel (*gasoil*) and petrol on S side of the

harbour. 0800–2000 in summer only. In winter the at-
tendant is at the second fuel station in the SW corner of
the harbour (☎ 95 60 73 82).
Water Water points on the quays and pontoons.
Electricity Supply points for 220v AC on quays and
pontoons.
Provisions In the season a supermarket and other shops to
W of the harbour can supply normal requirements. Out
of season it is necessary to go to Algajola 1·5M away.
Ice Available in the season once a day.
Garbage Rubbish containers on the quay.
Chandlery A shop in the shopping area open in the season
supplies chandlery.
Repairs Repairs to hull and engines can be effected by the
yard on the N side of the harbour also electronic repairs.
Post office A PTT office is established in the season in the
shopping area.
Hotels Hotels are being built. One ***, three ** and four
* hotels at Algajola.
Restaurants Several restaurants and café/bars in the season.
Yacht club The Yachting Club de Sant'Ambrogio (YCSA)
(☎ 95 60 70 88) has an office and clubhouse at the
Bureau de Port. It is primarily a dinghy club. Showers
and WCs Open April to September.
Showers At the *Bureau de Port*.
Information office At the *Bureau de Port*.
Visits Visits can be made to Algajola, a fortified village
which was the residence of a Genoese lieutenant-general
and it was ransacked by the Turks in 1643. Lumio,
which has a Roman church restored in the 18th century
can also be visited.
Beaches A small sandy beach close to the N side of the harbour which becomes very crowded in season with members of the Club Méditerranée. Another larger beach to
SE. There are also two excellent swimming pools.

Future development

Improvement of facilities are to be provided.

History

A recent development of a bay which has offered a good anchorage to local fishermen in the past.

⚓ Cala Stella

A small narrow creek with a housing estate behind, only room for dinghies or for a small yacht to moor with two anchors or lines ashore in 3m sand and rock, open to NW–N–NE.

Punta Spano (Pointe d'Espano)

A low but prominent point (29m) sloping gently upward and inland, with several islets covered and exposed rocks off its point. A ruined tower stands 400m to NE.

⚓ Portu a Diaghia looking SE

Punta Spano

Punta Spano (d'Espano) looking E

Iles de Spano (d'Espano)

One large islet 200m long 90m wide and 14m high, a small islet 5·9m high and many small exposed rocks. Fishing craft and dinghies can use the passage between these islets with care in calm weather.

⚓ Baie Algajola (Algajo)

An open bay with rocky shore and some small sandy beaches. Camping site on shore, houses in NE corner with road. Anchor in 5m sand, open to SW–W–NW–N.

⚓ Portu Algajola (Portu Algajo)

A small creek in the SE corner of the Baie Algajola with white sandy beaches. Sound carefully because it is shallow. Anchor in sand off beach, open to W–NW–N.

⚓ Portu a Diaghia

A small bay with rocks on S side. Anchor in 3m sand near head of bay open to W–NW.

Punta Caldanu (Carchincu)

A narrow pointed headland with a ruined tower on the S side of the promontory, houses and road also on top of the point. Three rocky islets off the point.

⚓ Portu Ricciaiu

A very small bay near the RC beacon for Calvi airport, approach from the SW because a reef (covered 0·7m) lies 80m to W. Several small rocky islets to W of the entrance. Anchor in 3m to S of the bay. Open to S–SW–W.

⚓ Golfe de Calvi

A 2M wide gulf which is 1M deep and has depths of up to 36m. It is backed by a very long sandy beach and pine woods. La Figarella and Fiume Seccu Rau rivers enter the gulf on the SE side. The bottom is mostly of sand and weed with a few patches of mud and one of rocks. It is open to NW–N–NE but somewhat protected from NW and NE by Pointe Revellata and Punta Spano. There is a nature reserve area see chart page 98. The usual anchorage is to S and SE of Calvi Citadelle in 5 to 6m sand and weed well clear of the harbour entrance but the holding ground is reported poor.

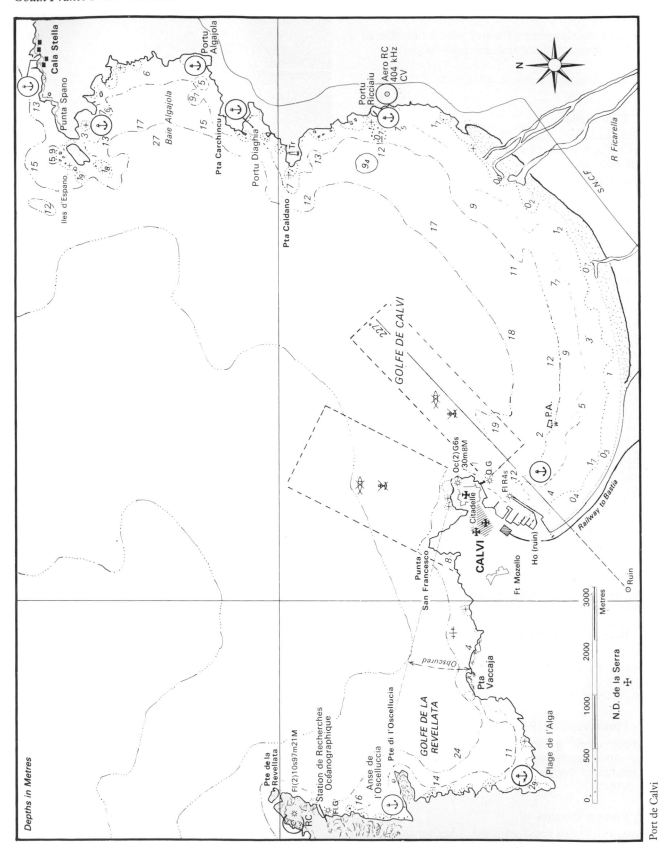

Depths in Metres

Cala Stella

Portu Algajola

Punta Spano

Baie Algajola

Iles d'Espano

Pta Carchincu

Portu Diaghia

Pta Caldano

Portu Ricciaiu

Aero RC
404 kHz
CV

R Ficarella

S.N.C.F

GOLFE DE CALVI

Oc(2)G6s
/30m8M

Q.G

FlR4s

Citadelle

CALVI

Punta
San Francesco

Ft Mozello

Ho (ruin)

Railway to Bastia

Ruin

P.A.
W

Obscured

Pta
Vaccaja

GOLFE DE LA
REVELLATA

Plage de l'Alga

Pte de la
Revellata

Fl(2)10s97m21M

Station de Recherches
Océanographique

Anse de
l'Oscelluccia

Pte di l'Oscelluccia

Fl.G

RC

N.D. de la Serra

Metres
3000 2000 1000 500 0.

Port de Calvi

98

3·8 Port de Calvi

20260 Haute Corse

Position 42°34'·00N 8°45'·60E
Minimum depth in the entrance 5m (16·4ft)
in the harbour 2 to 4m (6·6 to 13ft)
Width of the entrance 30m (98ft)
Number of berths 350
Maximum length overall 45m (148ft)
Population 3579
Rating 1–1–3

General

One of the most beautiful harbours on the island which is easy to enter under almost any conditions and which provides adequate shelter, though with strong winds from NW–N–NE the anchorage can become uncomfortable from the swell. Berths in the yacht harbour are well protected but there is some swell from NE gales. The harbour is very crowded in the season. Yachts from the French mainland usually make this harbour their first port of call. The Citadelle and the town are most picturesque and everyday requirements can be obtained from the shops. Parts of the harbour are reserved for commercial and fishing vessels. The whole harbour area has been recently dredged.

Data

Charts

Admiralty *1425*
French *6980, 7050*
ECM *1006*

Magnetic variation

0°35'W (1990) decreasing by 7' each year.

Marine radiobeacon

Pointe Revellata RV (·—·/···—) 294·2 kHz 100M every 6 mins. W Corsica group with La Garoupe GO.

Air radiobeacon

Calvi 42°35'N 8°48'E CV (—·—·/···—) 404 kHz.

Weather forecasts

Posted twice a day in the season at the *Bureau de Port*. Recorded forecast (French) (☎ 95 65 01 35 and 95 36 04 96).

Speed limit

3 knots.

Port radio

VHF Ch 9

Lights

Pointe Revellata Fl(2)W.10s97m21M White square tower, black top and corners obscured less than 060° RC.
Pointe Revellata Research Station Fl.G.4s5m6M White and dark green tower.
Citadelle NE side Oc(2)G.6s30m8M White metal framework tower, green top.
Pier head Q.G.10m8M White metal column, dark green top.
Digue du Large head Fl.R.4s6m7M White structure, red top.

Buoys

A large rusty unlit yellow warping buoy is located to S of the Citadelle close to the entrance to the yacht harbour.

Warning

The holding ground for anchors is not very good and with the SW *libeccio* or heavy gusts of wind will be experienced in this anchorage and berth. Anchors should be laid out with a good scope of chain. The commercial harbour including Quai Landry are forbidden to yachts without prior permission of the *capitaine du port*.

Restricted areas

A nature reserve lies to NNW of the coast between Pointe Revellata and Pointe Rossa it is 1M wide and extends 3M to seaward. Another area 400m wide and 1500m long stretches from Calvi in a NE direction, a similar area stretches from Calvi to NNE. Fishing, subaqua diving and anchoring is forbidden in these areas. See chart page 98.

Fire fighting planes

Large Canadair flying boats may use the Golfe de Calvi to load water for nearby fires. Important. See page 33.

Approach by day

From N The reddish orange coloured islands at l'Ile Rousse and its lighthouse are conspicuous as is the lighthouse at Pointe Revellata. The mass of holiday homes behind the harbour of Sant'Ambrogio will also be seen. In the closer approach the Citadelle and its fortifications will be recognised. In the approach from this direction the shoal patch Danger de l'Algajola which is marked by a small BR, 2 balls topmark, must be avoided. Topmarks missing and only a black rusty post remains (1990).

From S The very high, broken and mountainous coast continues N from the dark red rocky Ile di Gargalu which has a small lighthouse on it. The small village of Galéria and the signal station at Cap Cavallo together with the lighthouse at Pointe Revellata are easily recognised. The offlying small rocks and shoal patch, the Récifs des Scoglietti and the islets and rocks to S of Cap de la Morsetta are the only dangers.

Approach by night

The following lights may be used:
Ile di Gargalu Fl.WR.4s37m8/5M. White column, black top.
Ile Rousse Fl(3)WG.12s64m15/11M. White square tower and dwelling, green top. Shore-G-079°-W-234°-G-234°-shore. Green sector covers the Danger de l'Algajola.

Anchorage in the approach

Because this harbour is so easy to enter an outside anchorage is not necessary but if required anchorage is possible along the SE and S shores of the Golfe de Calvi in sand but the holding ground is not very good.

Pointe Vallitone   Pointe d'Espano

Approach to NW Corsica

Citadelle   *Pointe de la Re*

Calvi. Approach looking SW

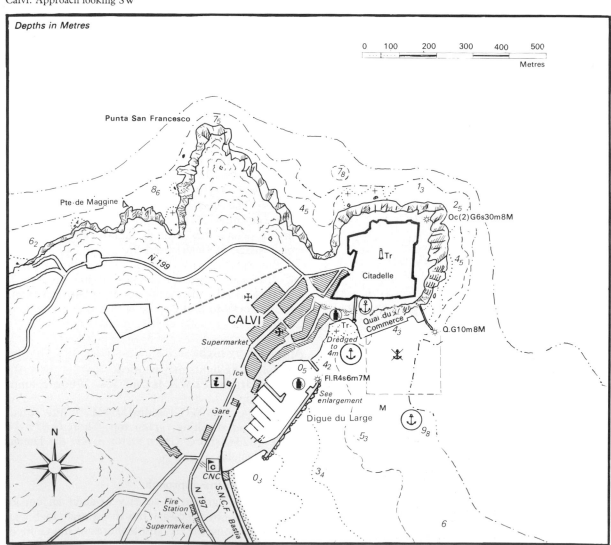

Port de Calvi

Golfe de Calvi   *Calvi Pointe Revellata*   *Cap al Cavallo*   *Cap Rosso*

Citadelle   *Pointe Revellata*

Calvi. Approach looking E

Citadelle

Calvi. Close approach looking SE

of breakwater   *Lighthouse*

Calvi. Close approach looking SW

Entrance

By day Approach the Citadelle which stands surrounded by high walls on a bare rock, round it, then round the head of a short breakwater leaving this 15m to starboard. Approach the yacht harbour to the SW leaving a yellow warping buoy to port and then the head of the entrance of the Digue du Large.

By night Approach Oc(2)G.6s leaving it 200m to starboard then follow the coast around closing it to pass Fl.G. to starboard at 15m then leave Fl.R to port.

Berths

On arrival yachts should secure to the *quai d'accueil* or near the fuel station on the port hand side of the entrance or in any vacant berth. Report to the *Bureau*

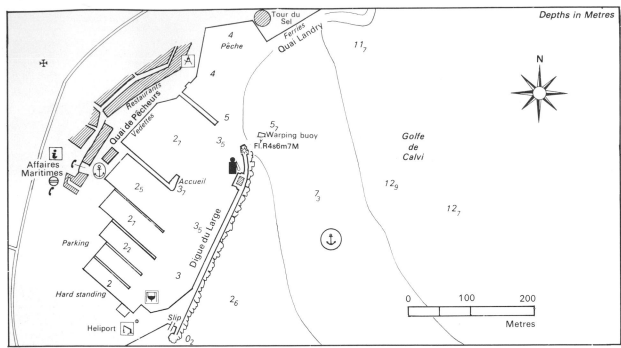

Port de Calvi

Calvi. Entrance to yacht harbour

Calvi looking S

de Port de Plaisance for allocation of a berth. Secure to pontoon or quay stern-to with bow-to chain (*pendillo*). When no ferry or commercial vessels are due, permission is sometimes given by the *Bureau de Port de Commerce* for a yacht to use the Quai Landry. Yachts may not secure to this quay without permission.

Anchorage
Anchorage is possible in most areas of the Golfe de Calvi, the best protected area being to SE of the yacht harbour in up to 6m sand and weed. Holding ground is not very good.

Prohibited anchorages
Anchoring is not permitted in the area extending 200m to the S of the Quai du Commerce (Quai Landry) where ferries and commercial vessel manoeuvre.

Formalities
If not allocated a berth on arrival take the yacht's papers to the *Bureau de Port de Plaisance* (☎ 95 65 10 60) located at the W side of the yacht harbour open in the season 0800–2000, out of season 0830–1200 and 1500–1800. The *Bureau de Port de Commerce* (☎ 95 65 10 60) is on Quai Landry to NE of the yacht harbour. The customs (☎ 95 65 00 69) have an office next to the *Bureau de Port de Plaisance* as do the *Affaires Maritimes* (☎ 95 65 01 71).

Charges
Harbour charges are made for the use of the pontoons and quays.

Quai d'Accueil   *Bureau de Port*

Calvi looking S-SW from the Citadelle

Facilities

Slips Two slips at S end of the harbour.

Hards A large hard standing for yachts at the S end of the yacht harbour.

Travel-hoist Travel-hoist 50 tonne, 7·5 wide at S end of yacht harbour.

Crane Mobile cranes of 7 and 35 tonnes are available.

Fuel Petrol and diesel (*gasoil*) are available from pumps on the port side of the entrance to the yacht harbour, at head of the Digue du Large (☎ 95 65 10 87) open 0800 to 2000 summer, winter 0830 to 1200 and 1500 to 1800. Diesel can also be delivered by bowser.

Water Water points on the pontoons and quays.

Electricity Supply points for 220v AC are established on the pontoons and quays.

Provisions A number of shops and three small supermarkets in the two roads to NW of the harbour. There is also a small market. A large supermarket lies to S of the harbour on the main road.

Ice Ice in small blocks from the supermarket in the season. Small lumps of ice for drinking (*glazones*) are obtainable all year round from the bars.

Duty-free goods Contact Toussaint-Nobili, rue Clemenceau.

Garbage Rubbish containers are to be found near the roots of the pontoons.

Chandlery A good chandler's shop opposite the PTT and an excellent one at N end of the Quai des Pêcheurs.

Repairs Repairs to wood or glass fibre hulls are possible and there are several workshops for the repair of engines. There is also a sailmaker and an electronic engineer.

Laundrettes Two in the town.

Post office The PTT is located near the W side of the yacht harbour.

Hotels Two ****, seven ***, nine **, six * and over seven unclassified.

Restaurants Nine restaurants and many café/bars.

Yacht club Calvi Nautique Club (CNC) (☎ 95 65 10 65) is only a seasonal dinghy club. M. Orsini, 23 Place du Marché (☎ 95 20 260) is president. The clubhouse is at the N end of the beach near the yacht harbour.

Showers At the *Bureau de Port de Plaisance*. 12 showers and 12 WCs. (It is forbidden to wash on the pontoons.)

Information office The Syndicat d'Initiative (☎ 95 65 16 67) has an office behind and above the *Bureau de Port de Plaisance*.

Medical Six doctors and three dentists.

Visits The 13th century Genoese Citadelle should be visited together with its cathedral and museum. There is a fine view from the ramparts. There are a number of interesting places to visit nearby including the 8th century village of St Antonio, the 4th century tomb of Ste Restitute and the church of Notre Dame de la Serra where there is a fine view.

Beaches There are miles of excellent sandy beaches all around the Golfe de Calvi.

Communications Rail and bus services to all parts of the island. Air services to Nice and Marseille and many other cities. Ferry service to Marseille, Nice and Toulon. *Vedettes* to Girolata and Porto.

Festivals Religious ceremonies and processions on Holy Thursday, Good Friday and 15th August. Pilgrimage to Notre Dame de la Serra on nearest Sunday to 8th September.

Future development

Plans exist for the improvement of facilities and the establishment of a Base Nautique.

History

Calvi has been a small fishing harbour since before recorded history. The Romans had a small garrison here and in AD 225 beheaded Ste Restitute. In 1268 the little village on the site of the Lower Town was rebuilt and the Genoese colonised it building the Citadelle to defend the place.

Calvi remained faithful to Genoa and the Citadelle held despite the two attacks by the French and Turks in 1553. This is recalled by a plaque over the gateway with the inscription *Civitas Calvi semper fidelis*. In 1795 the English fleet under Lord Nelson attacked and, after its surrender, entered Calvi. Over 4000 shells were fired into the town and the marks of them can still be seen on the dome of the church of St Jean-Baptiste. Nelson lost an eye during an opposed landing and a tablet to commemorate this event inscribed *Ici Nelson dirigeant le feu des batteries contre Calvi perdit un oeil, 12 Juillet 1794*, is to be found on a large rock at Macarona about 1M to W. His battery of two 26 pounders and a 12 inch mortar from HMS *Agamemnon* were landed at Port Agro 3M to SW. Even the patriot Pascal Paoli was unable to shake the inhabitants' faith in Genoa and he was forced to found and develop l'Ile Rousse in 1795 as an alternative to the 'Citadelle of the North.'

Christopher Columbus is reputed to have been born in this town and in 1793 Napoleon took refuge in the Citadelle when he was obliged to flee from Ajaccio. Plaques in the Citadelle commemorate these events.

In more recent years there has been a steady development of the tourist industry. Holiday camps and hostels are to be found all around the bay while at the same time cultivation and farming of the fertile area, the Balagne, inland has decreased. Since 1963 the French Foreign Legion have occupied the barracks in the Citadelle.

Punta San Francesco

A rocky-cliffed point to NW of the Citadelle of Calvi with the red roof tops of the town of Calvi showing behind. Steep-to.

⚓ **Golfe de la Revellata**

A small deep gulf with a bottom of sand, shell and weed. A small stony beach Plage de l'Alga lies in the S corner of this gulf. Anchor off this beach in 3m sand and weed open to N–NE. Track to road inland.

Punta di l'Oscelluccia

A narrow prominent rocky point (24m) providing a useful breakwater for an anchorage to its N.

⚓ **Anse de l'Oscelluccia**

A small bay with a white rocky and shingle beach. Anchor in 3m sand off this beach, open to N–NE–E. Track inland.

Station de Recherches Océanographique

A very small harbour with light tower white and green (Fl.G.4s5m6M) on the head of the jetty. A road leads inland. Anchorage is not permitted off this harbour. This harbour is open to E–SE.

Punta di l'Oscelluccia   *Station de Recherches Océanograph*

⚓ Anse de l'Oscelluccia and Station de Recherches Océanographique looking S

Passage Ile de la Revellata

Ile de la Revellata is a pointed rock (27m) lying just off Pointe de la Revellata. A passage only 15m wide and 2m deep lies between them. This passage should only be used by experienced navigators in calm conditions with great care and a careful lookout.

Pointe de la Revellata (Punta de la Revellata)

A conspicuous and prominent headland with a large white square tower on a house with corners and top picked out in black and a radio mast on top. The point and island are steep-to.

Pointe de la Revellata looking S

Pointe Rossa

A rocky-cliffed point forming the SW corner of Pointe de la Revellata.

⚓ Anse Margonaia

A small bay surrounded by rocky cliffs providing a temporary anchorage in calm conditions in 10m near its head avoiding a rock covered 1·4m. Open to SW–W–NW. Deserted.

Pointe Bianca

A similar headland to Pointe Rossa described above. Belloni (169m) with a black pyramid on its summit lies inland between these two points.

Pointe Bianca looking S

⚓ Porto Vecchió

A narrow 'V' shaped bay offering good protection but open to S–SW–W. Anchor in 5 to 3m sand and rock near its head in front of small stony beach. There is a rocky island (18m) in the mouth of the bay. Deserted.

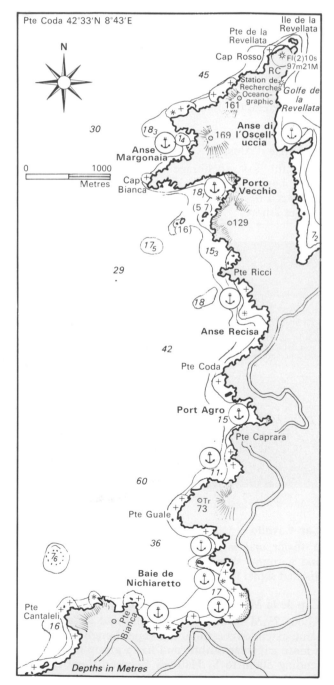

⚓ Porto Vecchio looking NE

⚓ Anse Recisa

Similar to Porto Vecchio but a wide bay open to S–SW–W–NW. An awash rock in the middle of the bay, anchor in 6m rock in calm weather. The coast road above. Deserted.

Anse Recisa

⚓ Port Agro looking E

⚓ Baie de Nichiareto looking SE

⚓ Port Agro

A narrow creek-type inlet with a stony beach at its head high sloping rocks on each side and track to coast road above. Anchor in 6m sand and rock open to S–SW–W–NW. Deserted. It was here Nelson landed his guns for the attack on Calvi in 1794.

Pointe Caprara

A round rocky-cliffed point sloping up inland to the coast road. It is steep-to.

Pointe Caprara S

A small bay to S of Pointe Caprara surrounded by sloping rocky hills. Anchor in 5m rock, open to SW–W–NW. Deserted, coast road inland.

⚓ Baie de Nichiareto

Anchorage in a large bay with four small sub bays and a long white sand and stone beach. Anchor off the beach in 4m sand and rock or in one of the sub bays in 6m rock. Open to W–NW. A track to coast road.

Pointe Cantaleli

A large rocky-cliffed headland some 80m high with rocks extending 100m in a NW direction from the point.

⚓ Anse d'Alusi

A useful little anchorage behind Cap Cavallo in a small bay with a rocky beach. Anchor in 4m rock and weed near head of bay, open NW–N–NE. Some houses ashore.

⚓ Anse d'Alusi looking SE

Cap Cavallo

A major and important headland with rocky cliffs and a round shape. Steep-to. It has a conspicuous disused signal station (322m) on the summit.

Cap de la Morsetta (Capo Mursetta)

About 2½M to S of Cap Cavallo and a part of the same extended coastline, this cape, though similar has a more irregular outline and has a group of islets extending 500m to S. Halfway between these capes is the conspicuous ruined Tour de Truccia (294m).

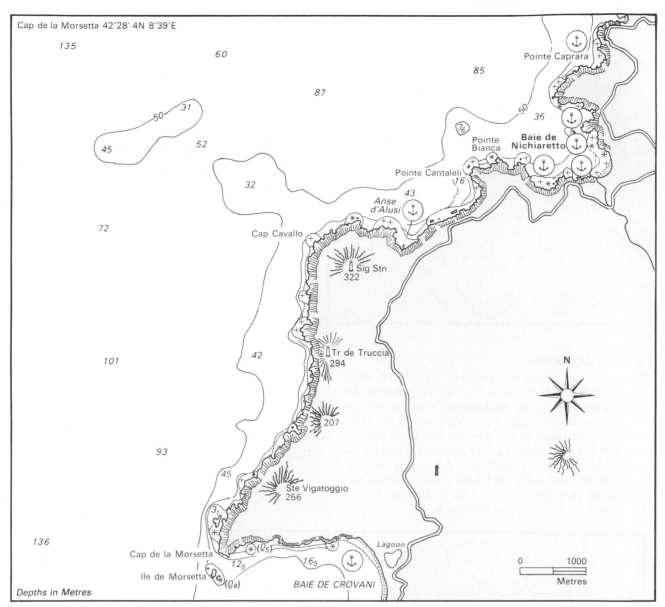

Cap de la Morsetta 42°28'·4N 8°39'E

135

60

87

85

50

35

50   31

45   52

32

43

Pointe
Bianca

Baie de
Nichiaretto

Pointe Cantaleli

16

72

Anse
d'Alusi

Cap Cavallo

Sig Stn
322

Tr de Truccia
294

207

101   42

N

Ste Vigatoggio
256

93

45

31

Pointe Caprara

136

Cap de la Morsetta

Ile de Morsetta   (0·4)

12·5   16·5

Lagoon

BAIE DE CROVANI

0   1000

Metres

Depths in Metres

Cap Cavallo looking S

L'Ile de la Morsetta and passage

This islet lies 300m to the S of Cap de la Morsetta
and is 16m high and 150m long, has awash and just
covered rocks on E–SE S–NW sides. An easy passage
100m wide least depth 17m lies between the isle and
the cape. This passage should be taken in an
ESE–WNW directions equidistant between the two.

Cap de la Morsetta looking N

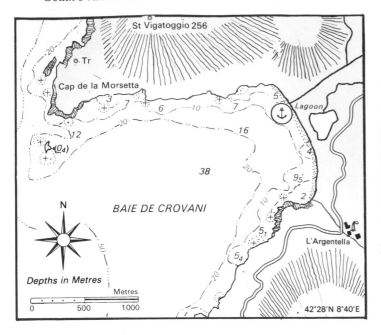

South France Pilot – La Corse

Baie de Crovani looking NE

⚓ Baie de Crovani

A spacious anchorage in a wide bay with a long white sandy beach, with beach restaurant. Surrounded by high mountains in the background. Anchor off the beach in 4–3m sand and stone open to SW–W–NW. Deserted. At the S end of the bay is a small landing stage with an overhead railway (disused) running via a small village and a factory at L'Argentella (1km inland) to the old silver and lead mines inland. The coast road runs through this valley. Another factory lies inland off the N end of the beach.

⚓ Baie de Martino

A bay which has a small cove with a sand and stone beach in its SE corner. Anchor off the beach in 2m sand open to W–NW–N. Exercise caution when entering there are two small awash rocks in the offing. Coast road inland. Deserted.

Pointe Ciuttone

A high prominent headland with red rocky cliffs, and one close inshore islet otherwise steep-to. Inland the point rises to 200m with a stony pyramid half way up the slope.

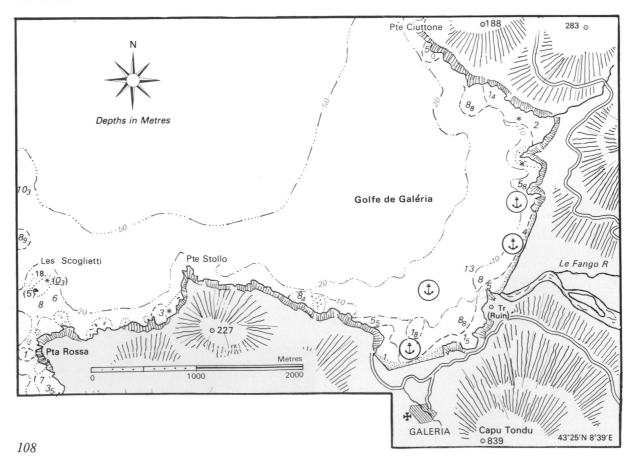

108

⚓ Golfe de Galéria N

This wide deep gulf has one long, one medium and several small sandy beaches. The N anchorage is off the N end of the long beach, Le Plage de Fango, in 4m sand open to W–NW–N. The area is backed by a wide river valley and The Tour de Galéria stands on a hillock at the S end of this beach and close to the river mouth. There is a conspicuous cemetery and caravan site inland and track to the beach.

⚓ Golfe de Galéria S

This anchorage is off the medium sized beach in the S of the bay. The village of Galéria which has an hotel, some shops and many houses stand behind the beach. There is also a caravan site. Road runs to the main coast road and a fuel station is 3M inland. Anchor in 3m sand, mud and rock off the beach and clear of moorings and paying attention in the approach to a 1·8m shallow patch off the centre of the beach. Open to W–NW–N. A deep anchorage lies 700m to N of this beach in 16m sand and mud. Offlying rocks 500 and 1000m to W.

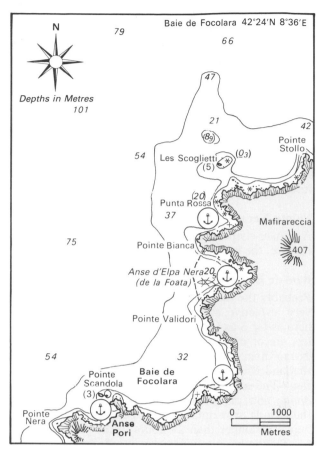

⚓ Golfe de Galéria S looking SE

Pointe Stollo

A small narrow rocky-cliffed headland steep-to and only visible when coasting close in.

⚓ Les Scoglietti and passage

An important and dangerous shoal area of islets, awash and covered rocks stretching up to 600m to NNW of Punta Rossa. The Ile Scoglietti is 5m high. A passage 200m wide and 8m deep exists between a group of islets lying off N side of Punta Rossa and a second group lying near Ile Scoglietti. Take the passage in NE–SW directions.

Punta Rossa

A broken rocky-cliffed point with offlying dangers – see above, sloping up to 100m high inland.

⚓ Punta Rossa S

A small bay with rocky cliffs anchor near head of bay in 4m rocks open to SW–W–NW. Deserted.

Pointe Bianca

A small headland similar to Punta Rossa, steep-to but sloping up to 408m.

⚓ Anse d'Elpa Nera (de la Foata)

A small rocky-cliffed bay. Anchor in 6m rock near head of bay, high land behind. Deserted. Fishing and subaqua diving forbidden. Open to SW–W–NW.

Pointe de Validori

A wide rocky-cliffed headland, a few small rocks close inshore otherwise steep-to.

⚓ Baie de Focolara

A wide deep bay surrounded by high rocky cliffs and a range of high tree covered hills. It is most attractive. Anchor near the centre of the bay just to N of a projecting rock in 4m rocks open to W–NW–N. Deserted. Small stream.

Pointe Scandola

A narrow rocky projecting point with Ilot Pori (31m) lying 200m to NW of the point.

Ilot Pori and passage

Ilot Pori (31m) which lies 200m to NW of Pointe Scandola and it has a small exposed rock 100m to its E. Pointe Scandola has two exposed rocks close inshore. A passage 50m wide lies between the rocks close to Pointe Scandola and the rock off Ilot Pori with a minimum depth of 16m. Take the passage in NE–SW directions with great care in calm conditions.

⚓ Anse Pori

A small rocky bay with an anchorage in 6m rocks at its head, open to W–NW–N. Deserted.

Pointe Nera

A square-shaped rocky headland with an islet close inshore, the land behind slopes up to 303m.

Baie de Elbo

Probably the most fantastic and beautiful area in the very attractive section of coast that stretches from here as far S as Cap Rossa. The cliffs, islands and islets are of dark red rock and their shapes are most extraordinary. The sea is clear dark blue and most of the land is covered with light and dark green vegetation. The area is a nature reserve, fishing, subaqua diving and camping are forbidden; also landing on the islands or mainland is not permitted and no boat may stay longer than 24 hours in the area. See page 112 for the boundaries of the area. In addition to the anchorage in the Marine d'Elbo there are many creeks, caves and fissures to explore in the area, some have vertical sides, an ideal place for fantastic photographs. Open to NW–N–NE.

Ile d'Elbo   Tour d'Elbo

Marine d'Elbo looking SE

Ile d'Elbo   Tour d'Elbo

⚓ Marine d'Elbo looking SE

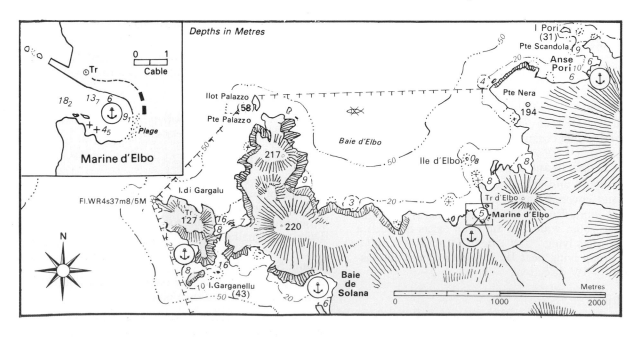

Ile di Gargalu

⚓ Marine d'Elbo

A small creek with a sand and stone beach used by fishermen. A line of rocky islets and awash rocks terminate at the rocky Ile d'Elbo. The Tour d'Elbo on the E side of the harbour is conspicuous. A lone awash rock lies 200m NW of the W side of the entrance. Anchor in 4m sand and weed in the centre of the creek, open to NW–N–NE, mooring to two anchors is advised. Track inland and a ruined hut near the beach. Deserted. Winds from SE–S–SW sometimes funnel down the valley behind the anchorage.

Pointe Palazzo

A high steep-sided point of very jagged aspect and with vertical striation. Steep-to with Ilot Palazzo (58m) off its NW corner and a smaller *îlot* off its N side.

Ile di Gargalu (Cargolo) and passage looking S
Ile di Gargalu

Ilot Palazzo

Pointe Palazzo and Ilot Palazzo looking SW

Ile di Gargalu (Cargolo) and passage looking N
Ile di Gargalu

Ilot Palazzo and passage

A simple little passage 45m wide and 22m deep between an almost vertical red rocky point and a steep-sided îlot 58m high. Take it in NE–SW directions in calm conditions. There is a smaller nameless îlot to the E of Ilot Palazzo with a narrow passage which can be used with great care by experienced navigators.

Ile di Gargalu (Cargolo) and passage

The largish red rocky Ile di Gargalu is 75m long and 45m wide, the highest point where there is a tower is 127m. There is an inconspicuous lighthouse on a neck of rocks that stretches out to NW (Fl.WR.4s 37m8/5M white column black top). There is a 40m long passage 10m wide and 2·5m deep to be taken in N–S directions; this passage should only be attempted in good conditions. The approach from the N is easy and 16m can be carried into the passage. From the S it is necessary to approach the entrance on a NW course carrying 16m into the passage. However three large rocks in mid passage reduce the depth to 2·5m and the width to 10m, care is necessary here and a good forward lookout is advised, the water is clear and the bottom can be seen, proceed slowly.

Ile di Gargalu (Cargolo) and passage looking S

⚓ Baie di Solana

A deep anchorage in a small rocky-cliffed bay in 16m rock open to S–SW–W. Use only in good conditions. Deserted.

'Dog Leg' passage

A passage with fantastic scenery around a small unnamed island in a creek, both the sides of the creek

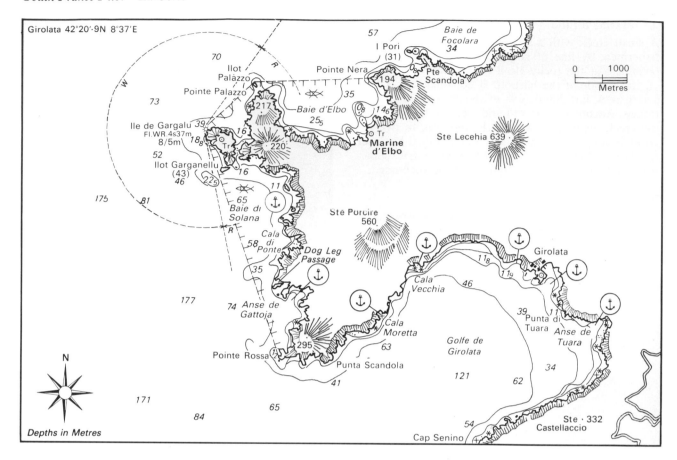

and the island have very nearly vertical red rock cliffs. The water is very deep 11 to 27m. This passage is just to N of the Anse de Gattoja and there is a pyramid shaped rocky islet on the S side of the S entrance. Keep a look out for tourist boats from Calvi.

⚓ Anse de Gattoja (Gattaghia)

An anchorage in a bay surrounded by high red rocky cliffs of extraordinary shape. There is a small rocky beach at the head of the bay. Anchor in 9m rock in good weather, open to S–SW–W. Deserted.

Pointe Rossa (Punta Muchillina)

A red rocky-cliffed point which is very prominent. There are awash and covered rocks extending 100m off shore.

Pointe Rossa looking N

'Dog Leg' Passage   ⚓ Anse de Gattoja

⚓ Anse de Gattoja and 'Dog Leg' passage

Pointe Rossa looking S

Pointe Scandola

A similar point to that above but pointing S. Do not mistake for a long thin unnamed point 500m from the Pointe Rossa.

⌓ Cala Moretta

A very useful anchorage in attractive surroundings but it has four small islets across the entrance and careful navigation is necessary to enter. A stone and sand beach at the head, anchor off this beach in 3m sand and weed. Open to E–SE–S. Deserted.

⌓ Cala Vecchia

A wide bay with a small beach of sand and stone at its head. The surroundings are striking with red rocky cliffs and the land sloping back to 446m. Some rocks on N side of the bay. Navigate with care. Anchor off the beach in 3m rock and sand open to E–SE–S. Deserted.

⌓ Girolata W

A small creek-type anchorage for two or three yachts. It is 500m NW of the Girolata fort. The creek has rocky-cliffed sides and a small sand and stone beach at its head. Moor with two anchors in 3m sand and rock off the beach open to S–SW. Track to Elbo and Girolata. Deserted.

3·9 Port de Girolata

20118 Corse du Sud

Position 42°20'·89N 8°37'·05E
Minimum depth in the entrance 16m (52ft)
in the harbour 10 to 0m (33 to 0ft)
Width of the entrance 200m (656ft)
Population 20 (approx)
Rating 1–2–4

General

Not really a harbour but a superb and beautiful anchorage which is reasonably safe under most conditions for yachts drawing less than 2m. The shelter for deeper draught craft is not good because they must anchor near the entrance and might have to leave in heavy SW winds. Approach and entrance are easy. Unfortunately this anchorage, which is a popular shelter between Calvi and Cargèse, becomes dangerously crowded in the season. Yachtsmen are advised not to use it during the months of July and August when there are over 100 yachts at anchor each evening and only the first 15 yachts will find good shelter. Late arrivals have to anchor at the mouth of the *cala* fully exposed to S–SW–W. Motor boats run daily trips from Calvi, Porto and Ajaccio and other harbours for tourists to this anchorage. The only facilities are several restaurant café/bars and a small shop ashore.

Data

Charts

Admiralty *1999*
French *7050*
ECM *1006*

Magnetic variation

0°20'W (1990) decreasing by 7' each year.

Buoys

Several small pick-up buoys belonging to the daily *vedettes*.

Warning

When approaching the coast in bad weather from the SW make quite certain that the yacht enters the Golfe de Girolata and not the Golfe de Porto. Both have towers on a pyramid-shaped peninsula at their

Fort

Girolata looking N

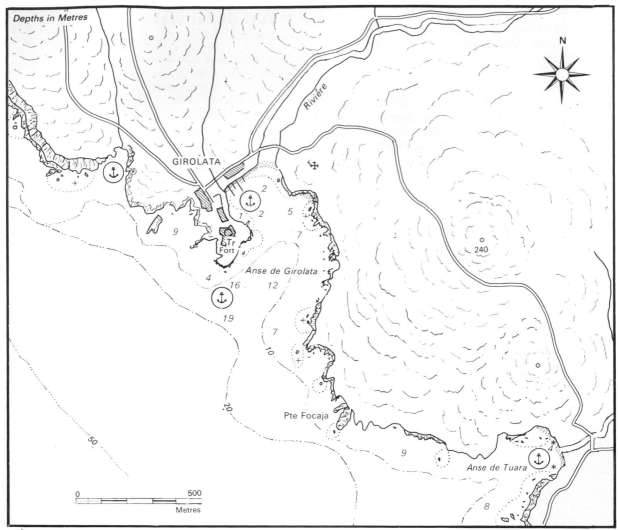

Port de Girolata

Golfes de Girolata and de Porto looking NE–E–SE–S

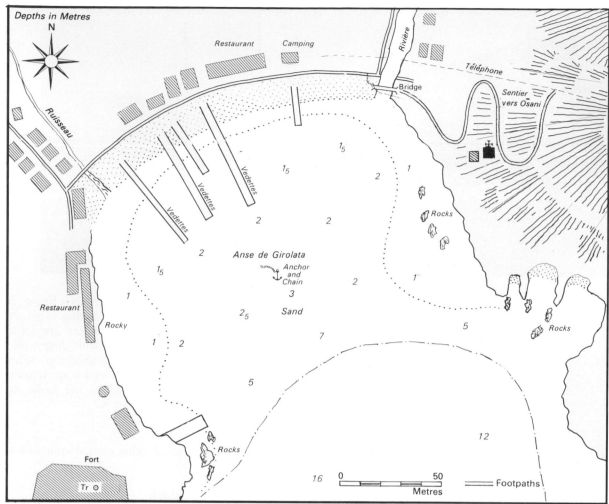

Depths in Metres
N

Restaurant   Camping

Rivière

Téléphone

Bridge

Sentier
vers Osani

Ruisseau

1_5

1_5

2

1_5

2

2

Vedettes

Vedettes

Vedettes

2

Vedettes

1_5

1

Anse de Girolata

Anchor
and
Chain

Rocks

Rocks

2

3

Restaurant

Sand

Rocky

2_5

1

1 2

7

5

5

12

Fort

Tr ⊙

Rocks

Rocks

1.6 0   50   ▬▬ Footpaths
                Metres

Girolata

head but Porto has no shelter and is very dangerous in these conditions. A very large anchor with lengths of heavy chain lies near the centre of this anchorage, an anchor tripline is essential. When approaching do not confuse Cap Rosso with Punta Rossa, the first being on the S side of the Golfe de Galéria and the other on the S side of the Golfe de Porto. (There are also other headlands of the same name.) Depths inside the harbour are approximate.

Approach by day

From N Round the easily recognised Ile di Gargalu which is of dark red bare rock with a small light tower, and follow the coast which is steep-to, as far as Pointe Rossa, a jagged sloping promontory with small islands very close to the point. Round this point onto a NE course and at the head of the Golfe will be seen a fort with a tower on a small pyramid-shaped promontory. Set course for this point.

Cap Rosso

115

Fort   Entrance

Girolata. Approach looking E

Fort and tower

Girolata. Approach looking NE

Fort and tower   Anse de Girolata

Girolata. Entrance looking NNE

From S Follow the indented coast to Cap Rosso, a promontory with a low-cliffed point sloping to a very high hill with a tower on its top. There are some small islands off the point. Cross the wide deep Golfe de Porto which has high jagged mountainous sides towards the high Punta a Scoppa and Cap Senino. The fort with tower at the head of the Golfe de Girolata will now be seen, head for it.

Approach by night

Due to lack of navigational lights a night approach is not advised.

Anchorage in the approach

The gulf is deep and the only anchorage in the approach is some 200m to S of the fort in 15m sand or in a small sandy bay 600m to SE.

Entrance

By day Round the S tip of this promontory on which stands the fort at 50m onto a N course and proceed very slowly towards the head of the bay sounding constantly.

Anchorage

Anchor with tripline as near to the NW corner as draught will permit if a SW *libeccio* is blowing or expected, otherwise near the centre of the bay. Mooring to two anchors or taking a line ashore is advised owing to restricted swinging room. At night the land breeze can be quite strong usually blowing from a NE direction down the valley. Except for the sides of the bay which are rocks and weed the bottom is coarse sand which does not offer very good holding ground. Heavy anchors of the fisherman-type with chain are advised. Alternative anchorage in Anse de Tuara 900m to SE but this is exposed to the SW *libeccio*.

Formalities

None.

Charges

None.

Landings

Four wooden cat walk-type piers at the head of the bay are used by the *vedettes* but can also be used for landing from dinghies.

Facilities

Slip It is possible to use parts of the beach as a slip if necessary.

Water The local restaurants and houses have a water supply piped from a cistern but are unlikely to be able to supply yachts except in an emergency. There is a cistern about 100m up the river where cans could be filled.

Garbage Because there is no place to dispose of rubbish and it cannot be collected by the local authorities, rubbish must be kept on the yacht and disposed of at the next harbour. Do not under any circumstances add to the mess ashore left by previous visitors.

Provisions Simple provisions available from a small shop which only opens on occasions.

Post office At Osani 2M direct but 5M by track. Mail delivered twice a week by mule.

Hotels One small pension-type.

Restaurants Four restaurant/bars.

Visits Climb up to the old fort for an excellent view. The long walks to Elbo or Osani are possible for the very fit.

Beaches A small beach on the E side of the harbour and another at its head.

Communications A mule and footpath to Osani 5M where there is a bus service and taxis.

⚓ Anse de Tuara

A small bay at the foot of a valley at the mouth of a small river with a beach of sand and stone at its head. Anchor in 5m sand and weed off the beach open to S–SW–W some rocks on the E side of the entrance. Track to Girolata and also to coast road. A useful alternative to Girolata.

Golfe de Porto

A wide mouthed deep bay surrounded by high hills and mountains mostly of red rock. Some of the cliffs on the S side of the gulf are especially spectacular. There are anchorages on both sides of the golfe and one at its head. These anchorages should be used with caution because the gulf is funnel-shaped with high sides, and this configuration is carried on inland up a valley at the head of the gulf. Because of this shape any SW–W–NW wind is speeded up as it passes up the gulf and the seas become very rough. Yachts will find it very difficult to leave the area and are, on occasions, driven ashore. With strong or gale force winds from the W quarter yachts should never attempt to enter this gulf but should keep well clear of the coast and eventually seek shelter in Calvi (20M) or Ajaccio (25M). In poor visibility or at a distance it is easy to mistake the Golfe de Porto for the Golfe de Girolata, careful navigation is advised.

Cap Senino (Osani)

An important red rocky headland rounded and facing NW, steep-to backed by the high pyramid-shaped Mont Senino (618m).

Cap Rosso (background), Cap Senino (foreground) looking SW

Pointe Scopa (Punta a Scoppa)

A similar feature to Cap Senino. Shallows to NW of this point.

⚓ Anse Lignaggia

A large bay with rocky cliffs and high (250m) land behind. Anchor in N corner in 5m sand, open to SE–S–SW–W, deserted.

⚓ Anse Gradelle W

A small bay with rocky cliffs and a beach of sand and stone at its head. A track leads up the valley, some houses behind the beach. Anchor off the beach in 5m sand avoiding an awash rock on the E side. Open to SE–S–SW.

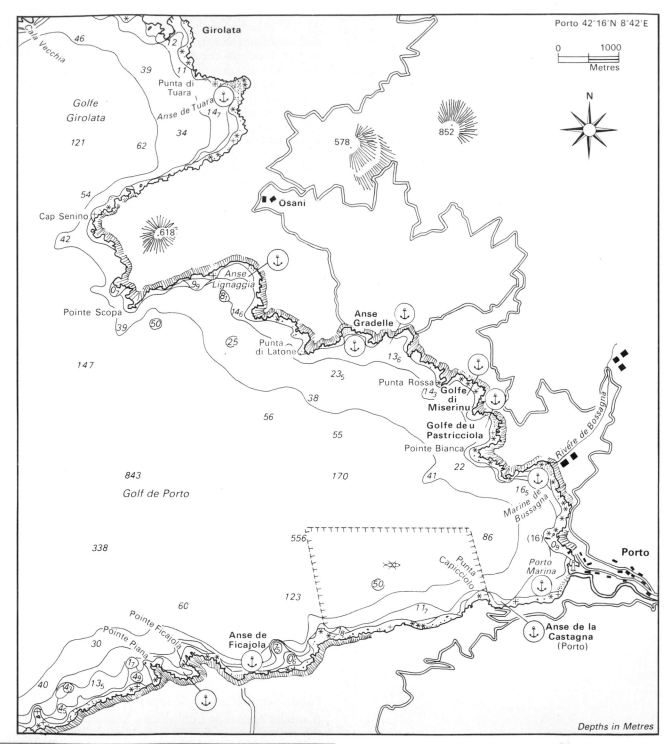

Porto 42°16′N 8°42′E

Depths in Metres

⚓ Anse de Gradelle W looking N

⚓ Anse Gradelle E (Pilatri or Caspio)

Exactly similar to Gradelle W but no houses and no awash rock. It is open to S–SW–W.

⚓ Golfe di Miserinu

A rocky-cliffed small bay. Anchor in NW corner in 5m rock. It is open to S–SW–W and deserted.

⚓ Golfe de u Pastricciola

Another rocky-cliffed bay which faces W. Anchor in N corner in 5m rock. Open to S–SW–W.

⚓ Anse de Gradelle E looking N

Pointe Bianca

A high rocky-cliffed point with rocky dangers extending 150m offshore. The land behind slopes up to 262m and a coast road runs across it.

⚓ Marine de Bussagna (Bussaghio)

A large bay with a long sand and stone beach. A river valley runs inland where there are a number of houses, small hotels and restaurants, a road joins the main coast road. There are beach restaurants and cafes. An awash rock is located just offshore in the middle of the beach. Anchor in N corner in 5m sand. Open to S–SW–W.

Porto

This beautiful fishing village in magnificent surroundings is being rapidly spoiled by the construction of cheap and nasty apartment blocks and hotels for holidaymakers and by the daily arrival of

⚓ Marine de Bussagna looking NE

hundreds of cars and coaches disgorging day-trippers. The harbour which is in the mouth of a river is only suitable for small fishing boats and dinghies. There is a quay with 1·5m alongside on the N side of a pinnacle rock with a small square fort on top. This is in frequent use by tourist boats from Calvi and sometimes by local fishermen. There are many restaurants and cafés. Everyday requirements can be obtained from the village. Marine engineer and chandlers. A restricted area lies to W of Porto between Punta Capicciolo and an unnamed headland 1½M to W where subaqua fishing is forbidden. (See chart page 118).

Quay   *River mouth*

⚓ Porto Marina looking E

⚓ Porto Marina

Anchor off the mouth of the river which is S of the pinnacle rock with a square fort on top or off the N end of the beach in 5m sand. Open to SW–W–NW. Be prepared to leave at short notice should the weather change. Shallow draught craft can enter the river where there are some wooden quays.

⚓ Porto (Anse de la Castagna)

A minute deserted anchorage in 5m sand tucked away behind Pointe Capicciolo open to N–NE and where some protection from the NW–W may be found. Two anchors are advised due to the wind swirling around the point and down the steep hills. The bay has steep sides and there is a small quay (2m) alongside with a road to Porto.

⚓ Anse de Ficajola E

Another small anchorage in beautiful surroundings at the foot of the Côte des Calanques. Anchorages and moorings to S of a small beach in 10m sand. A restaurant ¼M up a rocky path is open in the season, there are fishermen's huts on the beach. The anchorage is open to NW–N–NE but is still subject to a swell from W. At the top of the hill after a tremendous climb to NW lies the town of Piana where everyday supplies can be bought.

⚓ Anse de Ficajola looking S

Pointe Ficajola

A red rocky-cliffed promontory lying at 45° to the coast pointing NW. A 2·8m shallows to N of the point, otherwise steep-to.

⚓ Pointe Ficajola W

A small creek-like bay with high red rocky cliffs, anchor in 10m rock at head of bay open to W–NW–N. Deserted.

Pointe Piana

Similar to Pointe Ficajola described above.

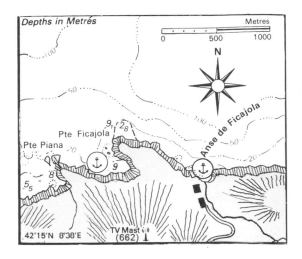

⚓ Pointe Ficajola W, Pointe Piana and ★ Pointe Piana W looking SE

Ilot Vardiola

A conspicuous islet 32m high of red rock which stands 200m off the coast.

⚓ Pointe Vardiola E

A V-shaped bay with high red rocky cliffs. Anchor at head of bay in 10m rock open to NW–N–NE.

Pointe Vardiola

A 200m tapered red rocky point steep-to but with rocky islets, rocks and awash rocks to its W extending the same distance from the coast.

⚓ Pointe Vardiola W

A spectacular anchorage for the skilled navigator. Enter between the two pairs of rocky islets on a SE heading, there is gap 100m wide, anchor at the head of the bay under high steep red rocky cliffs in 3m sand and rocky patches. Open to W–NW–N. Deserted.

Ilot Vardiola

⚓ Pointe Vardiola W and Pointe Vardiola looking SE

Cap Rosso (Cap Rossu)

An important headland of peninsula-shape with the conspicuous Tour de Turghio on top of a pointed hill (342m). The point is of high broken reddish rocky cliffs with an islet 100m to W and some rocky heads and shallows 200m to N.

⚓ Cap Rosso NE

A handy anchorage with fantastic surroundings, a 342m steep cliff to SW and two white sand and stone beaches. Anchor off the beaches in 3m rock and sand with care because there are a number of small rock heads close in. This anchorage is open to NW–N–NE. Deserted.

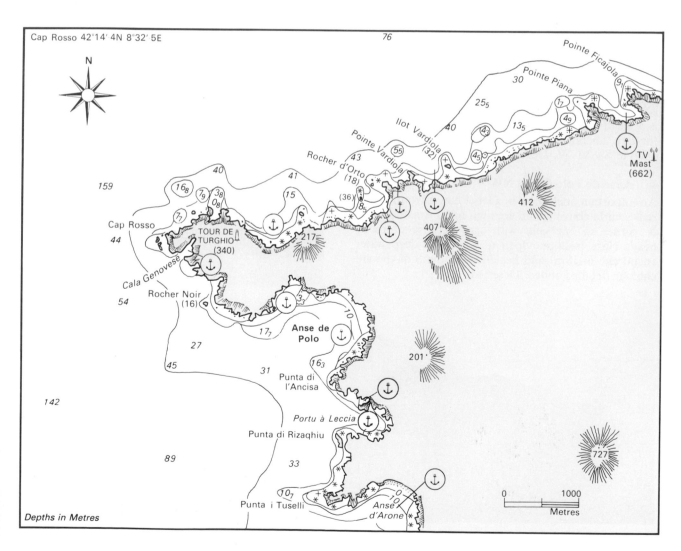

Cap Rosso 42°14′4N 8°32′5E

Depths in Metres

Entrance ⚓ *Cala Genovese*   *Tower*

⚓ Cap Rosso SW looking NE

Cap Rosso passage

A passage 250m long 3m deep and 75m wide at the N end. It lies between the 18m high and 200m long islet, Sbiro, off the W point of Cap Rosso. Use from S to N for the first time because the entrance is obvious from the S end. Navigate with care at slow speed with a bow lookout, in calm weather.

⚓ Cala Genovese

Another spectacular anchorage for the experienced navigator in calm weather. The entrance is close to W side of Cap Rosso and is 200m to S of the offlying islet. It has high steep red cliffs and is narrow, there is a small white sand and stone beach at the head of the bay, anchor off this beach in 5m sand and rock, open to S–SW–W. Deserted.

⚓ Anse de Polo (Palu) NW

An important anchorage in a large bay surrounded by rocky cliffs above which are high hills. Anchor in the N corner in 5m sand with care because of rocky heads close inshore. Open to S–SW. A deep water anchorage in 18m sand lies 700m to the S of the anchorage detailed above. Deserted.

⚓ Anse de Polo (Palu) E

Another anchorage in the same bay in 5m sand and weed open to S–SW–W. Deserted.

⚓ Porta â Leccia

A small anchorage in 6 to 10m rock and sand open to SW–W–NW. Road inland.

Pointe de Tuselli (Punta i Tuselli)

A hooked point with rocky cliffs and rocky dangers extending 400m W from the point, a hill (97m) stands behind the point.

⚓ Anse d'Arone

A long bay with black rocky-cliffed sides and a large sandy beach at the head. Some houses, a caravan site and a road inland stand behind the beach. The anchorage is off the beach in 4m sand, it is open to S–SW–W.

⚓ Golfe de Topiti (Orchino)

A deep bay sheltered from the S and SW by the mass of Pointe d'Orchino and with rocky cliffs around it. At its head are some small sand and stone beaches and an open valley. Anchor at the head of the bay in 5m sand, open to W–NW–N. Pay attention to some rocky heads near the shore.

⚓ Golfe de Topiti looking E

Golfe de Topiti

⚓ Anse de Polo NW looking NE

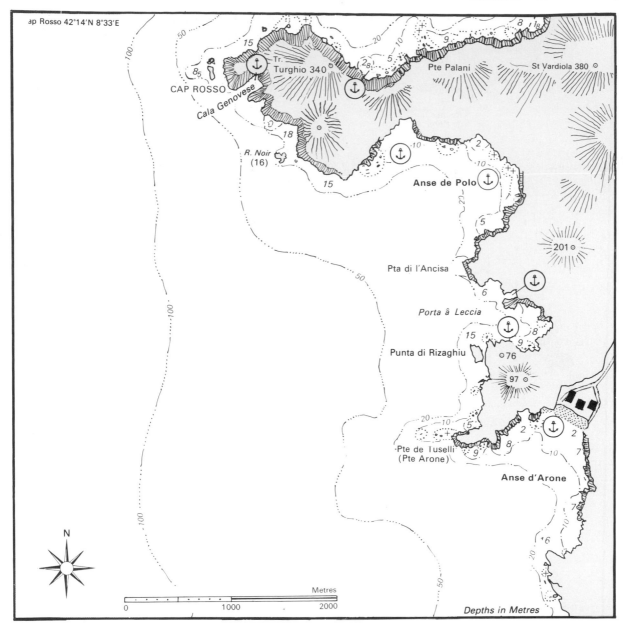

ap Rosso 42°14′N 8°33′E

CAP ROSSO

Cala Genovese

Tr. Turghio 340

Pte Palani

St Vardiola 380

R. Noir (16)

Anse de Polo

Pta di l'Ancisa

Porta â Leccia

Punta di Rizaghiu

Pte de Tuselli (Pte Arone)

Anse d'Arone

N

Metres

0   1000   2000

Depths in Metres

Pointe d'Orchino

A large prominent point 184m high inland where there is a conspicuous tower. A rounded point with an islet and rocky dangers extending W 200m.

⚓ Baie de Chioni

A wide deep bay with sandy beach at its head and behind it a conspicuous Club Méditerranée site with buildings that look like sails. Coast road inland. Anchor off beach in 5m sand open to SW–W–NW. A small bay on the S side of the bay provides a useful alternative calm weather anchorage in 6m rock.

Pointe d'Omignia

A long narrow low rocky promontory with a conspicuous tower near its point. A small rock and 0·9m shallows 75m off its point.

⚓ Pte d'Orchino looking NE

⚓ Baie de Chioni looking NE

123

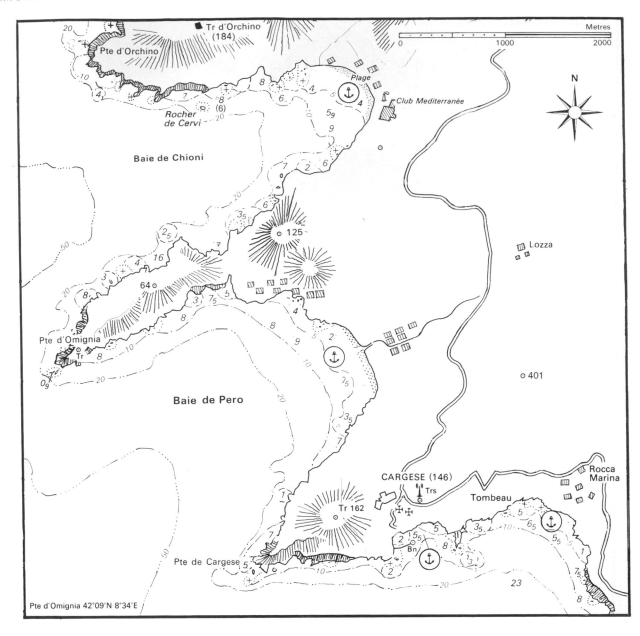

Metres
0   1000   2000

Tr d'Orchino
(184)

Pte d'Orchino

Plage

Club Mediterranée

Rocher
de Cervi

Baie de Chioni

N

125

Lozza

64

Pte d'Omignia
Tr

Baie de Pero

401

CARGESE (146)
Trs

Rocca
Marina

Tombeau

Tr 162

Bn

Pte de Cargese

Pte d'Omignia 42°09'N 8°34'E

⚓ Baie de Pero (Golfe de Peru)

A wide deep bay with sandy beach behind which are
sand dunes and the houses of Cargèse. There is also
a housing estate in the N corner. Anchor off beach in
4m sand. Open to S–SW–W.

Pointe de Cargèse

A pointed promontory with rocky cliffs and a conspicuous tower standing on a hill behind the point
162m high. The houses of Cargèse to NE of the
tower are easily seen.

Pointe d'Omignia looking E–SE. Pointe de Cargèse in background

⚓ Baie de Pero, Pte d'Omignia and de Cargèse looking NE

⚓ Baie de Pero and Pointe de Cargèse looking NE

Pointe de Cargèse looking SE

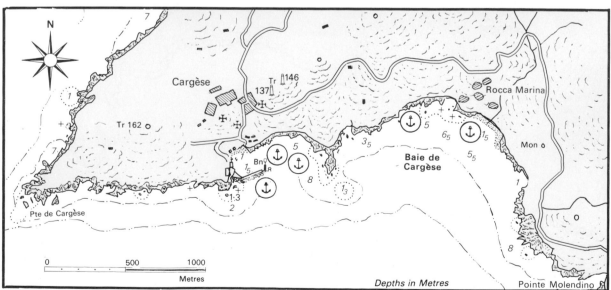

Port de Cargèse

3·10 Port de Cargèse

20130 Corse du Sud

Position 42°07′·90N 8°35′·90E
Minimum depth in the entrance 6m (20ft)
in the harbour 3 to 1m (9·8 to 3·3ft)
Width of the entrance 200m (656ft)
Number of berths 105
Population 989
Rating 3–3–3

General

A small fishing harbour which offers very limited space to yachts and becomes very crowded in the season. Easy to approach and enter but unless a berth can be obtained behind the jetty it can be uncomfortable with S to SW winds and swell and with strong SW winds dangerous to enter. Everyday requirements can be obtained from the interesting old village on the hill overlooking the harbour. Temporary anchorage is possible just outside the harbour entrance and a more secure one in the Baie de Ménasina about ¾M to E but both are open to S to SW.

Data

Charts

Admiralty *1985*
French *7050, 6821, 6942*
ECM *1007*

Magnetic variation

0°20′W (1990) decreasing by 7′ each year.

Warning

A shallow rocky area 1·3m (4·3ft) lies off the point just to the E of this harbour. The quay behind the breakwater has extended rocky feet.

Approach by day

From N The sloping, reddish, rocky promontory of Cap Rosso and the four points to the S, Pointes Tuselli, Orchino, d'Omignia (which has a conspicuous tower) and Cargèse, also with a conspicuous tower, are easily identified. Pointe de Cargèse has the town of Cargèse on a saddle just to NE of the tower. All of these points have offlying islands and rocks and should be given a 300m berth. An E course for 1M from Pointe de Cargèse brings this harbour abeam and the rocky breakwater will be seen.

From S Cross the wide and deep Golfe de Sagone on a N course from Cap de Feno, a low rocky-cliffed point with a ruined tower towards the far side of the golfe where the points listed above will be seen with Cap Rosso in the far distance. The nearer, Pointe de Cargèse has a tower on its summit and the town of Cargèse shows on the skyline just to the E of it. Below the town lies the harbour. The two church towers are conspicuous.

Approach by night

As there are no navigational lights a night approach and entrance are not advised.

Anchorage in the approach

It is possible to anchor 200m to S of this harbour entrance in 16m (52ft) rocks and boulders but the holding is poor.

Entrance

Enter on a NW course 15m from the head of the jetty at slow speed and sounding with care.

Berths

It may be possible to secure stern-to the inner side of the jetty with anchor and tripline ahead. There are some mooring buoys but these belong to the fishermen. Note that the foot of the jetty is shallow and rocky.

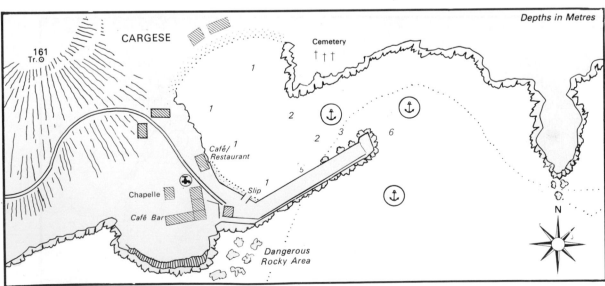

Port de Cargèse

Baie de Pero

Cargèse looking NE

Entrance   *Baie de Cargèse*

Cargèse. Approach looking N

Entrance

Cargèse. Entrance looking N

Anchorages

It is possible to anchor in 2m rock, sand and weed just inside the harbour but the holding is poor. A worthwhile alternative is to anchor in 3m sand off the beach in the Baie de Cargèse ½M to the E.

Formalities

Normally none.

Charges

Harbour charges are not normally levied.

Facilities

Slip A small slip at W side of the harbour.
Hard A sandy hard standing in the SW corner of the harbour.
Fuel Pumps for petrol and diesel (*gasoil*) in the town.
Water A water point from the café/bar.

Provisions Shops, supermarket and a market in the town which is at the top of the hill above the harbour. A stiff climb up a path or zig-zag road.

Garbage One rubbish container on the jetty.

Repairs A motor mechanic at the garage in the town.

Chandlery A shop in the town.

Post office A PTT in the town.

Hotels One ***, three ** and five * hotels and one unclassified.

Restaurants Several restaurant/bars and café/bars cater for the tourist trade and especially the bus-loads of holidaymakers from Ajaccio.

Information office Rue du Dr Dragacci (☎ 95 26 41 31).

Visits The Greek Orthodox church of Ste Marie, 19th century, and facing it the Roman Catholic church of the same name and period are worth a visit.

Beaches A rather poor beach inside the harbour with better beaches ¾M to N or E.

Communications Bus service along the coast.

Future development

Though no plans exist at the moment this harbour could easily be enlarged into a valuable yacht harbour. A part of the breakwater has been washed away and repairs were taking place in 1989. The breakwater head has been extended about 25m. Fuel pumps to be installed.

History

The history of this harbour is of particular interest in view of the present disharmony between the French Algerian settlers and the native Corsicans. In 1676 a group of Greeks from the Gulf of Colokythia in the Peloponnesus appealed to Genoa because they were being tyrannised by the Turks. The Genoese senate who were having difficulties themselves in crushing the Corsican resistance to their occupation of La Corse offered them the territories of Paomia, Reonda and Salogno located inland from Cargèse. In March 1676 some 730 Greeks arrived, settled in, and within a few years, due to their hard work, were becoming prosperous. Troubles commenced about three years later in 1679 when the Corsicans of Vice and Niolo, knowing the Greeks to be allies of Genoa and envying them their prosperity, murdered one of the Greeks. From this time on there was constant friction between the two groups ending in 1731 with the Greeks being driven out to take refuge in Ajaccio, and their villages being burnt to the ground. In 1768 when France annexed La Corse a new village, Cargèse, was built for the Greeks complete with their own church. The 110 remaining families who spoke only Greek and had kept their own religion, costume and customs, moved in and have remained there ever since. Over the ages they have intermarried with the native Corsicans and except for their religion and capacity for hard work, there is little to distinguish them from the native Corsican.

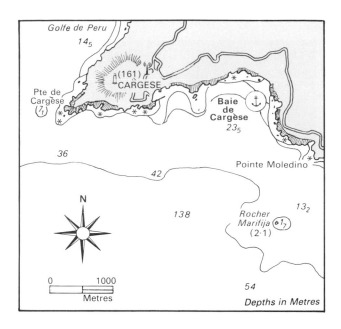

⚓ Baie de Cargèse looking NE

⚓ Baie de Cargèse

Two bays with a small rocky point and an offlying 1·8m shallows dividing them. Anchor in NE corner of either bay in 4m sand and rock open to SE–S–SW–W. Road runs above low rocky cliffs, a few houses. Landing very difficult due to rocks.

Pointe Molendino (Punta di Molendinu)

A small rocky-cliffed point with three small islets off the point otherwise steep-to.

Rocher Marifaja (Morifeja)

A small 1·8m isolated rock with a 1·7m shallow and some awash rocks close in. This rock lies 1000m SSW of Pointe Molendino.

⚓ Pointe des Moines N

A small bay with a sandy beach at its head, the sides are low with rocky cliffs, the coast road is a little way inland. Anchor off the beach in 3m sand open to S–SW–W. Some houses ashore.

Pointe des Moines

A small rocky point with awash and covered rocks extending 200m to S and W.

⚓ Plage de Ménasina (Marina de Monaccia)

A large open bay with a big sandy beach at its head and low rocky cliffs at each side with offlying rocks. A single awash rock is 100m off the N end of the beach. Anchor off the centre of the beach in 3m sand, open to SE–S–SW–W. The coast road runs behind the beach, with a few houses.

Pointe Puntiglione

A prominent pointed rocky-cliffed headland with 56m hill and coast road behind, a few rocky heads close in and a 2·7m rocky shallow 250m to S of the point.

Pointe de la Batterie

A prominent rocky-cliffed point which is easy to identify due to a conspicuous tower and battery just inland standing in some trees with the coast road in front. The cliffs have many dangerous rocks close in.

⚓ Plage de Ménasina looking NE

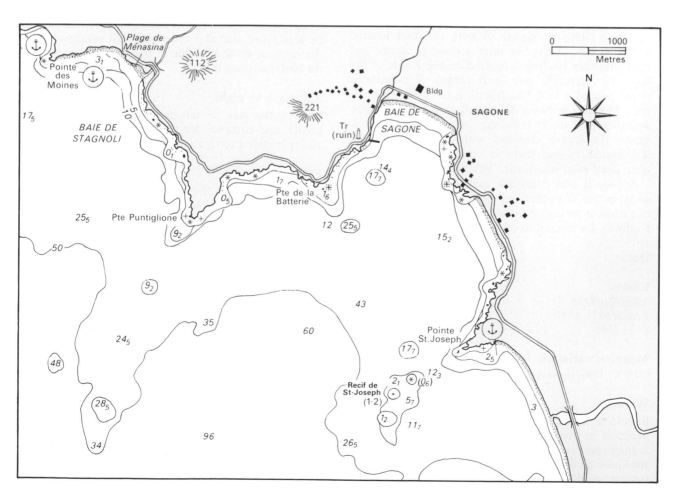

Pointe Puntiglione looking SE

3·11 Port de Sagone

20118 Corse du Sud

Position 42°06'·50N 8°41'·50E
Minimum depth in the entrance 12m (39ft)
 in the harbour 10 to 1m (33 to 3·3ft)
Width of the entrance ¾M
Number of berths 12
Population 100 (approx)
Rating 3–3–3

General

A bay open to S to SW lying at the head of the wide and deep Golfe de Sagone. A jetty and quay located at the W side of the bay offer a place to secure and land. Another landing is located on the E side of the bay. An attractive area with ranges of mountains rising behind a long beach with a river mouth at W end. The area is being developed as a holiday centre and there are many buildings being erected. In the season the area is crowded with camping sites and holidaymakers and there is constant traffic on the main coast road which runs behind the area.

Approach and entry are easy but even if tucked away in the W corner any heavy swell from the SW can make it an uncomfortable anchorage though safe. Facilities are limited to everyday requirements.

Data

Charts

Admiralty *1999*
French *6821, 6942*
ECM *1007*

Magnetic variation

0°28'W (1990) decreasing by 6–7' each year.

Warning

Should a strong SW wind get up and no space is available in the NW corner of the Baie de Sagone, it is important to leave this anchorage and work out of the Golfe de Sagone. If this is not possible some shelter can be obtained in the Baie de Liscia.

Approach by day

From NW Follow the N side of the Golfe de Sagone at 1M and outside the low (2·1m) Rocher Marifaja. When S of Pointe Puntiglione, a promontory that juts ½M out to sea, turn onto a NE course and enter the Baie de Sagone. The harbour lies close E to a conspicuous tower on the W side of the Baie.

From SW Round the low rocky-cliffed Cap de Feno with a ruined tower on its top, onto a NNE course passing outside the islet Piêtra Piombata and leaving the Récif de Paliagi and the Rocher de St Joseph well to starboard. The valley of the Rivière de Sagone will be seen from afar and the tower that stands close to the harbour on the W side of the Baie will be seen in the closer approach.

Approach by night

Due to the lack of navigational lights a night approach and entrance are not advised but possible for an experienced navigator.

Entrance

By day Approach the W side of the Baie on a N course and when identified approach the head of a small jetty.

Berths

Secure stern-to near the head of the jetty with anchor and tripline from the bow clear of local craft. The depth of water is nearly 10m at the head shelving back to about 3m at the root. A wood quay lies at 90° to the root of the jetty and is used by local fishing craft, it has rocky feet.

Anchorage

Anchor off the head of the jetty in 12m sand or near the moorings which lie to the N. A tripline for the anchor is advised.

Formalities

Normally none. A customs office is marked on the French charts but does not seem to exist.

Sagone. Approach to Baie de Sagone looking NE

Sagone. Approach to W side of Baie of Sagone

Sagone looking NNE

Charges

Harbour charges are not normally raised.

Facilities

Crane A crane of 5 tonnes is available.
Fuel Pumps for petrol and diesel (*gasoil*) in the village.
Water A water point on the quay.
Provisions Everyday requirements from a supermarket and other shops across the bridge over the river. Other shops in the village to the E.
Garbage A rubbish container on the quay.
Chandlery A shop in the village.
Repairs Repairs to hull and engine are possible.
Laundrette One located across the bridge.
Post office PTT in the village.
Hotels One *** and three ** hotels.
Restaurants Several restaurant/bars along the coast of the bay and in the village.
Information office Immeuble les Mimosas (☎ 95 98 06 36).
Visits The ruined cathedral and the statue-menhir beside the river should be visited.
Beach A long sandy beach at the head of the bay.
Communications A bus service.

Future development

A yacht harbour with two pontoons for fifty yachts is planned (which in La Corse may be a long time before construction).

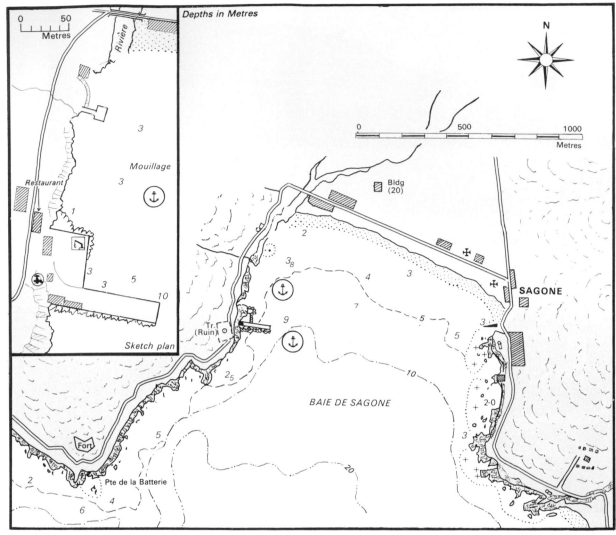

Port de Sagone

History

A very old town of importance and in the 6th century
the seat of an archbishop. Due to frequent raids by
Saracens and to its unhealthy site, the town and
cathedral were in ruins by the end of the 16th century and the archbishop was given permission to
move his seat to Vico, six miles inland. From Vico he
moved some fifty years later to Calvi. The cathedral,
built 1125, is of interest because it incorporates some
pagan 'Statue Menhirs' in its construction. In May
1812 seven French vessels at anchor close under the
tower were attacked by three British frigates which
were towed into range by their ships' boats due to
lack of wind. After a two hour engagement the
French ships blew up inflicting some damage to the
tower.

⚓ Baie de Sagone

This large deep sandy bottomed bay forms an excellent anchorage in depths of 3m up to 24m. It is
open to SE–S–SW but by thoughtful choice of anchorage the seas bought in by the SE and SW winds
can be considerably reduced. The bay has low rocky-
cliffed sides with a long sandy beach at its head, the
coast road runs around the bay and there is a road
running inland. Everyday requirements can be obtained from Sagone village – see also 3·11 Port de
Sagone page 130.

Pointe St Joseph

A sharp pointed rocky headland with an old battery
on top, rocky dangers extend 300m off the point, see
below.

Récif de St Joseph and passage

A shallow area with one awash rock and one rocky islet (1·2m) with depths of 1·3m to S. The awash rock
lies 900m to WSW of Pointe St Joseph. The reef is
400m wide extending 900m SSW from the awash
rock. The rocky islet lies near the centre of the reef.
A 500m wide passage lies between Pointe St Joseph

132

and this reef with a least depth of 9m, take the passage in NW–SE directions equidistant between the outer awash rocks of Pointe St Joseph and the awash rock in the reef.

Pointe St Joseph looking NE

Pointe de Locca looking SE

⚓ Plage de Liamone

A long sandy beach with the mouth of the Rivière Liamone and a road bridge near the centre. Opposite these features and 500m offshore lies a lone awash rock. Anchor in 3m sand off the beach, open to S–SW–W. The coast road lies behind the beach with a few houses.

Pointe Locca

A prominent sharp pointed rocky-cliffed headland with islet, rocks submerged and awash reaching 400m out from the point in a W direction. The Tour de Capigliolo on a hill 107m and an old tower 200m behind it are conspicuous.

⚓ Baie de Liscia N

A very wide bay with anchorage in a sub bay to NE also anchorages off a long sandy beach to S. The anchorage in the NE corner in 5m sand and weed is close to the village of Tiuccia, where everyday requirements can be bought. Several hotels here and a mechanic. There is a small exposed rocky islet in the approach and one awash near the shore, also near the shore are some permanent moorings. This anchorage is open to SW–W–NW. The village is famous for the Capraja Castle which belonged to the Counts of Ginarca who once ruled La Corse. This Castle lies to the S of the village. The other anchorages off the sandy beach are in 3m sand and open to SW–W–NW.

⚓ Baie de Liscia looking NE

Pointe Palmentojo

A pointed headland with rocky cliffs, the conspicuous Tour d'Orcino (40m) lies near the point with a hill sloping inland to 298m. Rocky islet, rocks awash and covered, extend 500m to NW.

⚓ Baie de Liscia looking NE

⚓ Baie de Liscia looking N

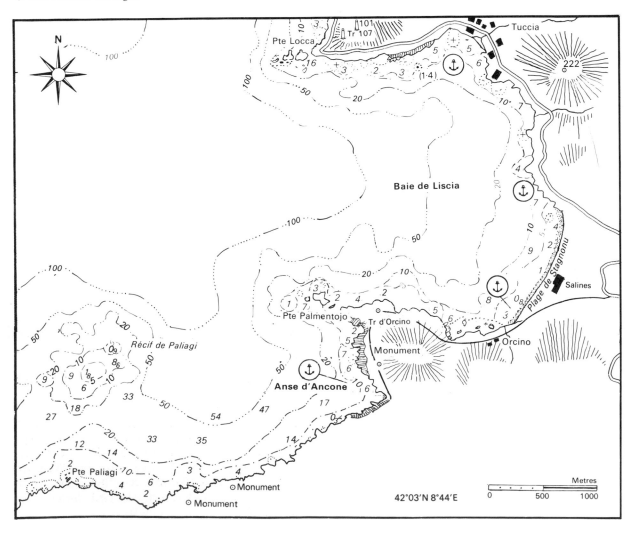

Pointe Pelusella looking SE

Iles de Pointe Palmentojo and passage

A short narrow passage about 50m long 40m wide and 2·5m deep exists between the islets off the Pointe Palmentojo and the small rocks close to the point to be taken in NE–SW directions. A reconnaissance by dinghy is advised first.

⚓ Anse d'Ancone

A small rocky-cliffed anchorage in 5m rock open to SW–W–NW in the E corner of a wide bay. Deserted.

Pointe Paliagi

A rounded headland of rocky cliffs, hills behind sloping up to 348m. Rocky islets extend 200m to N with a 2m depth 50m further on.

Récif de Paliagi and passage

This reef is centred 1200m to NNE of Pointe Paliagi, it has rocks covered 1m, 2m, 6m and 9m. A passage 1000m wide 60m long with a minimum depth of 10m lies 400m to N of the outer rocky islet off Pointe Paliagi to be taken in E–W directions.

Pointe Pelusella

A 90° point with rocky cliffs and sloping up to 111m. A ruined tower stands close to the point. An awash isolated rock (0·8m deep) lies 350m to NW of the point otherwise steep-to.

Port Provençale

The N corner of the Baie de Lava is referred to as Port Provençale but is only an anchorage that has many moorings laid for local fishing craft. There are good anchorages in 3 to 18m sand outside the moorings and off the sandy beach, open to SW–W–NW. There are many houses and several housing estates ashore, the village can provide everyday supplies also beach cafés, restaurants and hotels are available. There is a road to the main coast road. The S and SW coast of the Baie de Lava is foul with many rocks including a small islet, La Figiera 300m off the coast. Plans for a harbour exist.

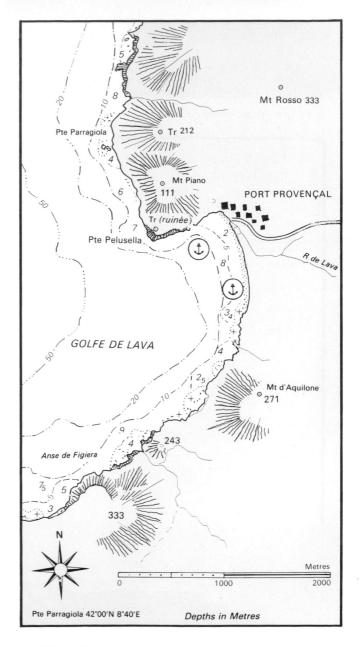

Pte Parragiola 42°00′N 8°40′E   Depths in Metres

Ile Piêtra Piombata and passage

A small islet lies 700m off the coast at the S side of the entrance to the Golfe de Lava. The islet is steep-to except for a rock 2m deep off the SE end of the islet. A 7m depth lies halfway between the island and the shore. A passage 200m wide, 100m long with a minimum depth of 10m lies 100m off the coast in E–W directions.

⚓ Port Provençale looking NE

Cap de Feno

An important and prominent point with high rocky broken cliffs and a conspicuous ruined tower standing on a 68m hill inland 200m from the point. The point has two close inshore islets on its W face and some small rocks extending 150m in a SW direction otherwise it is steep-to. In certain lights when approaching from the S the ruined tower has the appearance of a seated cat.

⚓ Anse de Fico N and S

Two popular anchorages. The N anchorage is in a rocky-sided bay off a white sandy beach in 6m sand and weed open to S–SW–W. A road and a track ashore, one house. This anchorage is the best of the two and offers the best protection. The S anchorage is in a small bay with rocky sides and a sandy beach. Anchor off the beach in 2m sand open to S–SW–W. Road ashore. Deserted. A rocky projection divides these two anchorages.

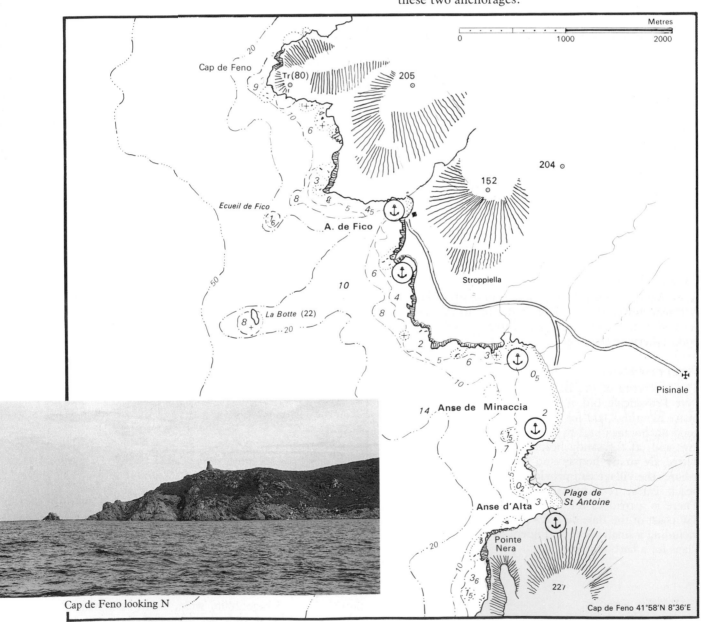

Cap de Feno looking N

Ecueil de Fico

A rock covered 1·6m is located 600m to WSW off a point (unnamed) that lies to the W of the ⚓ Anse de Fico N anchorage.

Ile la Botte

A 22m high island lies 1500m to WSW of Anse de Fico S. It is steep-to.

Ile la Botte looking W

⚓ Anse de Minaccia N and S

This large bay has a long sandy beach with anchorages at each end. Anchor in 3m sand off the beach open to S–SW–W. Sand dunes behind N end of the beach. Tracks behind the beach, a few houses and a housing estate behind the S end of the beach. Beach café. A rock covered 1·5m lies 50m off the S end of the beach.

⚓ Anse de Minaccia looking E

⚓ Anse d'Alta

A small bay with a sandy beach at its head, rocky sides. Anchor off beach in 3m sand open to SW–W–NW. Road and housing estate behind beach.

Pointe de la Corba

A small rocky point sloping up inland to 211m. Many small rocks extend up to 200m from the coast and an isolated rock 2m deep lies 400m to WSW of the point.

⚓ Anse de la Parata W

An open bay between Pointe de la Corba and Presqu'île de la Parata. Anchor in the corner off a small sandy beach in 3m sand, weed and rock. Open to SW–W–NW. Note that the rest of the bay has a low rocky cliff with many small rocks close in. There is a lot of weed on the beach.

⚓ Anse de la Parata W looking E

Iles Sanguinaires

An important attractive and dangerous feature which is similar to the Raz du Sein in Brittany but without the strong tidal streams. From NE to SW the high (283m) hills slope down to the Presqu'île de la Parata which consists of two distinctive parts, a low flat isthmus connected to a rounded feature with a small house and radio beacon mast on the top (86m). There is a road on the SE side leading to a restaurant. A second very low isthmus connects the first part to the second feature which is of a pyramid-shape (58m) with a conspicuous tower on top. It is essential to identify this feature if attempting the Passe de la Parata (des Sanguinaires).

SW of this pass lies Ilot Porre, two unnamed *îlots* and Ilot Cala d'Alga. Between these four *îlots* it is shallow and foul with rocky heads. The largest island Ile de la Grande Sanguinaire is the outer island, it has a white lighthouse black top and and white dwelling (Fl(3)W.15s98m27M) on the crest near the NE end. A signal station is located near the centre of the island and a tower stands near the SW end. There are rocks and shallows extending 500m SW from this point. The Ecueil du Tabernacle, an isolated rock 3m deep, stands 1300m to SE of the centre of this island and it is marked by a R pillar light buoy, □ topmark (Fl(3)R.12s).

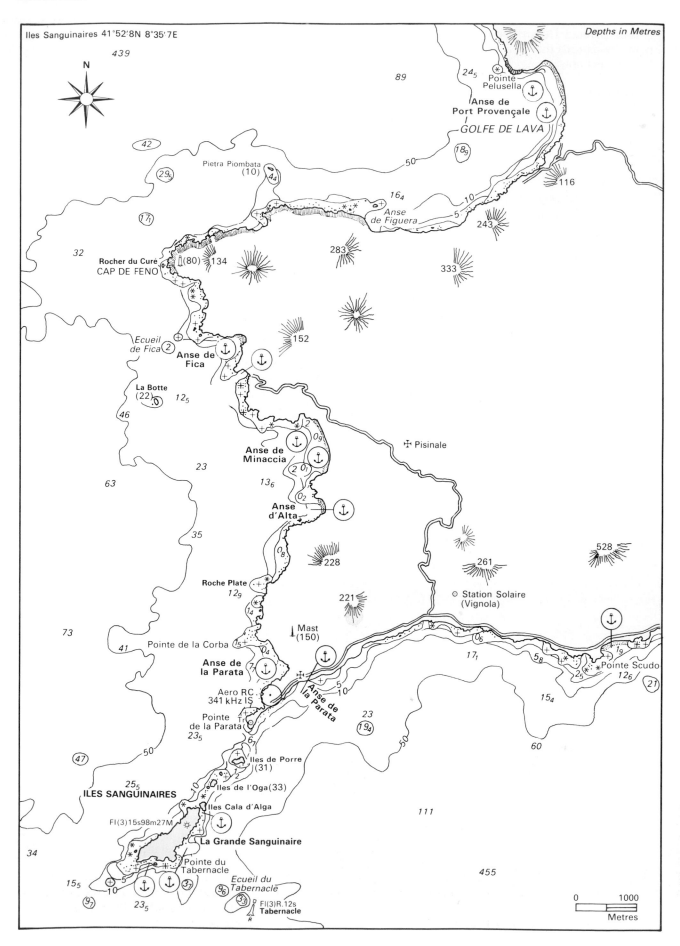

Iles Sanguinaires 41°52′8N 8°35′7E

Depths in Metres

439

42

29₅

Pietra Piombata (10) 4₄

17₁

32

Rocher du Curé (80) 134
CAP DE FENO

89

24₅
Pointe Pelusella
Anse de Port Provençale
GOLFE DE LAVA

18₉

50

16₄
Anse de Figuera

10

5

116

243

283

333

152

Ecueil de Fica 2
Anse de Fica

La Botte (22) 0

12₅

46

23

63

35

Anse de Minaccia
0₉
2 0₁
13₆
0₂

Anse d'Alta

✠ Pisinale

528

261

Station Solaire (Vignola)

0₈
228

221

Roche Plate 12₉
14

Anse de la Parata

Mast (150)

17₁

5₈
1₉
Pointe Scudo
2₅ 12₆
21

15₄

73

41
Pointe de la Corba 5
0₄
7

Aero RC 341 kHz IS

Pointe de la Parata
23₅

23
19₄

50

60

455

47

50

6₇
Iles de Porre (31)

25₅
2
ILES SANGUINAIRES
Iles de l'Oga (33)
Iles Cala d'Alga

Fl(3)15s98m27M

La Grande Sanguinaire

Pointe du Tabernacle

Ecueil du Tabernacle

111

34

15₅
5
10
9₇ 23₅

9₆
3₃ Fl(3)R.12s
Tabernacle
R

0   1000
Metres

Torre de La Parata   *Ilot Porre*   *La Grande Sanguinaire*

Iles Sanguinaires looking SE

Passages des Sanguinaires

The main passage is the Passe de la Parata (des Sanguinaires) between the Presqu'île de la Parata and Ilot Porre, it is 200m long, 200m wide with a minimum depth of 7m. Take the passage in E–W directions about 50m from the La Parata and 150m from Ilot Porre. For yachts drawing 2m or less the passage is 400m wide with a minimum depth of 2·8m. Currents of up to 3 knots can be experienced in the area and these frequently set across the passage. Under conditions of heavy seas and strong winds the use of this passage is not advised, round La Grande Sanguinaire keeping over ½M to SW and pass outside the Ecueil du Tabernacle light buoy. There are two other narrow passages for small boats to use in calm weather with care and a good lookout forward.

1. The passage SW of the Ilot Porre, minimum depth 1m, take in NW–SE directions.
2. This passage is to NE of the Ilot Cala d'Alga minimum depth 3·5m take in E–W directions.

⚓ La Grande Sanguinaire

There are three small anchorages on the SE side of this island.

⚓ La Grande Sanguinaires looking W

1. A very small anchorage in a little bay between the Ilot Cala d'Alga and the NE end of La Grande Sanguinaire, anchor in 3m sand and rock open to NE–E–SE–S.
2. A large anchorage just N of the Pointe du Tabernacle which projects in a SE direction from the middle of the island. There are two 3m deep rocks and also small rocks close in along the coast. Anchor in 2m rock open to NE–E–SE. There is a small landing stage used by *vedettes* which unload tourists.
3. A very small anchorage just below and to SE of the tower on SW end of La Grande Sanguinaire in 4m rock open to E–SE–S–SW. Small stony beach.

⚓ Anse de la Parata E

A bay partly sheltered by the Les Sanguinaires open to E–SE–S. Anchor in 3m sand and rock near the isthmus. Road ashore, bus service, cafés and restaurants, some houses, huts, a chapel, tennis courts (conspicuous lamp standards, etc.)

⚓ Anse de la Parata E looking N

Pointe Scudo

A small flat headland on a straight section of the coast, exposed, awash and covered rocks extend 300m S from the point.

⚓ Pointe Scudo E

A small anchorage in 3m sand open to E–SE–S–SW. Close to E side of Pointe Scudo. Road ashore and some houses.

Rocher La Botte

An awash rock marked by a R pole beacon □ topmark.

Rocher La Guardiola

A R round beacon tower □ topmark and light (Fl.R.2.5s6m2M) erected on a small group of rocks just over 1M to SW of Ajaccio Citadelle and 500m offshore, covered by the red sector of the Citadelle light. Give it a 200m berth either side.

⚓ Anse Maestrello (Maestrellu)

A bay open to E–SE–S–SW with a road and many houses and apartment blocks behind. Anchor off the sandy beach in 3m sand. See Port de Ajaccio page 142 for details of facilities available.

Rocher Citadelle

A R round beacon tower □ topmark and light (Fl(4)R.10s7M) lies 400m S of the Citadelle marking a rock and with shallows 3m lying 100m to N and 3·5m lying 200m to W. Pass to S of this beacon.

Section C – Ajaccio to Porto Vecchio

The coast

The section of coast between Ajaccio and Porto Vecchio is impressive by normal standards but cannot be compared with the exceptional section of coast to the NW. In general the actual coastline is lower and the land slopes up more gently to the high mountains which lie inland and this gives a less dramatic impression to the yachtsman coasting southwards.

By the shortest route this section only measures some 31M but if the actual coastline is followed into the multitude of gulfs, bays and estuaries a distance of well over 100M would be sailed.

The coast consists of broken rocky cliffs often with rocky islets and dangers close inshore. The heads of most of the gulfs, bays and estuaries have small beaches many of which are of sand. These breaks in the cliffs and in the coast form a series of delightful anchorages and because many are deserted and have no paths or roads to them, they form a perfect cruising ground for the yachtsman who likes to 'get away from it all'.

The major ports of Ajaccio, Bonifacio and Porto Vecchio offer easy entrance and protection under most conditions with adequate facilities ashore. The minor harbours of Porto Pollo, Propriano and Figari offer only limited protection and facilities but are of use in settled weather.

In the N the wide and deep Golfe d'Ajaccio is bounded by the long chain of islands, Les Iles Sanguinaires and Cap Muro, a prominent headland. The sides of the golfe are broken and rugged and the coast at its head is low with a long sandy beach. A road follows the coast around and there are a number of housing estates and some campsites especially near the heads of the many small bays where there are beaches.

Between Cap Muro and the Pointe de Senetosa lies another deep gulf, the Golfe de Valinco, again offering anchorages. Some of these are deserted and the only centres of population are near the two harbours of Porto Pollo and Propriano, though some housing development is taking place around the golfe notably at Campo-Moro.

An almost deserted section of coast lies between Pointe de Senetosa and Cap de Feno which although they are only 9M apart contain dozens of delightful anchorages. There are some offlying dangerous rocks in this section, notably Les Moines, which is marked by a beacon and covered by special light sectors from two lighthouses.

The section of white cliffs from Cap de Feno to Cap Pertusato is unique and only includes the port of Bonifacio and two anchorages. The channels between La Corse and Sardinia, Les Bouches de Bonifacio, and the two French islands are given separate treatment in this text because they are of a complex nature. The Corsican islands are low and rocky and have many offlying dangers, the Italian islands which lie to the S are not described.

From Cap Pertusato to Pointe Araso at the far side of the Golfe de Porto Vecchio the coast is interspersed with large gulfs and bays. The hills and mountains have a more rounded tree-covered appearance in contrast to the markedly jagged appearance of the W and SW coast. The Iles Cerbicale and some isolated rocks and shallows lie offshore and are only marked by two buoys. The main road runs inland along this section of coast and there are campsites, holiday centres and sailing schools at the head of many of the bays though some of the anchorages still remain deserted.

3·12 Ports d'Ajaccio

20000 Corse du Sud

Position 41°55'·13N 8°44'·61E
Minimum depths Vieux Port in the entrance 17m (56ft)
　　　　　　　in the harbour 6 to 3m (20 to 9·8ft)
　　　　　　　L'Amirauté in the entrance 12m (39ft)
　　　　　　　in the harbour 12 to 1m (39 to 3·3ft)
Width of the entrance 350m (1148ft)
Maximum length overall 50m (164ft)
Number of berths Vieux Port 313
　　　　　　　　L'Amirauté (Cannes) 726
Maximum length overall Yachts under 15m (49ft) can use
　　　　　　　　pontoons.
Population 60,000
Rating 2–1–3

General

A large commercial, fishing, naval and yachting port, it is the second largest city and port in La Corse and the capital of the island. It is an attractive city in a pleasant setting which has good facilities. There are two yacht harbours which can be approached and entered under almost any conditions and shelter found, but with strong winds from S and SE the swell enters the main harbour and is reflected by the Quai de la République into the Vieux Port making it very uncomfortable and occasionally dangerous. In the season these yacht harbours become very crowded.

Data

Charts

　　Admiralty *1424, 1985*
　　French *6821, 6851, 6942*
　　ECM *1007*

Magnetic variation

0°15'W (1990) decreasing by 6–7' each year.

Air radiobeacons

Ajaccio, Campo del'Oro (41°54'·01N 8°36'·80E) IS(··/···) 341 kHz 50M.
Ajaccio, Pte Senetosa (Pte Aquila) (41°33'·50N 8°47·90E) SNE (···/—·/·) 394·5 kHz 15M.

Port radio

VHF Ch 9, 16 (both yacht harbours). Pilot (☎ 95 21 42 28) Ch 06.

Coast radio

Ajaccio VHF Ch 16, 24. Continuous.

Speed limit

4 knots.

Traffic signals

Shown from a mast at the head of the Jetée de la Citadelle.

Day	*Night*	*Meaning*
Red flag	Red light	Entry forbidden
Green flag	Green light	Exit forbidden
Red and green flag	Red and green light	Entry and exit forbidden

Weather forecasts

Posted each day at the *capitaineries*, Vieux Port and Port de l'Amirauté. Also from the Met. Office, Aerodrome d'Ajaccio, Campo del'Oro (☎ 95 21 05 81) or from an automatic recorded forecast (☎ 95 21 05 81 and 95 20 12 21).

Lights

Ecueil de la Citadelle Fl(4)R.15s10m7M Red truncated tower, 'Citadelle' in white.
Citadelle Fl(2)WR.10s19m20/16M White tower, red top. 045°-R-057° covers Ecueil de la Guardiola, obscured when bearing 057°, 057°-W-045°.
Jetée de la Citadelle head Oc.R.4s13m8M White tower, red column.
Jetée des Capucins Fl.RG.4s8m7/7M White column, 110°-R-271·5°-G-065°.
Port des Cannes S breakwater head Fl(2)R.6s5m6M White tower, red top.
Jetée de Margonajo Fl(4)Vi.15s7m1M White column. F.W and F.R lights from 3 towers. 1M E occasional.
Darse d'Aspretto Outer Jetée head Q.RG.8m7M White column, green top. 035°-G-300°-R-035°. Occasional.
Darse d'Aspretto Jetée Intérieur head Fl.R.4s7m9M Occasional, white column red top.

Beacons

La Campanina BRB beacon tower, 2 balls topmark, 2½M to S of the harbour marks isolated danger, rock 0·3m (1ft) deep.
La Botte R beacon post, □ topmark, on a rock 2M to SW of the harbour.
Ecueil de la Citadelle R beacon tower, □ topmark, ¼M to S of the harbour (Fl(4)15s) rock 3·3m (13ft) deep.
Ecueil de la Guardiola R beacon tower, □ topmark, stands on a rock 1¼M to SW of the harbour covered by the R sector of the Citadelle lighthouse (Fl.R.2·5s6m2M).

Buoys

Ecueil de Tabernacle R light buoy (Fl(3)R.12s) with □ topmark, ½M to SE of Ile Grande Sanguinaire over a rock 3m (10ft) deep.
Mouillage de la Ville Two warping buoys one located at the head of the Baie d'Ajaccio both of which are unlit.

Warning

The Golfe d'Ajaccio has several shallow patches of foul ground extending up to 500m from the shore in places. There are some large unlit buoys in the Baie d'Ajaccio. The wash from manoeuvring commercial craft can affect yachts in the Vieux Port. Ferries, commercial vessels and naval vessels have priority over yachts.

Fire planes

Large flying boats may land in the Golfe d'Ajaccio to pick up water for fire fighting. It is important to see page 33.

Approach by day

From N Round Cap de Feno, a sloping rocky headland with a ruined tower, keeping outside the small rocky islet of La Botte to avoid the shallows off Fico. Take the Passe des Sanguinaires between the Pointe de la Parata and Ile Porre in a NW–SE direction keeping nearer to the Pointe de la Parata and making allowance for the currents that are sometimes strong

Depths in Metres

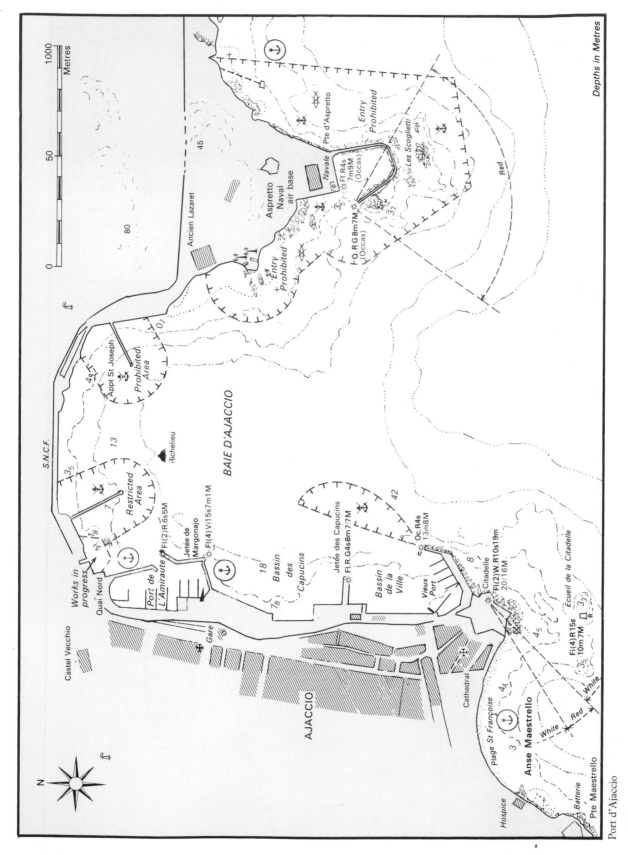

N

1000

50

0

Metres

S.N.C.F.

Castel Vecchio

Works in progress

Quai Nord

Port de
L'Amirauté

Appt St Joseph

Prohibited
Area

Restricted
Area

Richelieu

BAIE D'AJACCIO

Jetée de
Margonajo

Fl(2)R.6s5M

Fl(4)Vi15s7m1M

18

Bassin
des
Capucins

Gare

AJACCIO

Jetée des Capucins

Fl.R.G4s8m7·7M

Bassin
de la
Ville

Oc.R4s
13m8M

42

Ancien Lazaret

80

45

Aspretto Naval
air base

Entry Prohibited

Entry
Prohibited

Pte d'Aspretto

Navale

Fl R4s
7m9M
(Occas)

Fl.Q.R.G8m7M
(Occas)

Les Scoglietti

Red

Entry
Prohibited

Cathedral

Vieux
Port

Citadelle
Fl(2)W.R10s19m
20/16M.

Ecueil de la Citadelle

Fl(4)R15s
10m7M.

R

Plage St Françoise

Hospice

Anse Maestrello

Batterie

Pte d'Ajaccio

White

Red

White

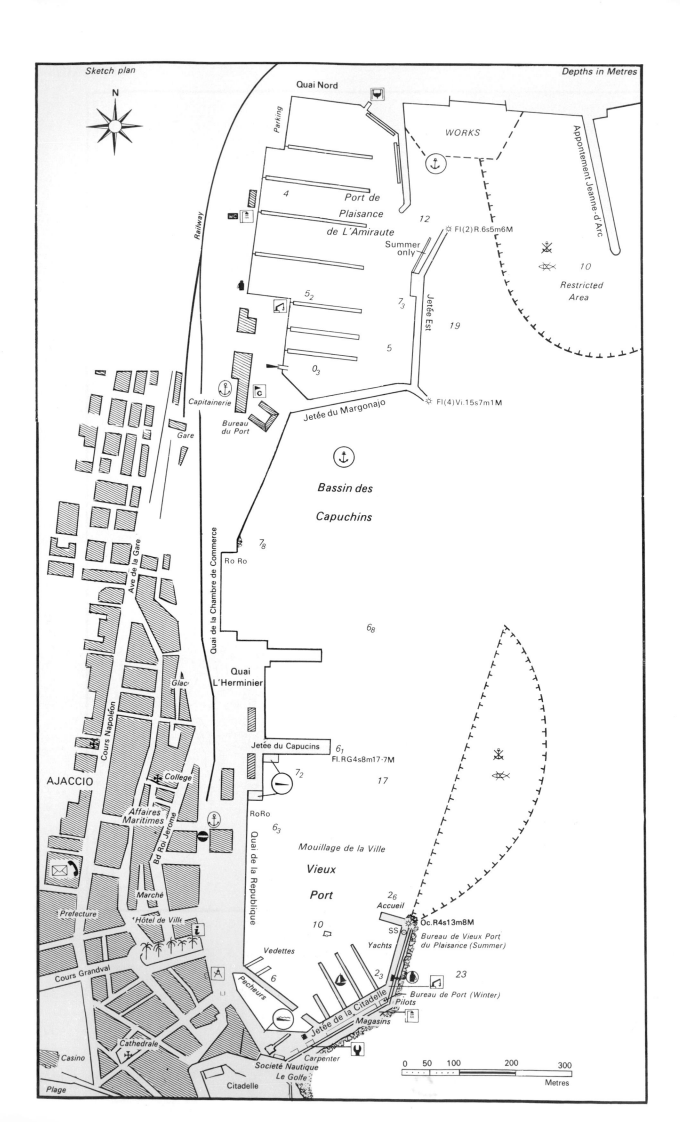

Sketch plan

Depths in Metres

N

Quai Nord

WORKS

Parking

Appontement Jeanne-d'Arc

Railway

4

Port de
Plaisance
de L'Amiraute

12

☼ Fl(2)R.6s5m6M

Summer
only

WC

⚓

🗡

10

Restricted
Area

5_2

7_3

Jetée Est

19

3

5

C

Capitainerie

⚓

0_3

Bureau
du Port

Gare

Jetée du Margonajo

☼ Fl(4)Vi.15s7m1M

⚓

Bassin des

Capuchins

7_8

Ro Ro

Quai de la Chambre de Commerce

Ave de la Gare

6_8

Cours Napoléon

Glac

Quai
L'Herminier

Jetée du Capucins

6_1

Fl.RG4s8m17·7M

College

7_2

17

AJACCIO

Affaires
Maritimes

⚓

RoRo

6_3

Bd Roi Jerome

Mouillage de la Ville

Vieux

✉

Port

2_6

Marché

Accueil

Oc.R4s13m8M

Prefecture

10

SS

Bureau de Vieux Port
du Plaisance (Summer)

Hôtel de Ville

i

Yachts

23

Vedettes

6

2_3

Bureau de Port (Winter)

Cours Grandval

A

Pilots

Pecheurs

Jetée de la Citadelle

Magasins

Casino

Cathedrale

✝

Carpenter

0   50   100   200   300

Societé Nautique

Plage

Citadelle

Le Golfe

Metres

Beacon Ecueil de la Guardiola

Ajaccio. Approach looking NE

Citadelle   *Head of Jetée de la Citadelle*

Ajaccio. Approach looking N. Beacon – Ecueil de la Citadelle

in the pass. In the distance La Parata appears as an island but in the close approach the low isthmus which joins it to the mainland will be seen. In severe weather the Passe des Sanguinaires can be dangerous and it is advisable to round the whole group of islands at least ½M to S keeping outside the Ecueil du Tabernacle marked by a R conical buoy, □ topmark, (Fl(3)R.12s). Now follow the coast at ½M in an E direction leaving the La Botte R beacon, □ topmark and the beacon towers La Guardiola and La Citadelle to port. The high-rise blocks of flats around Ajaccio will be seen from afar.

From S Round Cap Muro a rocky-cliffed point with a conspicuous lighthouse on its S side at ½M onto a NNE course leaving the following all more than ½M to port:

Pointe de la Castagna, a rocky peninsula with a tower on top.

La Campanina, a BRB beacon tower with 2 balls topmark.

Pointe de Sette Nave, a lower tree and house covered peninsula with a tower.

The high-rise blocks of flats and houses of Ajaccio will now be seen. Set course towards the church towers and the Citadelle which will be seen towards the E side of the blocks of flats.

Approach by night
The following lights can be used:

Iles Sanguinaires, Grande Sanguinaire, Fl(3)W.15s 98m27M White square tower, black top, white building.

Cap de Muro Oc.W.4s57m9M White square tower with name in black.

Entrance Vieux Port de la Citadelle

By day Approach the head of the Jetée de la Citadelle on NW course and round it at 25m having first checked that no commercial vessels are entering or leaving. Secure to the small pontoon at the head of this jetty for berthing instructions.

By night Leaving Fl(4)R.12s and Fl(2)WR.10s to port, approach Oc.R.4s on a NW course. Round it leaving it 50m to port and then secure to the small pontoon at the head of the Jetée de la Citadelle for berthing instructions.

Entrance Port de l'Amirauté (Cannes)

By day Approach the NW corner of the Baie d'Ajaccio and leave the head of the Jetée du Margonajo with a white tower 7m to port. Follow along the Jetée Est on a N course for 150m and then round its head at 25m entering the harbour. Secure to the first pontoon to port and report to the *capitainerie* at the root of the jetée.

By night Approach NW corner of the Baie d'Ajaccio leaving Fl.RG.4s 400m to port and then Fl(4)Vi.15s, 25m to port. Follow along the Jetée Est on a N course for 150m round Fl(2)R.6s at 25m entering the harbour. Secure to first pontoon to port on entering. The lights listed above are difficult to pick out against the lights of the town.

Port de l'Amirauté (Cannes)

Ajaccio looking N Vieux Port de la Citadelle in the foreground

Pontoon d'Accueil

Ajaccio. Port de l'Amirauté looking SW–W–NW from head of
Jetée Est

Head of Jetée Est

Ajaccio. Port de l'Amirauté entrance looking W–NW

Berths – Vieux Port de la Citadelle

Yachts normally berth stern-to the pontoons on the NW side of the Jetée de la Citadelle. These pontoons have 'fingers' and anchors must not be used. Larger yachts secure stern-to the Jetée de la Citadelle between its head and the fuel pumps with anchors from the bow, a tripline is advised. In the season the overflow is berthed stern-to along the outer side of the wall protecting the Port Abri de Pêche.

Berths – Port de l'Amirauté (Cannes)

Berth stern-to the pontoons which have 'fingers'. There are two groups of pontoons, one group on N side of Jetée de Margonajo and the other along the Quai de la Defence Mobile. Changes are to be expected, see plan.

Anchorages

Anchorages in the N half of the Mouillage des Capucins in 6 to 16m sand and off the Port de l'Amirauté (Cannes) in 4 to 13m sand is possible, and also in the bay to E of the Citadelle. Triplines are advised.

Prohibited anchorages

It is forbidden to anchor in the Mouillage de la Ville and in the S half of the Mouillage des Capucins as these areas are used by commercial traffic. Anchoring is also forbidden between these areas and Pointe d'Aspretto (see chart). The Mouillage d'Aspretto may be used outside a 200m band extending along the W side of the harbour wall and the coast provided a red or blue light is not being shown from a signal mast at Pointe d'Aspretto.

Formalities

Vieux Port

On arrival in summer secure just inside the port on the port hand. Report to the Bureau du Vieux Port de Plaisance at the head of the Jetée de la Citadelle (☎ 95 21 28 01 and 95 51 21 80) open 0800–2000. In winter report to the *bureau* located just beyond the fuel station on the Jetée de la Citadelle (same phone numbers) open 0800–1200 and 1400–1800.

Port de l'Amirauté

On arrival at the Port de l'Amirauté (Cannes) secure to the *quai d'accueil* just inside the entrance on the port hand, report to the *Bureau de Port* (☎ 95 22 31 98) on the opposite side of the harbour. Customs (☎ 95 21 00 31 and 95 21 28 01) at 3 Parc Cunéo. *Affaires Maritimes* (☎ 95 21 55 53) at 1 rue Saint Roch.

Charges

There are harbour charges based on overall length of yachts and these are high in the season.

Facilities

Slip A long slip on the S side of the Port Abri de Pêche located behind the Vieux Port.
Cranes Cranes of 8 and 20 tonnes plus mobile cranes of 40 tonnes available at the Vieux Port.
Travel-hoist Two 40-tonne travel hoists to be provided at the Port de l'Amirauté (Cannes).
Fuel Petrol and diesel (*gasoil*) are available from pumps located on the Jetée de la Citadelle and in Port de l'Amirauté (Cannes). Open 0700–2100 in summer, 0500–1900 in winter (☎ 95 21 51 23).
Water Water points are to be found on the pontoons and on the quays in both harbours.
Electricity Outlets for 220v AC are provided on the pontoons and on the Jetée de la Citadelle also in Port de l'Amirauté.
Provisions Many shops for all types of provisions and a good daily market nearby with a separate fish market alongside. Several supermarkets.
Ice In season this is obtainable from the Société Nautique 'Golfe d'Ajaccio' and at other times from the warehouse behind the garage just N of the root of the Jetée des Capucins.
Duty-free goods These can be obtained. Contact G. Luigi at fuel pumps on Jetée de la Citadelle.
Garbage Containers for rubbish are located at the roots of the pontoons and on the Jetée de la Citadelle.
Chandlery Several shops on the Jetée de la Citadelle and in the town.
Repairs Several excellent yards can repair wood and fibre glass yachts and many workshops for the repair of engines.
Laundrette Several in the city.
Post office The PTT is a large building on the far side of the Cours Napoléon about ¼M to NW of the yacht harbour.
Hotels Three ****, eleven ***, fourteen **, seven * and four unclassified. There are many more around the Golfe d'Ajaccio.
Restaurants Over one hundred and very many café/bars.
Yacht club The Société Nautique 'Golfe d'Ajaccio' near the root of the Jetée de la Citadelle (☎ 95 21 35 75) is more of a café/bar than a normal yacht club. It has showers, and ice in the season. A new club at the Port de l'Amirauté is to be built for the Circle de Voile d'Ajaccio (CVA) (☎ 95 20 22 24).
Showers Modern showers and WCs are located in the buildings along the Jetée de la Citadelle. 40 are to be provided in Port de l'Amirauté.
Information office The Syndicat d'Initiative has an office in the SE corner of the Hôtel de Ville located on the far side of Place Foch, a square with trees close to Quai Napoléon (☎ 95 21 40 87 and 95 21 53 39).
Lifeboat A *vedette* 1st class lifeboat and a pneumatic inshore rescue craft are stationed here (☎ 95 21 44 45).
Medical Hospital, doctors and dentists available.
Visits The chief places to visit in Ajaccio are the various displays connected with Napoleon. His birthplace, Casa Bonaparte, the Musée Napoléon in the Hôtel de Ville, the Musée Fesch, the Chapelle Impériale where members of his family are buried and Les Milleli, their country house.
   Further away may be seen the Château de la Punta which was a copy of a pavilion in the palace gardens of the Tuileries and was built using its original stones. The hills behind the city provide a spectacular view of the gulf and coast, a narrow road runs to the top. Many other places to visit are described in leaflets provided by the information bureau.
Beaches A small sandy beach lies beside the root of the Jetée de la Citadelle and others lie to the W of the city.
Communications Rail and bus services over the island. Air services to Paris, London (via Lyon), Marseille and Nice. Ferry services to Nice and Marseille.

Festivals 18th March, festival in honour of Our Lady of Mercy, patroness of the town. Good Friday, procession by night through the town. 1st to 15th August, festival of dramatic art. 15th August, celebration of the anniversary of the birth of Napoleon. 2nd June, festival of St Erasmus, patron of fisherman, with a procession. First fortnight in November, the Rally of 10,000 Bends. An international motor rally organised by the Automobile Club de la Corse. Leaves from Ajaccio and Bastia in alternate years.

Future development

A major redevelopment of the Port de l'Amirauté (Cannes) is taking place and completion is due in 1992. The new layout is shown on page 144.

History

The name of this old fishing village probably originated from the Latin *adjacium* meaning a resting place and it was sited to the N of the Citadelle. In the 10th century it was destroyed by the Saracens and later reconstructed by the Genoese. The Citadelle dates from 1554 as does the Cathedral. The birth of Napoleon Bonaparte on 15th August 1769 in the Casa Bonaparte, a few hundred yards NW of the Citadelle is the local event of importance. The fact that Pascal Paoli's partisans chased him out of his house and forced him to flee to Calvi is not so well known. They confiscated his house and used it as an arms depôt.

Ajaccio, which has a pleasant temperate climate, became one of the first towns to be visited by the Victorians seeking to escape the horrors of the English winter and was developed as a resort along with Cannes, Nice and Palma de Mallorca all of which have similar architecture.

Pointe d'Aspretto

A low flat wide promontory extending to S with naval air base buildings on the top where it slopes up to 50m. A spur of shallow water extends 600m to S of the buildings, and around this spur there is an enclosing breakwater of a small harbour. The entrance is at the NW corner with depths of 3·2m to 1·5m inside. This is a naval harbour and should only be used in an emergency. The whole of this point including the islands Les Scoglietti, which are a mass of small islets and rocks lying to the S of this harbour, is bounded by a 200m wide band which is forbidden to all except naval personnel.

⚓ Pointe d'Aspretto E

This is an anchorage area for large vessels but is rarely used. Anchor 350m from the naval base in 7m sand and weed or in deeper water, open to SE–S–SW. This anchorage is close to the Aéroport d'Ajaccio–Campo del'Oro and can be noisy. Alternative anchorages in 5m sand off the sandy beach that stretches for 3M SSE. Do not anchor in line with the runway which is marked by two light buoys, W cardinal and E cardinal, 400m from the coast.

⚓ Pointe de Porticcio NE

An open shallow anchorage separated by a line of exposed rocky heads from the Pointe de Porticcio. Anchor off sandy beach but outside permanent moorings in 3m sand, open to W–NW–N. Many private houses ashore, road down to the coast. Yacht Club, small jetty, chandler and yard 1M away. Some shops. An area is set aside especially for sailing yachts to anchor.

Pointe de Porticcio

A small low (36m) rocky-cliffed headland with rocky dangers extending 200m to W. Three large white buildings on the point, tree covered with houses inland.

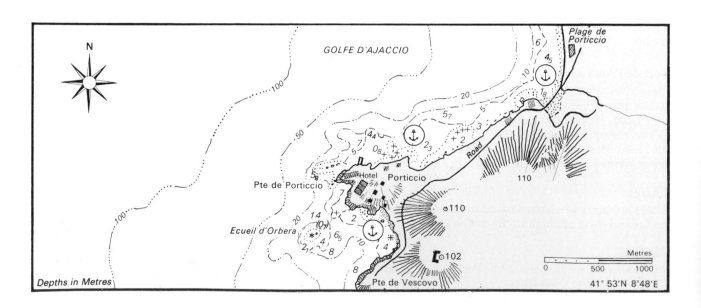

Pointe de Porticcio looking NE

Ecueil d'Orbera

Pointe de Porticcio looking N

Ecueil d'Orbera

An area of rocky heads awash and some 3 to 4m deep 500m to SSW of Pointe de Porticcio.

⚓ Pointe de Porticcio SE

Anchor in the small bay off a sandy beach to SE of this point in 5m sand, open to SW–W–NW. Pay attention to some rocky islets close inshore, and to Ecueil d'Orbera 700m offshore.

⚓ Plage d'Agosta

A sandy beach 1M long. Anchor off the beach in 4m sand, open to SW–W–NW. Coast road ashore. Tour Molini stands 500m inland.

⚓ Anse Ste Barbe

Anchorage either side of a shoal area with rocky heads that jut out in a N–NE direction from the coast 400m to E of an unnamed islet. Approach with care and anchor in 4m sand outside moorings, open to W–NW–N. Coast road ashore, two large slips, beach huts, houses in trees.

Pointe de Sette Nave

A rocky-cliffed prominent tree covered point with outlying rocky dangers 300m to W and 400m N. The Tour de l'Isolella stands on a 66m hill behind the point and can be seen from afar there are many private houses and a coast road.

Pointe de Sette Nave looking E

⚓ Anse Ste Barbe looking SE

⚓ Anse Medea

An anchorage in 5m sand and rock in a small bay with rocky sides and a sandy beach tucked in behind Pointe de Sette Nave, keep clear of moorings. Pay attention in the approach to La Campanina beacon, to rocky shallows on the E side of the bay and to two small rocks in the middle of the beach. Open to S–SW.

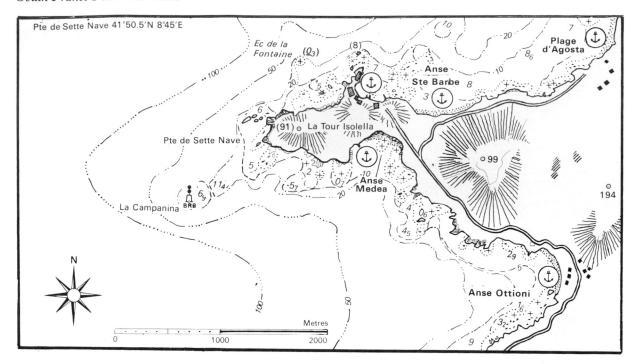

⚓ Anse Medea looking E

ground off the enclosing points. Main road and camps behind the beach. Small jetty, a small quay and a beach café.

⚓ Ile Piana E and Port de Chiavari looking E

La Campanina beacon

A BRB tower with two globes topmark, located ½M to SW of Pointe de Sette Nave marks a rock covered 0·3m. Deep water within 100m of the beacon.

⚓ Anse Ottioni

A small and stony beach (Plage de Ruppione) at the head of a gulf with rocky shores. Anchor off the beach in 4m sand, open to SW–W–NW. There are rocks at both ends of the beach. Coast road, trees and many houses and beach huts behind the beach.

Port de Chiavari

An anchorage not a port, in a wide bay open to W–NW–N. Anchor off a beach in 4m sand. Keep to the N half of the beach as there are rocks off the S half. Enter the bay on a SE heading as there is foul

⚓ Ile Piana E and Port de Chiavari looking S

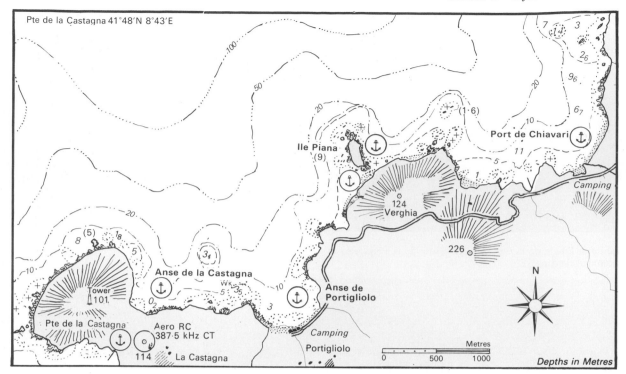

⚓ Ile Piana E

A beautiful little anchorage on the E side of the Ile Piana in 5m sand open to NW–N–NE, rocky cliff and small sandy beach ashore. An isolated rock lies 50m to NE of the N end of this islet. Very popular in the season and at weekends.

⚓ Ile Piana SW

A similar anchorage to that detailed above but not so spacious. There are many rocky dangers extending 50m from the W coast of this islet. Anchor in 5m sand and rock to SW of the S end of the islet, open to SW–W–NW.

⚓ Anse de Portigliolo

A fine sandy bay open to W–NW–N with a camping site ashore and a road leading to a small village. Anchor in 5m sand about 200m offshore due to rocks near the beach.

⚓ Pointe de la Castagna NE

A small bay behind the Pointe de la Castagna, rocky cliffs and trees ashore with some houses, a track to the road, a small sandy beach and huts on the beach. An 0·2 shallow area inshore and rocky heads close in. Anchor in 5m sand and rock clear of moorings, open to NW–N–NE. Small village inland.

Pointe de la Castagna

A conspicuous promontory with a 91m hill behind the point with a conspicuous tower and an Aero RC mast on the next hill inland. Rocky dangers and shallows extend 500m to W and SW.

Anse de la Pointe de la Castagna NE (Anse de la Portigliolo in background) looking E

⚓ Anse de la Portigliolo looking S

⌁ Anse de la Pointe de la Castagna NE (Anse de la Portigliolo in background) looking SE

⌁ Pointe de la Castagna SE looking E

Pointe de la Castagna looking S

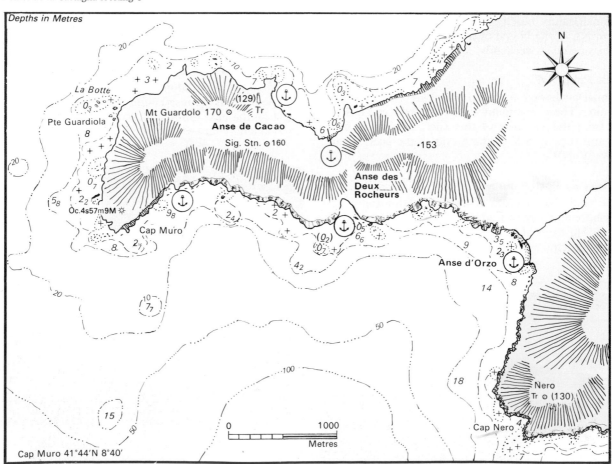

152

⚓ Pointe de la Castagna SE

A similar anchorage to that on the NE side of the point except yachts should anchor in 8m rock in the E side of the bay to avoid offlying rocky dangers. This anchorage is open to S–SW–W.

Carapono radio mast

A radio mast (625m) (F.R Lts) lies 3M to SE of Pointe de la Castagna.

⚓ Anse de Cacao (Cacau)

A pleasant and useful anchorage to NE of Cap Muro which is open to NW–N–NE. Anchor in 5m sand in the S corner off a small sandy and stone beach or in the NW corner in 7m rock. A ruined tower stands to the W of the bay. Offlying rock at each side of the bay. Deserted.

⚓ Anse de Cacao looking E

Pointe Guardiola and passage

The NW part of Cap Muro is called Pointe Guardiola. It has offlying rocky dangers including the islet La Botte. A 100m wide passage 4m deep and 200m long exists between La Botte and the point if taken in NE–SW direction. However when at the NE end of the passage N–S directions must be taken to pass to W of three isolated rocks which have only 2m depths between them and the shore.

Cap Muro (Capo di Muru)

A large and important headland rising to 167m, there is a tower on the NE side and on the SW point is a lighthouse, white square tower, black top (Oc.W.4s57m9M). A statue of the Madonna is carved into the cliffs on the S point.

⚓ Cap Muro E

A wide bay open to E–SE–S–SW with small rocks close inshore. Anchor in NW corner in 7m sand and weed. Deserted.

⚓ Anse des Deux Rochers

A small anchorage on the opposite side of the peninsula to Anse de la Cacao, with rocky-cliffed sides and a small stone and sand beach. Approach with care because there are 0·7 and 0·2 shallows 400m to SSW of the entrance and two islets 300m to SE. Approach the Anse on NNW course and with a good look out. Near the entrance there are two ball shaped rocks. Anchor in 3m sand off the beach, open to SE–S–SW. Track along coast. Deserted.

⚓ Anse de Deux Rochers looking NE

⚓ Anse d'Orzo

A wide bay with rocky sides and a sand and stone beach. Scrub covered hills behind with signs of housing development and tracks inland. Camping and beach cafés behind beach. Anchor in 3m sand in the NE side of the bay, open to S–SW–W, pay attention to two lone rocks about 100m offshore.

Cap Muro looking S

153

⚓ Anse d'Orzo looking NE

⚓ Anse d'Orzo looking E

Cap Nero

A major promontory with a rounded blackish rocky-cliffed point and rocky dangers extending 300m offshore. Tour Nero stands on a ridge close to the point amongst green scrub. There are tracks around the headland.

Cap Muro   Capo Nero

Cap Nero looking NW. Cap Muro in the background

⚓ Baie de Copabia (Cupabia)

A large bay open to S–SW–W which has good space for anchorage. There is a long sandy beach on the NE side of the bay with a monument standing behind it. Anchorage is available along the beach in 3m sand. To the S of this area an anchorage in 10m sand clear of the rocky shallows can be used. Anchorage is also possible in 17m further out. A track runs inland from the beach, some houses and a road have been built.

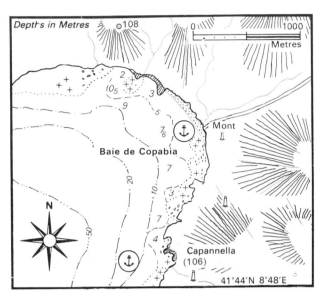

⚓ Baie de Copabia NE and S looking SE

⚓ Pointe de Porto Pollo W

A deep bay sheltered by the spur of land running out to the Pointe de Porto Pollo, a second spur of shallow water with islets and rocky heads projects SW on the other side of the bay. The sides of the bay have exposed rocks close in and there are sand and stone beaches at the head. Deserted except for three houses. Anchor off the longest beach in 6m sand, open to S–SW–W. Care necessary because charts do not show all dangers.

Pointe de Porto Pollo

Care is needed when rounding this point due to extensive offlying rocky reefs and islet. One reef extends 500m SW from the SW point another extends 1000m to SE from the SE corner of the point. This reef has two islets (3m) near its S extremity, if the outer islet is given berth of 200m and a course E–W adopted the other reef will be cleared. The point is covered with woodland and scrub. Two ruined towers stand on the crest inland but are partially hidden in the trees.

⚓ Pointe de Porto Polo W looking NE

Pointe de Porto Pollo looking ESE

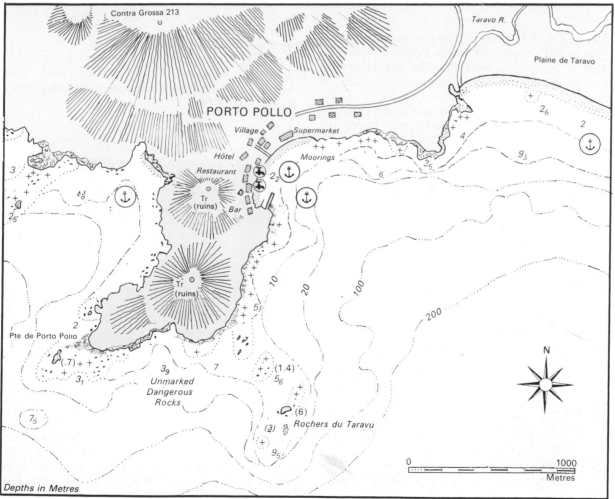

Port de Porto Pollo

3·13 Port de Porto Pollo

20140 Corse du Sud

Position 41°42′·41N 8°48′·91E
Minimum depth in the entrance 20m (66ft)
in the harbour 15 to 2m (49 to 6·6ft)
Width of the entrance 200m (656ft)
Population 200 (approx)
Rating 3–2–4

General

Not really a harbour but a large well protected anchorage with a short breakwater, easy to approach and enter. The anchorage is open to E–SE–S. Limited facilities ashore but everyday requirements are available. Many houses surround the anchorage including an ugly apartment block but otherwise a pleasant anchorage.

Data

Charts

Admiralty *1424*
French *6942, 7162*
ECM *1008*

Magnetic variation

0°15′W (1990) decreasing by 7′ each year.

Warning

A line of small rocky islands and foul ground extends some ½M to SSE, S and SW of the Pointe de Porto Pollo and is unmarked. Note that the two ruined towers on the Pointe de Porto Pollo are surrounded by trees and cannot be seen easily from the sea.

Fire planes large flying boats may land in the Golfe de Valinco to pick up water for fire fighters. Important to see page 33.

Approach by day

From NW Round the broken rocky-cliffed Cap Muro which has a small lighthouse on its S side and then Cap Nero which has blackish cliffs and a conspicuous tower, keep on a course towards the low Pointe de Porto Pollo. This headland must be given a berth of over ½M because of small rocky islets with foul ground between, that stretch SSE, S and SW from the point which are unmarked. Do not turn towards this anchorage until it bears NW.

From S Round the low rocky-cliffed Pointe de Senetosa which has a conspicuous lighthouse on its S side and pass well outside Pointe d'Eccica which has rocky islands extending some ¼M offshore. The Pointe de Campo Moro which has a conspicuous squat tower and offlying rocks should be left ½M to starboard, and a NNE course set across the deep Golfe de Valinco towards a cluster of houses. In the closer approach the low Pointe de Porto Pollo must be left at least ¼M to port because of outlying rocks and foul ground. When the anchorage lies to NW, an approach can be made.

Approach by night

An approach and entrance by night is not advised due to lack of adequate navigational lights. Using the following lights an approach to the area is possible in conditions of good visibility:

Cap de Muro Oc.W.4s57m9M White square tower with name in black.
Propriano, Rocher Longo Jetée head
  Oc(3)WG.12s16m15/12M White tower green top.
Pointe de Senetosa Fl.WR.5s54m20/16M Two white towers black tops and a white building. 306°-R-328°-W-306° RC.

Porto Pollo looking N

Porto Pollo. Approach looking NW

Porto Pollo. Approach looking N

Porto Pollo. Entrance looking NNW

Entrance

By day Approach the NW corner of the bay where there are several larger houses. In the close approach a group of permanent moorings will be seen.

By night In the close approach only the light at Propriano (Oc(3)WG.12s) is visible and care must be exercised.

Anchorage

Anchor just outside the moorings in 10m (33ft) weed, sand and stone with a tripline to the anchor. Smaller craft may be able to find a space inshore of the moorings. The holding ground is not very good.

Landing

On sandy beach or alongside wooden jetty.

Formalities

None.

Facilities

Fuel Petrol and diesel from pumps at the village garage.
Water From restaurant.
Provisions Several simple shops in the village including a supermarket.
Hotels Six * hotels.
Restaurants Several restaurants and several café/bars.
Information office 17 rue Gen-de-Gaulle (☎ 95 76 01 49).
Visits The Stone Age archaeological site circa 3500 BC at Filitosa is 5 miles away and should be visited.
Beach A long sandy beach lines the bay.
Communications Bus service to Propriano.
Festivals Procession for St Erasmus, the patron saint of fishermen, on 2nd June.

Future development

Possible development as a yacht harbour.

⚓ Orimeto Plage

A long sandy bay, anchor off the beach in 3m sand, open to SE–S–SW. Marsh and lakes behind beach, many campsites and caravans. Mouth of Rivière Taravo to E.

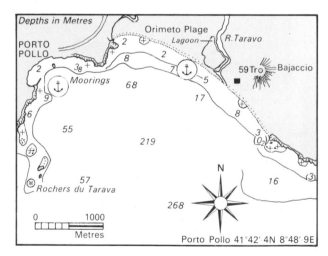

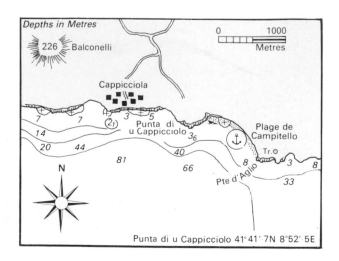

157

⚓ Plage de Campitellu (Campitello)

A sandy bay with wreck and lone rock at the NW end. Anchor in 3m sand near the centre of the bay, open to S–SW–W. Coast road behind the beach. Wreck in NE corner.

Pointe d'Agliu

A small rocky headland with a tower, tree and scrub covered hills and coast road behind.

⚓ Plage de Baracci

A deep sandy beach at the head of the Golfe de Valinco, usually crowded in the summer, beach cafés and coast road behind. The mouth of Rivière Boracci lies at the N end of the beach. Anchor in 4m sand off the beach, open to W–NW.

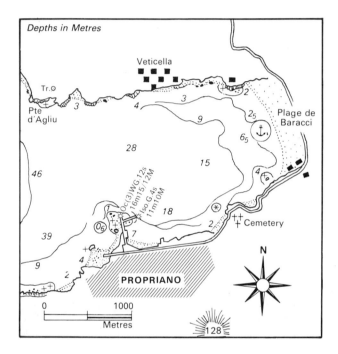

3·14 Port de Propriano

20110 Corse du Sud

Position 41°40'·63N 8°54'·32E
Minimum depth   in the entrance 7m (23ft)
               in the harbour 7 to 1m (23 to 3·3ft)
Width of the entrance 80m (262ft)
Maximum length overall 32m (105ft)
Number of berths 380
Population 2102
Rating 3–3–3

General

A commercial, fishing and yacht harbour in attractive surroundings near the head of the deep Golfe de Valinco. The Port de Commerce is not fully enclosed and with strong winds from SW–W–NW the swell can be unpleasant. In very severe weather it can be dangerous berthed to the quay. A yacht harbour, the Port de Plaisance, has been constructed to the E of Port de Commerce, and this offers good protection. Approach and entrance are easy. The small town can provide everyday requirements, it caters for thousands of tourists who pack the area in the season. The harbour also becomes very crowded.

Data

Charts

Admiralty *1424*
French *6851, 7162*
ECM *1008*

Magnetic variation

0°18'W (1990) decreasing by 7' each year.

Speed limit

3 knots

Port radio

VHF Ch 9.

Weather forecasts

Posted twice a day at *Bureau de Port*. Recorded forecast (☎ 95 20 12 21 and 95 21 05 81).

Lights

Rocher Longo Jetée head Oc(3)WG.12s16m15/12M White tower, green top. 070°-W-097°-G-137°-W-002°.
Jetée Nord head Iso.G.4s11m10M White column dark green top.
Port de Plaisance Digue Ouest W head Fl(2)W.6s2m. Red structure. 285°-unintens-045°.
Port de Plaisance Digue Ouest E head Fl(3)G.12s5m6M. White structure, dark green top. 285°-unintens-045°.
Port de Plaisance Jetée Est head Iso.R.4s1m1M strip light.

Buoys

Two large warping buoys (unlit) are located in the Port de Commerce.

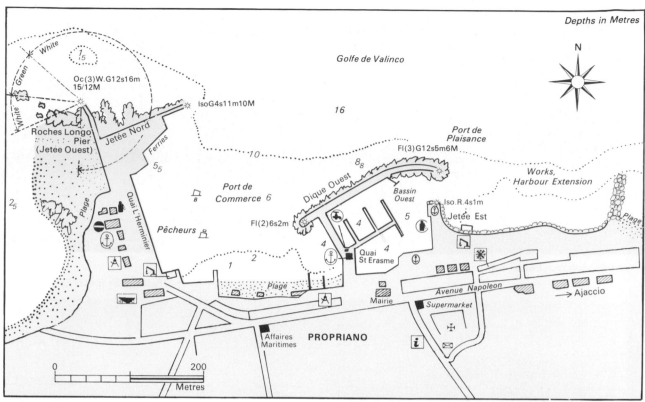

Port de Propriano

Entrance to yacht harbour

Propriano. Approach looking SE

Warning

In the event of a heavy swell entering the Golfe de Valinco the Quai l'Herminier in the Port de Commerce can become dangerous and yachts should enter the Port de Plaisance. Large ferries use the Port de Commerce and have powerful blow thrusters to manoeuvre.

Restricted areas

A nature reserve lies to W of Propriano along the S coast of the Golfe de Valinco from Portigliolo to Campo Moro extending 1M to N. Fishing, subaqua diving and anchoring in the area is forbidden, see chart page 162.

Fire planes

Large flying boats may land in the Golfe de Valinco to pick up water for fire fighting. Important, see page 33.

Approach by day

From N Round Cap Muro, a broken rocky-cliffed point with a conspicuous lighthouse on its S side, onto an ESE course and pass two more headlands, Cap Nero and Pointe de Porto Pollo, the latter has some off-lying rocks which should be given a ½M berth. The houses around the town will be seen from afar and the lighthouse and jetty in the closer approach. The cemetery on a point to the E of the town may also be observed.

From S Round Pointe de Campo Moro which has offlying rocky shallows giving it a ½M berth. There is a small village in the bay beyond the point. Proceed up the Golfe de Valinco on an ENE course keeping ½M off the coast. The harbour and town of Propriano are not visible until the closer approach though the lighthouse and a part of the jetty may be observed earlier.

Approach by night

Use the following lights:

Cap Muro Oc.W.4s57m9M White square tower, black top with name in black.

Pointe de Senetosa (**Pointe Aquila**) Fl.WR.5s54m 20/16M Two white towers, black tops, with house between. 306°-R-328°-W-306° RC (not visible inside the Golfe de Valinco).

Propriano. Approach looking NE

Head of Jetée Roches Longo

Propriano. Approach looking E

Fuel Head of W breakwater

Entrance

By day Approach the lighthouse on Rocher Longa Jetée head leaving it 200m to starboard to clear a 1·1m rocky patch which lies 100m to NW of it. When the lighthouse bears S alter course to round the head of the Jetée Nord Est at 20m leaving it to starboard onto a ESE course towards the entrance to the Port de Plaisance.

By night Approach Oc(3)WG.12s in the G sector until 400m away from it when divert to pass at least 200m to N of the light. When this light bears S alter course to round Iso.G.4s at 20m leaving it to starboard, then steer ESE towards Fl(3)G.12s and Iso.R.4s(strip light) and enter between.

Notes
1. In the approach these lights are reversed.
2. In the approach to Port de Commerce the lighthouse tower on Rocher Longo obscures the light at the head of Jetée Est from 094°-095°.

Berths

Report to the *Bureau de Port de Plaisance* to S of the entrance to this harbour. Yachts have to berth stern-to the quay or pontoons with 'fingers' in the Port de Plaisance. If not required for commercial vessels the

Propriano. Entrance to yacht harbour looking S

Quai l'Herminier may be used with prior permission of the *capitaine de port de commerce*. It is usually free during the winter months.

Anchorage

Yachts may anchor in 10m sand/mud 200m to NE of the entrance to the Port de Plaisance.

Entrance to yacht harbour

Propriano looking S

Prohibited anchorage

Area opposite the Quai d'Herminier extending some 300m. This is in effect the whole of the Port de Commerce. Anchoring is not permitted here from 1st June to 30th September.

Formalities

The *Bureau de Port de Commerce* is on Quai l'Herminier (☎ 95 76 10 40) open 0800–1200 and 1400–1800 hours. Customs office is also on Quai l'Herminier (☎ 95 76 05 30) and the *Affaires Maritimes* office is at the W end of the Avenue Napoleon (☎ 95 76 06 07). Prior permission from the *capitaine du port* is required if wishing to secure to the Quai l'Herminier. The *Bureau de Port* of the Port de Plaisance is S of the entrance (☎ 96 76 10 40) open winter 0800–1200 and 1400–1800, summer 0600–1200 and 1400–2000.

Charges

Harbour charges are levied but visits of 2 hours duration are not charged.

Facilities

Slip A small slip on Quai l'Herminier.
Elevator 18 tonnes
Crane 15 and 35-tonne mobile cranes are available.
Fuel A fuelling point is established on the Quai l'Herminier for diesel (*gasoil*) and petrol, also E side of Port de Plaisance (☎ 95 76 01 17 and 95 76 03 43).
Water Water points are on the quay and pontoons in the Port de Plaisance.
Electricity Electric points are provided on the pontoon and on the quay 220v AC. Application has to be made to the *Bureau de Port* before these can be used.
Provisions Many shops in the town can provide all normal requirements, several supermarkets.
Ice In season blocks of ice are available from *Una* Supermarket and from fuel station.
Garbage A few rubbish bins are to be found on the quay and the jetty.
Chandlery A shop at the W end of the Avenue Napoléon, one on the quay and one near the yard to W.
Repairs Repairs to hull and engines can be carried out by four yards.
Showers Showers and WCs near *Bureau de Port de Plaisance*.
Laundrette One in the town.
Post office The PTT lies up a side street off the middle of the town.
Hotels Four ***, three ** one * and five pensions.
Restaurants Sixteen bar-restaurants and twelve café/bars.
Yacht club There is only a dinghy club, the Club Nautique de Valinco (CNV) (☎ 95 76 04 26) and the Club des Loisiers Nautiques de Propriano (CLNP) (☎ 95 76 12 56).
Information office The Syndicat d'Initiative (☎ 95 76 01 49) has an office next to the Hôtel de Ville in the centre of the town.
Lifeboat A *vedette*, 2nd class, and an inshore rescue inflatable lifeboat are stationed here.

Medical Doctors and dentists.

Visits The most interesting place to visit is Sartène located some 8M away which has been described as the most typical Corsican village in La Corse. The 3500 year old *menhirs* and 6000 BC year old village of Filitosa is only 5M away and worth the visit.

Beaches A good beach at the head of the bay and another just W of the harbour.

Communications A bus service and a small airfield for light planes with a service to Ajaccio.

Future development

Improvements to the facilities at the Port de Plaisance and extension to E providing 350 extra berths and a new office building for the *capitaine*.

History

A little fishing settlement which the Turks destroyed in 1583, 1590 and again in 1660. Most of the town is of recent origin created when tourism came to the area.

Cap Laurosu

A low headland with rocks, stones and rocky heads extending 200m offshore.

⚓ Plage de Laurosu (Tavaria)

A long sandy beach at the delta of the Rivière Rizzanese. An islet surrounded by rocky dangers lies 400m off this beach near its centre. Anchor in 2m sand off the village, open to SW–W–NW–N. Sound carefully in the approach due to uneven bottom. A light aircraft landing strip lies behind the beach.

⚓ Portigliolo

A protected anchorage at the S mouth of the Rivière Rizzanese. A village is located nearby. Anchor in 2m sand off village, open to W–NW–N. Approach on a S heading to avoid many offlying dangers to W.

⚓ Portigliolo looking SE

⚓ Campo Moro

A very popular anchorage in a large bay surrounded by tree and scrub covered hills with a long sandy beach with rocks at each end and a village behind. There is a conspicuous tower on the Pointe de Campo Moro which also has outlying dangers, see below. Anchor in 6m sand and weed open to NW–N–NE.

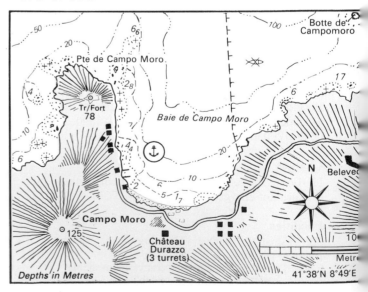

er on Pointe de Campo Moro

⚓ Campo Moro looking SE

⚓ Campo Moro looking SE

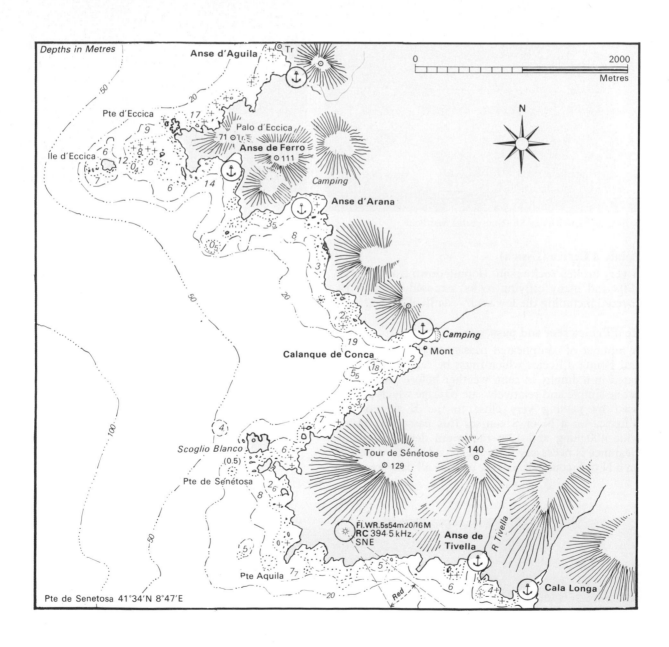

Depths in Metres

0   2000
Metres

N

Anse d'Aguila   Tr
Pte d'Eccica
Palo d'Eccica
71 Tr
Anse de Ferro
111
Ile d'Eccica
Camping
Anse d'Arana
Calanque de Conca
Camping
Mont
Scoglio Blanco
Tour de Sénétose
140
129
Pte de Sénétosa
Fl.WR.5s54m20/16M
RC 394 5kHz
SNE
Anse de Tivella
R Tivella
Pte Aquila
Cala Longa
Red
Pte de Senetosa 41°34'N 8°47'E

163

Pointe de Campo Moro

A prominent headland at the mouth of the Golfe de Valinco, with a conspicuous fort and tower just inland of the point, the hills rise to 116m behind. Rocky dangers extend to 250m in a NW direction and 500m to the NE, the latter partially obstructing the entrance to Campo Moro bay.

⚓ Anse d'Agulia

A remarkable anchorage ½M to NE of Pointe d'Eccica (Essica) in a narrow rocky-sided cove with sand and stone beach at its head. Enter on an ESE course and moor with two anchors in 3m sand and rock, open to W–NW. Track inland, deserted.

⚓ Anse de Ferro

A small bay tucked away behind Pointe d'Eccica on its S side with high rocky tree covered hills around it. Enter on a NE course to avoid rocky dangers. Anchor off head in 5m rock and weed paying attention to rocks close inshore, open to S–SW–W. Deserted.

⚓ Anse d'Arana

A bay surrounded on two sides by tree and scrub covered rocky hills with a sandy beach at its head, a housing estate the NW side. Approach on a NE course, anchor in 3m sand rock and weed off the head of the bay. Open to S–SW–W.

⚓ Anse de Ferro looking SE. Note yachts near Point

⚓ Anse de l'Arana looking E

Pointe d'Eccica (Essica)

A very broken rocky point sloping down from 71m to cliffs and many offlying rocks, exposed, awash and covered including the low rocky isle Ile d'Eccica.

Ile d'Eccica reef and passages

A number of complicated passages exist between Ile and Pointe d'Eccica which must be carefully investigated in a dinghy in calm weather before use. There is one simple and relatively safe passage which can be used by passing very close to the E side of Ile d'Eccica on a N or S course, this passage is 150m wide 400 long and 12m minimum depth. A 300m clearance is necessary from the W side of Ile d'Eccica on a N or S course if passing outside all dangers.

⚓ Calanque de Conca

An attractive anchorage in a narrow V-shaped cove at the mouth of a small river, it has rocky sides with coastal rocks and a sandy beach at its head. Approach on an E course and anchor near the bend in the channel in 4m sand, open to SW–W–NW. Track inland. Deserted except for campers.

Rocks off Pointe d'Eccia   *Tour de Senetosa*   *Pointe de Senetosa*

Pointe d'Eccia and Pointe de Senetosa looking S

⚓ Calanque de la Conca looking NE

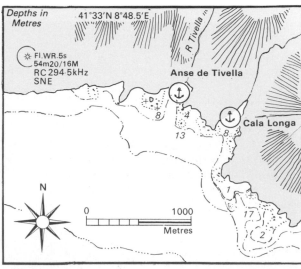

⚓ Anse de Tivella looking NE

Pointe de Senetosa (Sénétose) and Pointe d'Aquila

The Massif de Senetosa has a grey tower on its peak (129m). It slopes downwards to WNW to Pointe de Senetosa and SSW to Pointe d'Aquila. The land is scrub covered. Pointe de Senetosa has two longish islets off its point, Scoglio Blanco (white rock) is the larger of the two and furthest to NNW, between this islet and the point are a mass of rocky dangers. Pointe d'Aquila has a long thin promontory, there is a conspicuous lighthouse consisting of a white house with two white towers (Fl.WR.5s54m20/16M). The point has rocky dangers extending 500m to W. Give the whole headland a 1000m berth when rounding these two points. Aero RC established here.

⚓ Pointe d'Aquila E

A useful anchorage protected by the promontory of Pointe d'Aquila for use with care. Anchor in 3 to 6m sand and rock, open to SE–S–SW. Pay attention to isolated rocks to NE. A mooring buoy which belongs to the lighthouse services may be available.

⚓ Anse de Tivella

A small bay with sandy beach at its head, some rocks at the E side of the bay. The sides of the bay are of rock with scrub. Deserted. Anchor off beach in 5m sand, open to SE–S–SW–W.

⚓ Cala Longa

A long narrow cove with rocky sides and a small sandy beach at its head, surrounded by scrub covered rock, deserted. Anchor in 3m sand off the beach, open to S–SW–W.

⚓ Anse de Bercajo

A small bay, rocky sides with sand and stone beach at head of the bay. Pay attention to rocks close to the shore on both sides near the beach. Anchor off the beach in 3m sand, open to SE–S–SW. Deserted but with tracks inland.

Pointe de Senetosa and Pointe Aquila looking NW

⚓ Anse de Tivella and Cala Longa looking N

⚓ Anse Bercajo looking N

⚓ Anse de Tromba looking NE

⚓ **Anse de Tromba**

Exactly the same as Anse de Bercajo (above) except the approach must be on a NE course and the anchorage is open S–SW–W.

⚓ **Port de Tizzano**

Not a port at the moment but an attractive and useful anchorage in a narrow estuary which has silted up near its head. This silting continues but the plans are in hand to dredge it and to extend the breakwater by 40m. Completion is expected in mid 1991. There are many buildings surrounding its rocky shores and a road to the main coast road. The houses and old fort can be seen from afar. Enter on a N course and leave a short breakwater to port, anchor in 3m sand near a jetty, open to S–SW. There is a small quay, restaurant/café and a mobile food shop. Yacht club de Tizzano (YCT), Hameau de Sartène, Tizzano.

⚓ Port de Tizzano looking N

⚓ **Baie de l'Avena**

A bay with rocky sides and a sandy beach at its head. The bay is well protected by the Massif of Pointe Latoniccia. Approach the S end of the beach on an E course, the N end of the beach has offlying rocks. Anchor in 4m sand, open to SW–W–NW. Road near N end of the beach. Deserted.

Pointe Latoniccia (**Cap de Zivia**)

A large promontory with hills reaching 146m a short distance inland. It has rocky dangers close inshore. On the S facing point there are three patches of rocky heads which extend 100m.

Jetée

⚓ Port de Tizzano looking N

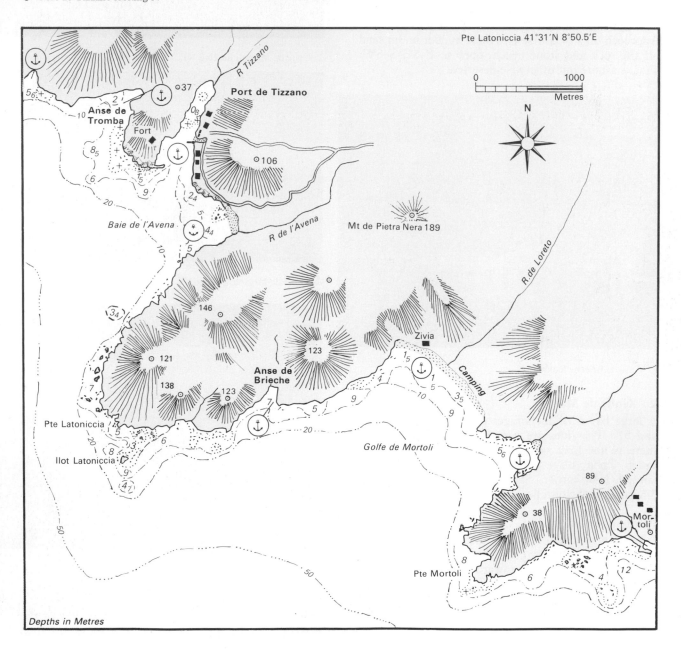

Pointe Latoniccia looking NW

Ilot Latoniccia and passage

The Ilot Latoniccia (La Botte de Tizzano) (20m) lies 300m offshore and has rocky dangers to its N. A passage 100m wide, 200m long with a minimum depth of 3m to be taken E or W halfway between the Corsican shore and the îlot detailed above. Use with care and with a good lookout.

⚓ Anse de Brieche

A small bay on the E side of the Massif de Latoniccia. It is surrounded by scrub covered rocky hills. Approach on a N course enter and anchor in 3m sand off the rock and stone beach, open to E–SE–S–SW. Tracks ashore but otherwise deserted.

⚓ Golfe de Mortoli looking NE

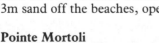

⚓ Anse de Brieche looking N

⚓ Golfe de Mortoli

A large bay with anchorages off the beaches to NW and SE. The sides are very broken rocky cliffs and there is one long sandy beach and one short sandy beach. Zivia village with a few houses and a road inland in NW corner. Summer campsites. Anchor in 3m sand off the beaches, open to SE–S–SW–W.

Pointe Mortoli

A point with a hill 38m high inland rising to 89m, it has a broken rocky-cliffed coastline with rocky dangers projecting 200m towards SW.

⚓ Golfe de Mortoli looking NE

⚓ Golfe de Roccapina looking N

⚓ Golfe de Roccapina

A large open bay at the foot of a wide valley of the Rivière l'Ortolo. There is a group of rocks 1M to E

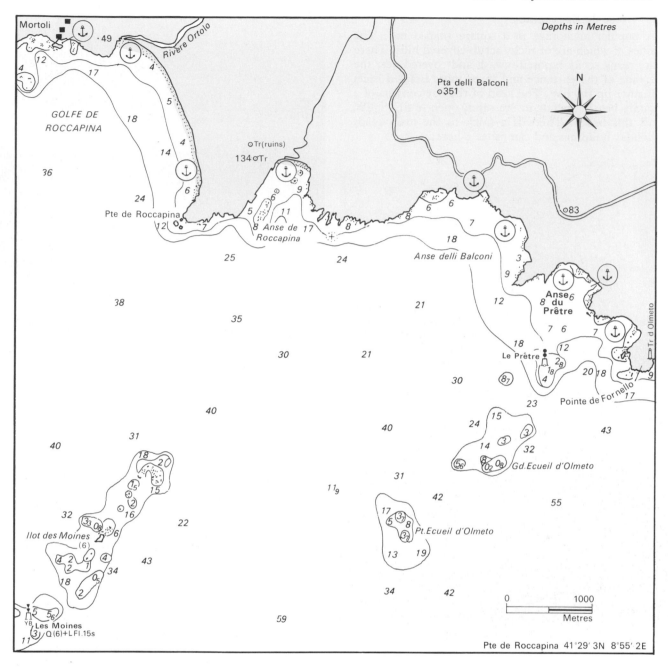

Depths in Metres

Mortoli

Rivère Ortolo

·49

GOLFE DE ROCCAPINA

Pta delli Balconi
∘351

N

36

Tr(ruins)∘
134 ∘Tr

Pte de Roccapina

Anse de Roccapina

Anse delli Balconi

Anse du Prêtre

Tr d'Olmeto

Le Prêtre

Pointe de Fornello

Gd.Ecueil d'Olmeto

Pt.Ecueil d'Olmeto

Ilot des Moines

YB Les Moines
Q(6)+LFl.15s

0   1000
Metres

Pte de Roccapina 41°29′3N 8°55′2E

of Pointe Mortoli and the coast in the W part of this bay has rocky dangers close in. The E half consists of a long sandy beach, anchorage is available off this beach in 3m sand, open to SE–S–SW–W. There is a beautiful one or two yacht anchorage by the village of Mortoli behind a small rocky projection for use by very experienced navigators. There is a track to the main coast road from here.

Pointe de Roccapina

A high (134m) narrow promontory with a forked point and rocky dangers extending 200m to SW. The crest of the hill behind the point has the appearance of a lion from some directions and in certain lights. There is also a tower and a ruined tower nearby also on the crest.

Pointe de Roccapina looking E

⚓ Anse de Roccapina

A popular anchorage in a square shaped bay. The sides of which are of rocky scrub covered hills. There are many rocks exposed, awash and covered near the E side of the entrance and three more isolated islets further up the bay. The head of the bay consists of a sandy beach, anchor in 3m sand, open to SE–S–SW off this beach. There is a track to the main road, holiday buildings and campsites ashore.

Tower   Tower

⚓ Pointe and Anse de Roccapina looking NE

⚓ Pointe and Anse de Roccapina looking NW

Ecueil des Moines (Islets, reefs and passage)

A dangerous area of islets, exposed, awash and covered rocks lying between 1½M and 3M to SSW of Pointe de Roccapina. The Ilot des Moines (6m) lies near the centre of the group. There are many exposed rocks at the N end and Les Moines beacon tower S cardinal, YB ▼ topmark, (Q(6)+LFl.15s) marks the S end. There is a NW–SE passage minimum depth 11m halfway between the Ilot de Moines and the beacon tower.

⚓ Anse delli Balconi

A wide bay with rocky edges and two small sandy beaches one at the centre of the head of the bay and one on the NE side. Two small rocky islets lie in the middle of the bay, anchor in 3m sand and weed off the beaches. Open to S–SW–W. Tracks to main road from beach, mountain delli Balconi (351m) behind road. Deserted area.

Le Prêtre

Anse du Prêtre looking N

⚓ Anse du Prêtre N

A small bay, rocky shores with many coastal rocks extending 50m from the shore. Anchor or moor in 3m sand and weed, open to S–SW–W. Tracks to main road, one house otherwise deserted.

⚓ Anse du Prêtre NE

A second and smaller bay lying immediately to SE of Anse du Prêtre N with rocky sides and extending 100m from the E shore. Narrow sandy beach at head of bay. Anchor or moor in 3m sand and rock near middle of bay, open to S–SW–W.

Pointe de Fornello

A low rounded rocky point with the conspicuous Tour d'Olmeto on its SE side. Rocky dangers on the W side extend up to 150m and on its SW side up to 250m.

Ecueils d'Olmeto and Le Prêtre and passages

Three shallow areas lying in a line approximately SSW of the Pointe de Fornello. Le Prêtre lies 800m from this point with shallows of 1·7 and 1·8m and an awash rock. This rock was marked by a BRB beacon tower with two spheres as a topmark but it has been partially destroyed (1989), ¾M further out from Le Prêtre beacon lies the Grand Ecueil d'Olmeto which has depths of 0·2 and 0·8m with shallows of 3 and 5m on the landward side of them. 1¼M still further out the Petit Ecueil d'Olmeto has shallows of 3·7m.

The passage between Le Prêtre and the Corsican shore is 600m wide and should be taken in SSE–NNW directions to avoid dangers extending 250m from the Pointe de Fornello. Keep about equidistant from the ruined beacon and this point.

The passage between Le Prêtre and the Grand Ecueil d'Olmeto is about 900m wide and should be taken in NW–SE directions equidistant between the ruined beacon and the broken water over the 0·2 and 0·8 shallows at the S end of the Grand Ecueil d'Olmeto.

Tour d'Olmeto   *Le Prêtre*

Pointe de Fornello looking E

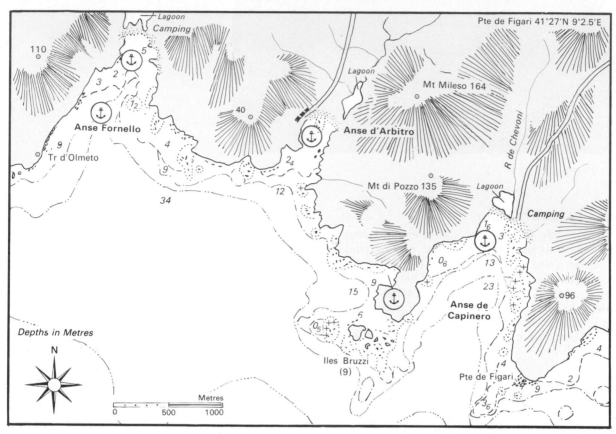

The passage between the Grand and Petit Ecueil d'Olmeto is 1¼M wide and should be taken in NW–SE directions. Except in heavy seas the Petit Ecueil d'Olmeto can be ignored by yachts drawing less than 3m.

⚓ Anse Fornello

A large pleasant V-shaped bay with rocky low hills tree and scrub covered. The Torre d'Olmeto on Pointe de Fornello on the W side of the entrance is conspicuous. There is a 1·2m deep rock near the centre of the bay halfway in. The E shore has rocky outliers extending 50m. Anchor in 3m sand and weed off a sandy beach at the head of the bay, open to SE–S–SW. Summer campsites, track to main road otherwise deserted.

⚓ Anse Fornello looking N

⚓ Anse Fornello and Tour d'Olmeto looking N

⚓ Anse d'Arbitro looking N

⚓ Anse d'Arbitro (Albitru)

A small bay with a low rocky coast line and a large sandy beach at its head but with some rocks extending 150m out from the centre of the beach. Anchor in 3m sand and rock, open to S–SW. There is a large red house on the W side of the bay and some smaller apartment blocks and houses behind the beach. Tracks leading inland, usually deserted. Behind the beach is a lake and marshes fed by the Rivière Agninaccio.

⚓ Iles Bruzzi

A small bay to the N of these islands tucked away behind the large spur which forms the W side of the Anse de Capinero. It has rocky-cliffed sides and there are many rocks close to the shore. There is a small beach at the head of the bay. Anchor in 3m sand off this beach, open to SW–W.

Iles Bruzzi

A group of one large and eight small rocky islets with many rocky heads and shallows covering a dog leg shape 1000m NW–SE and 1000m N–S. Located 200m off the unnamed headland that lies between the anchorages at Iles Bruzzi and Anse de Capinero, as detailed above and below. There is a passage between the headland and Iles Bruzzi for small yachts and dinghies in calm conditions. Larger yachts should keep at least 1000m from the headland and preferably 1500m in bad weather.

⚓ Iles Bruzzi looking NE. Note Iles Bruzzi in bottom right and Anse de Capinero above

⚓ Anse de Capinero

A large bay with low rocky sides and a big sandy beach at its head. There are many offlying rocks close inshore on the W side of the bay and another group extends 150m from the centre of the beach. Two isolated rocks lie 300m to the S and SW of Pointe de Figari. The Iles Bruzzi (see above) obstruct direct entrance to this anchorage from SW–W–NW. Enter on a N course. Anchor in 3m sand and weed off the beach, open to SE–S–SW. Summer campsite and track inland otherwise deserted.

Pointe de Figari

A rocky headland with two islets and many rocky heads extending 300m to S and SW.

3·15 Port de Baie de Figari

Position 41°26'·98N 9°03'·45E
Minimum depth   in the entrance 16m (52ft)
                  in the harbour 16 to 1m (52 to 3·3ft)
Width of the entrance 200m (656ft)
Population 100 (approx)
Rating 2–3–5

General

Not really a port but a very important and useful anchorage. A comparatively deserted long narrow estuary and the surroundings are not spectacular. Some care is necessary when approaching and entering due to outlying rocky dangers and shallows. In very strong winds from S–SW entrance would be dangerous. Good protection is available once inside particularly at the head of the estuary where there is only limited space available. Facilities are virtually non-existent, the nearest village being over a mile away.

Data

Charts

Admiralty *1213*
French *7096*
ECM *1008*

Magnetic variation

0°10'W (1984) decreasing by 7' each year.

Warning

There are a number of isolated rocky dangers well offshore in the approach and care should be exercised. The navigable channel inside the estuary has steep sides. Very thick weed on the bottom in the N half. Care should be exercised in anchoring. Unmarked mussel farms around the estuary.

Fire planes

Large flying boats may land in the bay to pick up water to fight fires. Important see page 33.

Approach by day

From W Follow the very indented coast along from Pointe de Senetosa which can be identified by its lighthouse on the S side. The tower and *Le Lion* rock on Pointe Roccapina, the beacon tower *Le Prêtre* BRB with 2 balls topmark, partially destroyed (1989) and *Les Moines* YB ⩒ topmark, Q(6)+LFl.W.15s 26m9M mark a series of rocky islets and shallows can also be recognised.

Care is necessary near these rocky dangers which can be passed inshore, through the middle, or offshore as required. The Tour de Olmeto at Anse Fornello, the inshore Iles Bruzzi and, in the closer approach, the grey tower at Figari are conspicuous. Make for a position S of this latter tower and 1M away.

From SE Round the low rocky point of Cap de Feno that has a conspicuous lighthouse on its point give it a 300m berth and onto a NNW course. In the closer approach the tower at Figari will be seen. Navigate to a position where this tower is 1M due N.

Approach by night

Due to unmarked offlying dangers and the lack of suitable navigational lights a night approach and entrance are not advised.

Entrance

By day From an area about 1M to S of the Tour de Figari bring it into line with a large group of rocks on a hill just over 1M behind the tower at 008°. Close the tower on this bearing until it is 500m distant then divert to a course of 040° and follow it up the bay sounding carefully.
By night Not recommended.

Anchorages

Several anchorages are marked on the chart but it is possible to anchor almost anywhere to suit draught. The bottom is mud, sand and weed. The N anchorages offer the best protection but swinging room is restricted and a line may have to be taken to the Ilot du Port.

Landings

There are two landing pontoons either side of the head of the bay with tracks inland, also some small shallow private landings around the bay.

Formalities

None.

Rear (rocks)   Front (tower)

Figari. Approach looking NE. Leading marks

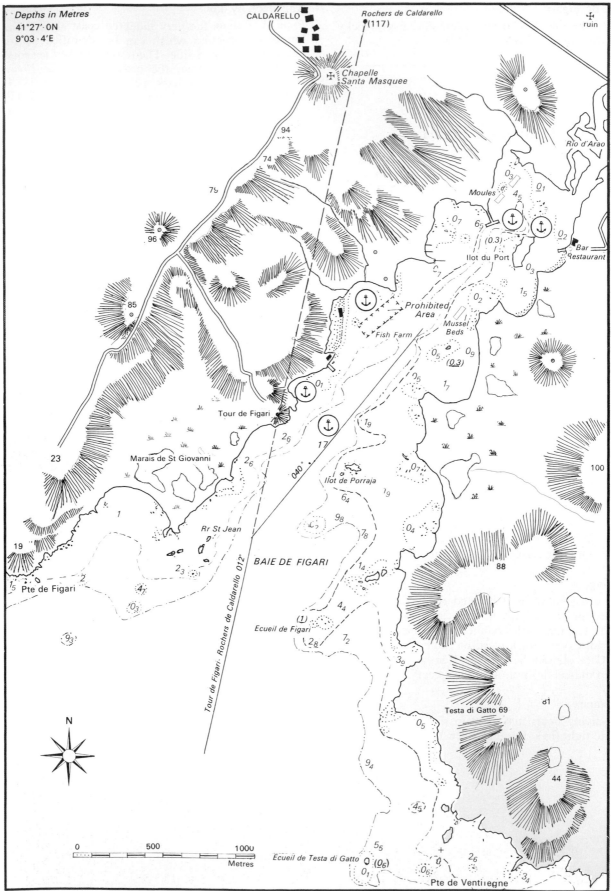

Depths in Metres
41°27′·0N
9°03 ·4′E

CALDARELLO

Rochers de Caldarello
•(117)

⊕
ruin

Chapelle
Santa Masquee

94

74

79

96

85

Rio d'Arao

Moules

0·3

4·5

0·1

0·7

6·5

(0.3)

0·2

Bar
Restaurant

Ilot du Port

0·3

1·5

0·7

0·2

Prohibited
Area

Fish Farm

Mussel
Beds

0·5

0·9

(0.3)

0·5

1·7

23

0·1

Tour de Figari

2·6

1·7

1·9

Marais de St Giovanni

2·6

040°

0·7

Ilot de Porraja

1·9

6·4

1·9

19

1

Rr St Jean

9·8

7·8

0·4

100

2·3

BAIE DE FIGARI

1·4

88

1·5   Pte de Figari

2

4·7

4·4

0·3

Ecueil de Figari

(1)

9·3

2·8

7·2

3·9

Testa di Gatto 69

61

0·5

Tour de Figari: Rochers de Caldarello 012°

44

N

9·4

4·5

0
500
1000
Metres

5·5

Ecueil de Testa di Gatto

(0·6)

2·6

0·1

0·6

3·4

Pte de Ventilegne

Baie de Figari

Tower · Rocks

Figari. Entrance looking NW. Leading marks

Tower · Anchorage

Figari looking SW–W

E landing · Ilot du Port

Figari. Head of the bay looking SE

Charges

None.

Facilities

None in the Baie de Figari with the exception of a small beach restaurant/bar opposite the Ilot du Port. The nearest village Caldarello, over a mile away has small shops for everyday requirements. The village of Pianottolo a mile further on is on the main road and offers more choice of goods and services.

Visits There are some prehistoric troglodyte dwellings in the rocks near the two villages.

Beaches Some rather poor small beaches around the estuary.

Communications Bus service along the main road ½M to N of the head of the estuary.

Future development

A 65m breakwater 1·5m high with wooden quay is to be built for landing.

⚓ Pointe de Ventilegne

An inconspicuous headland with foul ground extending 700m from the shore in a SW direction and 500m in a S direction.

⚓ Anse de Piscio Cane

A smallish V-shaped bay with a lagoon behind it. Both rocky shores have some close inshore rocks. Anchor in 5m sand and weed off head of bay, open to S–SW. Deserted. Main road ¾M inland.

Anse de Piscio Cane

⚓ Anse de Piscio Cane looking NE (left side of photo) and N shore of Golfe de Ventilegne

⚓ Golfe de Ventilegne

A large gulf which has several anchorages around its head for use with care due to shallows and several areas foul with rocky heads. The bay is open to SW–W. The coast road runs behind this gulf.

⚓ Iles de Tonnara

A group of three rocky islets extending up to 600m from the coast with outlying rocky dangers. A small anchorage lies between the NE island which is the largest, and the coast where there are several ruined houses and a sandy beach. Approach this anchorage from the Golfe de Ventilegne on a S course with care. Anchor in 3m rock and sand, open to NW–N. Road to main coast road, usually deserted.

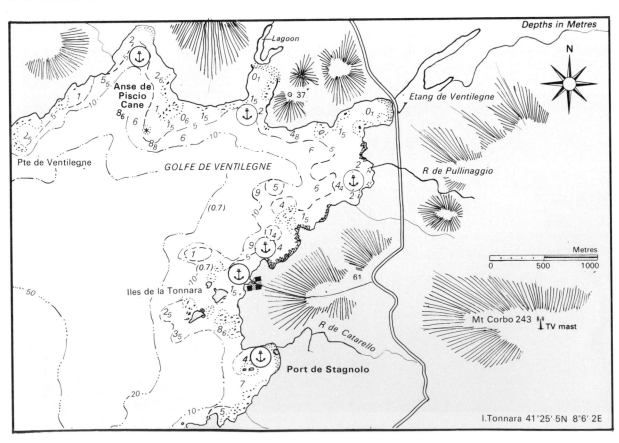

⚓ Iles de la Tonnara looking NE

⚓ Port de Stagnolo

A bay with rocky coast and sandy beach at its head. There is a small islet in the entrance of the bay. This is not a port but a deserted anchorage. Pass N or S of this islet and anchor off the beach in 3m sand, open to SW–W–NW. Track to main road.

⚓ Anse Grande

A fantastic very small anchorage on the W side of Cap de Feno in a rocky-sided bay. The E side of the bay has some close in rocky heads and there is an exposed rock in the centre of the bay. Enter on a NNE course close to the W side of the bay with a good lookout forward. Anchor or moor in 3m rock and sand short of the head of the bay where there is a sand and rocky beach. Open to S–SW. It may be necessary to take a line ashore. Footpath, deserted.

Cap de Feno

An important broken rocky promontory sloping up to 114m inland with irregular cliffs. Two small rocky dangers 200m to W of lighthouse and a 3m shallow 200m to S. The lighthouse is a white square squat tower with a black top marked 'Feno' (DirFl(4)W.15s21m21M). The W section covers the Les Moines beacon tower (109·4°-114·4°), second light (Fl(4)WR.15s(sync)23m7/4M). The W sector covers the safe approach to Cap de Feno (270°-150°).

⚓ Anse de Paragano

A long thin bay, high broken hills with two towers to W, light grey cliffs to E and a white sandy beach at the head of the bay. It is popular with summer visitors and tourist boats. A patch of rocky heads extend 100m on the W side of the entrance. Anchor off the beach in 3m rock and sand, open to S–SW. Road to main road.

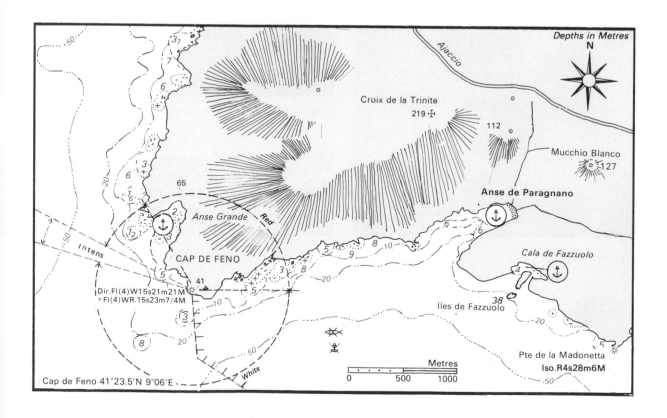

⚓ Port de Stagnolo – Iles de la Tonnara (on left side of photo) looking NE

⚓ Anse de Paragnano looking N

⚓ Iles et Anse de Fazzuolo (Fazziolu)

A fantastic small creek and bay with two islets almost blocking the entrance leaving two entrances/exits, the W entrance is the wider and deeper of the two. The sides are of layered whitish grey cliffs and there is a small beach at the head of the bay. Yachts should use the W entrance and smaller boats can use the E entrance. Anchor to N of the islet in 2·5m sand, open to S–SW. There is a path to Bonifacio and in summer there are many visitors who come by land or by tourist boats.

⚓ Anse Grande looking NE

⚓ Iles et Anse de Fazzuolo looking N

⚓ Anse Grande looking NE

⚓ Iles et Anse de Fazzuolo looking N

Cap de Feno looking SE

3·16 Port de Bonifacio

20169 Corse du Sud

Position 41°23′·41N 9°07′·44E
Minimum depth in the entrance 17m (56ft)
in the harbour 10 to 1m (33 to 3·3ft)
Width of the entrance 200m (656ft)
Maximum length overall 18m (59ft)
Number of berths 350 (approx)
Population 2433
Rating 1–2–2

General

This commercial, fishing and yachting harbour which is the only harbour on the S coast of La Corse almost defies description. It is certainly the most spectacular and attractive natural harbour in La Corse and probably in the Mediterranean. The narrow, deep, fjord-like inlet with high almost vertical sides of white rock crowned by a medieval walled town and Citadelle is certainly unique. The approach and entrance are easy and almost complete shelter is available once inside. The facilities for yachtsmen are good but unfortunately the harbour becomes very crowded in the season. There are two *Bureaux de Port*, the Club Nautique (a private affair) and the Port de Plaisance (the municipality).

Data

Charts

Admiralty *1213, 1424*
French *7024, 7096*
ECM *1008*

Magnetic variation

0°10′W (1990) decreasing by 7′ each year.

Weather forecasts

Posted twice everyday at the Club Nautique. Recorded forecast (☎ 95 21 55 53 and 95 20 12 21).

Speed limit

3 knots.

Port radio

VHF Ch 9. 24 hour watch. Call Centre Nautique or Port de Plaisance.

Lights

Pointe de la Madonetta Iso.R.4s28m6M Red square tower, grey corners with name in white.
Pointe Cacavento Fl.G.4s6m5M White pyramid, dark green top.
Jetée du Grand Débarcadère Oc.G.4s7m7M White 8-sided column, dark green top and base.
Pointe d'Aranella Oc(2)R.6s9m3M Red tower on grey base.

Warning

Large commercial craft use this harbour and yachts must keep out of the way. The pontoons on Quai Jerome are to be changed.

Restricted area

A nature reserve lies along the coast from Cap de Feno to Ile St Antoine and extends 1M seawards. Fishing, subaqua diving and anchoring is forbidden in this area. See chart page 187.

Approach by day

From NW Follow the very ·indented coast from Pointe de Senetosa outside Les Moines shallows marked by a S cardinal beacon tower, YB ☟ topmark, (Q(6)+LFl.W.15s) with two down-pointed cones as a topmark. Round the low rocky Cap de Feno with a conspicuous small lighthouse onto an E course when a square red light tower to E 2M away will be seen. The harbour entrance lies beside it and is almost invisible from this direction though the houses of the old town will be seen on top of the cliff beyond the entrance.

From E The routes through the Bouches de Bonifacio are described on page 186. Round Cap Pertusato, a white-cliffed point with a conspicuous signal station and lighthouse on it. A NW course for 1M will bring the entrance abeam and in the closer approach the red square lighthouse tower with grey edges will be seen at the entrance. The houses on the cliff to the E of the Citadelle and entrance are very conspicuous.

Approach by night

Use the following lights:
Pointe de Senetosa Fl.WR.5s54m20/16M Two white towers, black tops and house 306°-R-328°-W-306° RC.
Ecueil Les Moines Q(6)+LFl.W.15s26m9M. Black tower, yellow top, ☟ topmark.
Cap de Feno DirFl(4)15s21m21M. White square tower, black top. 109·4°-intens-114·4°.
Cap Pertusato Fl(2)W.10s100m25M White square tower, black top and corners. 239°-vis-133°.
Iles Lavezzi Oc(2)WRG.6s27m15/11M White square tower and white house, red band. 053°-W-111°-G-237°-W-278°-G-334°-W-346°-R-053°.
Capo Testa (Sardinia) Fl(3)W.12s67m17M White square tower and house. 017°-vis-256°.
Note There are other lights on the Sardinian coast and islands.

Entrance

By day Enter on a NE course leaving the steep-to white-cliffed Pointe de la Madonetta with a red square lighthouse tower on its top 100m to port and the similar steep-to white-cliffed Pointe du Timon which has a large cave 100m to starboard. Follow the inlet around to starboard in mid-channel. If sailing it will be found that the wind may baffle between the steep sides of the inlet or the hills may screen it all together. If available, the engine should be ready for use or plans made to warp the yacht in by using the warping bollards which are located at short intervals on both sides of the harbour.
By night Approach Iso.R.4s on a NE course and then leave it 50m to port. Set course for Oc(2)R.6s and

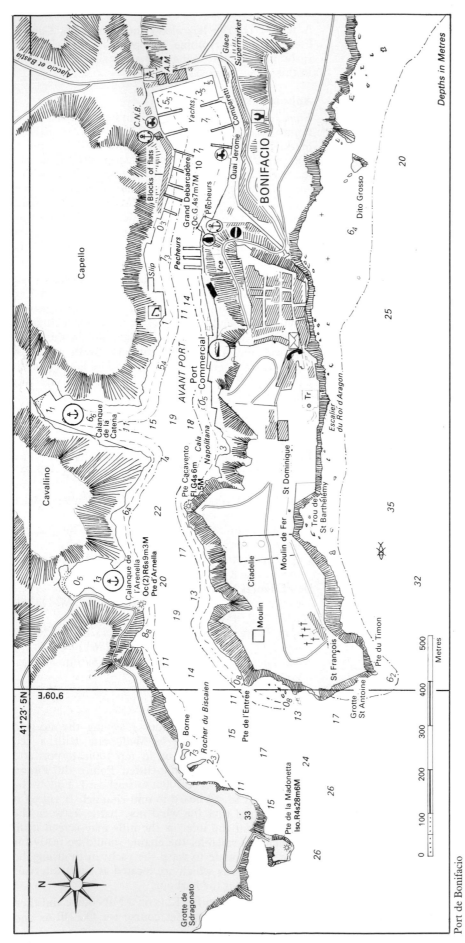

Port de Bonifacio

Bonifacio. Approach looking E–NE

Bonifacio. Approach looking NW

Bonifacio. Entrance looking NNE

when 50m short of it proceed on an E course up the inlet leaving Fl.G.4s and then Oc.G.4s to starboard.

Berths

Yachts berth near the head of the harbour. The N section is administered by the Centre Nautique and has the usual facilities. The S section is controlled by the municipality. In the N section yachts secure stern-to the quay or pontoons with bow-to small buoys or stern to pontoons. In the S section yachts secure stern-to the quay or pontoon with anchor from the bow. Pontoons have fingers for berthing. Changes are expected. The use of anchors is forbidden.

Lighthouse

Bonifacio. Entrance looking NE

Bonifacio looking E up the harbour level with the Port de Commercial

Pointe de l'entrée

Bonifacio. Inside the entrance looking E

Bonifacio looking E up the harbour level with the Citadelle

Grue (crane)   *Port de Commerce RoRo*

Bonifacio looking E up the harbour

Centre nautique

Bonifacio. Head of the harbour looking NE

Anchorages

There are two secluded anchorages in the harbour both with poor holding. The Calanque de la Catena with a mud bottom of 15m sloping to 0·5m and the much shallower Calanque de l'Arenella 10m rapidly sloping to 0·5m. This anchorage is not so sheltered as the Calanque de la Catena.

Formalities

If secured in the NE section report to the Bureau du Centre Nautique (☎ 95 73 03 13 and 95 73 03 78). The clubhouse is close by, open summer 0700–2100 winter 0800–1200 and 1400–1800. If berthed in the S section report to the *Bureau de Port* (☎ 95 73 10 07), 8 Quai du Commerce, on the corner below the ramparts open summer 0700–2200 winter 0800–1200 and 1330–1730. The customs (☎ 95 73 03 53 and 95 73 00 50) have an office in a large building on Quai Jerome Comparetti. *Affaires Maritimes* (☎ 95 73 01 10) is located in a building at the head of the harbour. Customs officers are stricter here than elsewhere due to the proximity of the Italian island of Sardinia.

Charges

There are charges for the use of its quays, pontoons and facilities.

Facilities

Slip A slip on the N side mid-way along the harbour.
Cranes A 30-tonne mobile crane is available, midway along the N side of the harbour (☎ 95 73 01 86).
Fuel Petrol and diesel (*gasoil*) is available from pumps at the Quai de Commerce.
Water Available at the Centre Nautique by hose, from the front of the club also from a point on the Quai Jerome Comparetti, there are taps on the pontoons.
Electricity 220v AC is available at the Centre Nautique and on the pontoons.
Provisions A number of shops along the quayside and others in the old town on the hill, a supermarket to SE of head of the harbour.
Ice In the season it is available from the supermarket near the head of the harbour and from the fuel station on the Quai de Commerce.
Garbage Refuse bins at the Centre Nautique.
Chandlery A shop next to the Centre Nautique and two others near the harbour.
Repairs Repairs to hulls and engines are possible. Electronic expert, sailmaker, woodworking yard next to Centre Nautique.
Post office Located at the top of the hill in the old town. Another is located on the road to the Citadelle in summer.
Hotels Four ***, one **, three * and one unclassified.
Restaurants Thirty-six restaurant/bars and sixteen café/bars.
Yacht clubs The Yacht Club de Bonifacio (YCB) (☎ 95 73 02 13 and 95 73 03 78) is located at the clubhouse of the Centre Nautique. Lounge, bar, showers & WCs etc. are available to visitors using their quays.
Information office The Syndicat d'Initiative office on the road to the old city (☎ 95 73 03 48) and on the W side of the old city, rue des Deux-Moulins (☎ 95 73 11 88).
Lifeboats An all weather lifeboat and an inshore rescue craft kept here.

Crane (grue)   *Bureau de Port de Plaisance*   *Clubhouse*

Bonifacio. Head of the harbour looking NW

Medical Four doctors and two dentists practise here.
Visits The Museum in a part of the bastion and the old town itself are well worth the visit. There are six churches, the most interesting is probably Sainte Dominique which was built by the Knight Templars between 1270 and 1343 which is in the Citadelle and permission to visit must first be obtained from the Guard House at the gate. In fair weather a dinghy trip along the coast to visit the many caves and bays is rewarding.
Beach A small crowded beach at the head of the Calanque de l'Aranella and an even smaller one at the head of the Calanque de les Catena.
Communications Bus service and a ferry service to Italy and Sardinia. Airport at Figari.
Festivals Good Friday processions of various groups with traditional singing. Other processions are held on 3rd May, 2nd and 24th June, 22nd July, 24th and 29th August and 14th September.

Future development

Plans exist for the development of the whole of the head of this harbour into a yacht harbour. The commercial harbour has already moved halfway down the harbour in preparation. A new yacht quay is to be constructed and floating pontoons are being replaced by concrete pontoons.

History

This superb natural harbour must have been used by local fishermen since time immemorial but the real foundation of the town dates from 828 AD when Bonifacio, Marquis de Toscane, arrived here on his return from an expedition against the Saracens. In 1195 during celebrations after a marriage ceremony, a force of Genoese seized and occupied the town driving out all of the inhabitants. They have held the town virtually ever since and even today many of the inhabitants still speak a Genoese dialect. In 1420 Alfonso of Aragon arrived with a strong force at the request of the local Corsican lords who had succeeded elsewhere in driving the Genoese out of the island

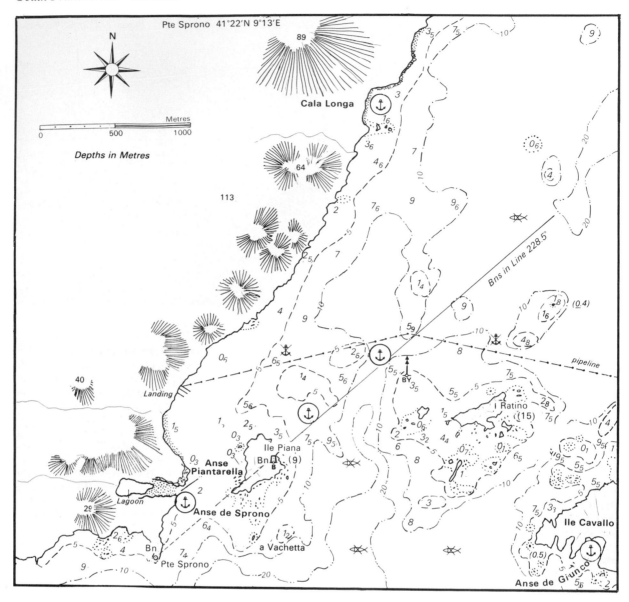

Pte Sprono 41°22'N 9°13'E

N

Metres

0   500   1000

Depths in Metres

89

Cala Longa

64

113

2

Bns in Line 228.5°

(9)

0.6

4

20

0.6

20

7₆

9

9₆

10

7

2.5

7

1₄

9

4

9

10

9

0.8

(0.4)

1.6

48

5₉

10

8

pipeline

0₆

6₅

2₆

5

5₅

5₅

7₅

2.8

Landing

40

1₄

5

5₆

5₅

Ratino

(15)

7₅

10

4

1₅

9₅

0.1

9₅

5₅

5₆

0.1

BY

3₅

5₉

5₅

0₆

I

Anse
Piantarella

0₃

2₅

3₅

7₅

9₅

Bn
B

Ile Piana
(9)

2

3₂

4₄

6

8

0.7

0.1

1

7₅

5₅

Lagoon

2₉

0₃

0₃

0₃

2

Anse de Sprono

10

1

9

3

10

8

10

7₅

3₃

Ile Cavallo

6₄

a Vachetta

1₂

8

(0.5)

Bn

4

2₆

7₄

5

5

Pte Sprono

9

10

20

20

Anse de Giunco

5₆

2

Rear leading mark

⚓ Pointe de Sprono W looking NW. Note rear leading mark on
Pointe and Cap Pertusato in background)

Cap Pertusato looking SE

but their attacks on Bonifacio failed. The population of the town was decimated in 1528 by the plague and in 1554 a combined French and Turkish force captured the town but it was returned to Genoa by a treaty a short time afterwards.

In 1963 the French Foreign Legion took over the barracks in the Citadelle and in subsequent years the development of the tourist industry has slowly taken place.

Cap Pertusato

A major headland of whitish grey rock 86m high with an offlying islet St Antoine, which has a chapel on its top. The outer rock of this cape is shaped like a French Marines cap. There is foul ground to W of the cape extending 100m. The lighthouse stands 400m to E of the cape and is housed in a white square tower with black top and corners (Fl(2)W.10s100m25M). A conspicuous signal station stands 800m to NNW of the cape. Contact by flag, light or VHF Ch 10 or 16 and (☎94 73 00 32), permanent watch.

Ile St Antoine and passage

This islet is 150m long 80m wide and 30m high of layered whitish-grey rock. There is a 30m wide passage between this islet and the cape about 1·5m minimum depth, it is most spectacular. Take in NE–SW direction when the sea is calm and with great care. Boats with tall masts cannot get through due to overhanging rocks.

Le Prêtre beacon looking N

Le Prêtre beacon

A pole beacon RW stripes 6m high sphere topmark, is located on a 4·6m shoal.

⚓ Pointe Sprono W

A small anchorage on the W side of Pointe Sprono which can easily be recognised because the rear mark (a wall) of the transit for the Passage de la Piantarella stands on the point. Anchor in 3m sand in the NE corner, open to S–SW–W. Track ashore.

⚓ Anse Piantarella

A small shallow cove with white sandy beach and small river at its head. Caution is necessary when approaching due to shallows between Ile Piana and the Corsican coast, depths can also change during storms, deep water is usually near the Corsican coast. Anchor in 2·5m sand near the mouth of the cove, open to NE–E–SE–S. Track ashore, popular with summer visitors.

⚓ Ile Piana NE

An open anchorage 300m to NE of the Ile Piana in 8m sand just N of the transit for the Passage de la Piantarella. An alternative anchorage is 1000m from this island and again N of the transit in 12m sand, this second anchorage is opposite the Tignosa di Ratino beacon. Keep clear of the power cable further N. Both anchorages are open to NE–E–SE–S–SW.

Landing Ile Piana NW

Three jetties are located on the Corsican coast 500m to N of Anse Piantarella, they are used by ferries and boats from Ile Cavallo and Iles Lavezzi. Main road ashore.

⚓ Cala Longa

A small bay on the high rocky coast that stands out to Pointe Cappiciolo like a finger. Anchor in 2·5m sand off the centre of the bay, open to E–SE–S. A few houses ashore and a road inland. A group of rocks extend 150m from the shore from SW corner of the bay.

Landing opposite Ile Piana (Ile Piana extreme right)

3·17 Les Bouches de Bonifacio

General

The 3¼M passage between La Corse and Sardinia is considered as a separate section because of the numerous offlying dangers and the adverse weather that is sometimes encountered here. Experienced navigators, especially those used to a similar type of coast such as is found in North Brittany and around the Channel Islands should experience no difficulty. The less experienced should take extra care and should avoid the area in poor weather conditions. The passages between the Italian islands off Sardinia are not described. The large scale French charts 7024 and/or 4595 (obsolete) are advised for those exploring this most attractive and challenging area.

The passages

There are six passages on the N or Corsican side and they are as follows:
1. Grande Passe des Bouches (Bocas Grande in Italian) which is the main deep water commercial route running between Sardinia and the Ecueil de Lavezzi. 3M wide, 3M long, 19m deep.
2. The pass between the Ecueil de Lavezzi and Iles Lavezzi, a deep water route useful for yachts. 1M wide, 1M long, 5m deep.
3. The pass between Iles Lavezzi and Ile Cavallo, a fair weather route for use only by very experienced navigators in daylight. Under 100m wide, 100m long, 1·2m deep.
4. The pass between Ile Cavallo and Ile Ratino, a fair weather route for yachts by day. 300m wide, 800m long, 3m deep.
5. The Passage de la Piantarella, a daytime passage between Ile Ratino and Ile Piana in normal weather. 300m wide, 2M long, 3·5m deep.
6. The passage between Ile Piana and the Corsican coast which is only suitable for shoal draught craft by day in good weather. 200m wide, 2M long, 1m deep (approx).

Data

Charts

Admiralty *1213*
French *7024*
ECM *1008*

Magnetic variation

0°10′W (1990) decreasing by 7′ each year.

Currents

During and after a NW–W gale, E-going currents of up to 3 knots can be experienced. Strong winds from NE–E create weaker W-going currents. In winter this W-going current is semi-permanent.

Lights

Cap Pertusato Fl(2)W.10s100m25M White square tower, black top and corners. 239°-vis-133°.
Capo Testa (Sardinia) Fl(3)W.12s67m17M White square tower and two storied house. 017°-vis-256°.
Pointe Becchi (Iles Lavezzi) Oc(2)WRG.6s27m15/11M Square tower, red band and white house. 053°-W-111°-G-237°-W-278°-G-334°-W-346°-R-053°. Partially obscured 138°-218°.
Ecueil de Lavezzi Fl(2)W.6s18m9M Black tower, red band. Topmark 2 balls vertical.
Perduto Rock Q(3)W.10s16m11M Wind generator, BYB ♦ topmark. Racon.
Isola Razzoli Fl.WR.5s77m13/9M. Truncated conical stone tower. 022°-W-092·5°-R-106·5°-W-237°-R-320°.
Note There are other lights on the Sardinian coast and islands which are not listed here.

Buoys

Ecueil de Lavezzi S cardinal light buoy, YB ⍒ topmark, (Q(6)+Fl.15s) moored just over ½M S of Ecueil Lavezzi beacon. Perduto W cardinal light buoy, YBY ⍓ topmark, VQ(9)10s), marks the NW extremity of the shoals off Perduto Island.

Beacons

The *Sémillante* pyramid tower marks the SW point of the Iles Lavezzi.
Le Prêtre beacon, BRB with topmark 2 balls marks a 4·6m rocky patch ¼M to SW of Pointe Sprono.
Tignosa di Ratino N cardinal post BY ⍒ topmark is located ¼M to NW of Ile Ratino.
Passage de la Piantarella leading mark beacons: front, a white wall on Ile Piana; rear, a white wall on Pointe Sprono bearing 228·5°.

Warning

In bad weather especially from the NW–W–SW the seas and wind can be considerably increased by the funnel effect between the high hills of La Corse and Sardinia. Currents of 2 to 3 knots can be expected with strong winds which are sometimes against the prevailing wind creating a savage sea.

La Grande Passe des Bouches

A 3M wide deep-water pass for commercial shipping and the easiest and safest route. There is a local magnetic anomaly 2M to S of Cap Pertusato with a maximum deflection of 3°.

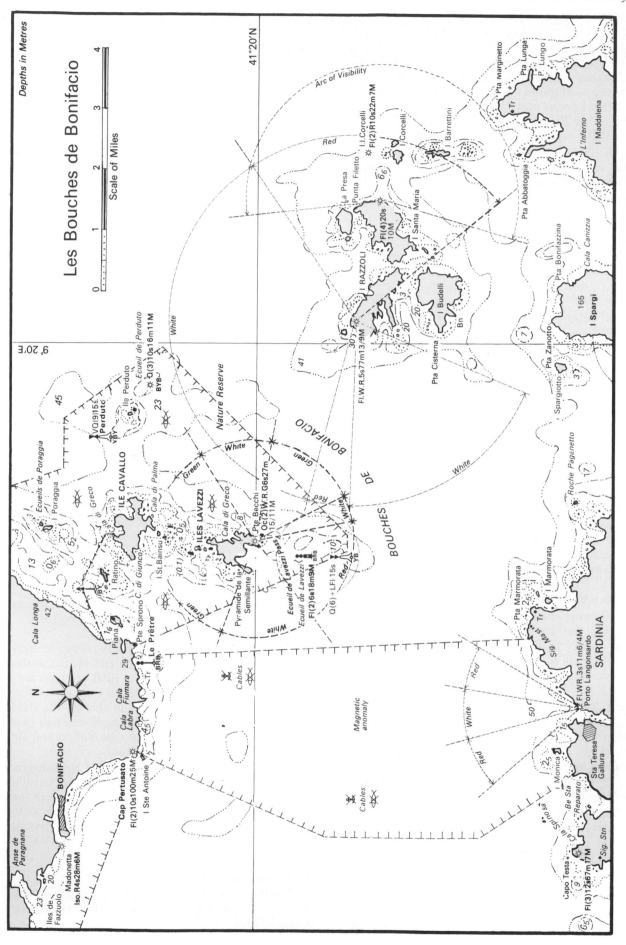

Les Bouches de Bonifacio

Depths in Metres

Scale of Miles

0 1 2 3 4

Approach by day

From W Approach the pass on an E heading approximately 1M to N of the Sardinian coast and 1M to S of the Ecueil de Lavezzi marked by a S cardinal buoy and a beacon tower, BRB 2 balls topmark. When this has been passed round onto a NE course and pass between Iles Lavezzi and Isola Razzoli and then leave the Ecueil de Perduto marked by a E cardinal light buoy, BYB ♦ topmark, 1M to port.

From E The directions given above are taken in reverse order but it is essential to make a positive identification of Iles Lavezzi and Isola Razzoli before entering the area.

Approach by night

From W Approach Isola Razzoli (Fl.WR.5s) on a course between 80° and 85° in a white sector. When Iles Lavezzi (Oc(2)WRG.6s) changes from white to red (053°) turn to a 90° course until it changes back to white (346°) when set a 045° course. When Ecueil Perduto (Q(3)10s) is abeam the passage has been completed.

From E Enter the pass on a SW course with the Capo Testa light (Fl(3)W.12s) on 236° showing halfway between Isola Razzoli (Fl.WR.5s) in the white sector and Iles Lavezzi (Oc(2)WRG.6s) in the white and green sectors. Leaving Perduto Rock (Q(3)W.10s) over 2M to starboard. When Iles Lavezzi (Oc(2)WRG.6s) changes from white to red change to a W course leaving Ecueil de Lavezzi (Q(6)+LFl.15s) close to starboard which ends the passage.

Iles Lavezzi – Ecueil de Lavezzi pass

This pass is very suitable for yachts though in bad weather it will be rougher than the Grande Passe due to the shallower water. The pass is 1M wide minimum depth 5m.

Approach by day

From W Enter the pass on an E course halfway between the Iles Lavezzi and the Ecueil de Lavezzi beacon tower, BRB, two balls topmark. When Pte Becchi bears NW change course to NE and leave the Ecueil de Perduto E cardinal, BYB ♦ topmark, 1M to port.

From E The reverse course holds good provided positive identification of Iles Lavezzi has first been made.

Approach by night

From W Enter the pass by approaching the light on Isola Razzoli (Fl.WR.5s) on 106° on the junction of the red and white light. When the red sector of the Iles Lavezzi light (Oc(2)WRG.6s) turns green change course of 70° and remain in the green sector changing to white sector at (278°) of this light passing 1M to SE of Perduto Rock (Q(3)W.10s).

Note Do not mistake the red/white junction on 106° from Fl.WR.5s with the white/red junction on 092°.

From E Approach Ecueil de Lavezzi (Fl(2)W.6s) on a WSW course until the light on Isola Razzoli (Fl.WR.5s) turns from white to red, turn onto 286° and keep on the junction of the red and white lights astern.

Ile Cavallo – Iles Lavezzi pass

A fair weather pass for yachts in daylight that requires very careful navigation and should only be used by very experienced yachtsmen. A forward lookout is essential as the channel is narrow and it is necessary to pass close to various rocks. The pass is in 100°-280° direction and runs close to the S end of the small Ile San Bainsu located off the S side of Ile Cavallo.

From W The approach on this bearing is clear of nearby dangers but having passed 50m off the S point of Ile San Bainsu it may be necessary to divert slightly to avoid the odd rock and care is necessary.

From E It is important to approach on an accurate 280° towards a point 50m to S of Ile Saint Bainso. This course passes between two small groups of rocks which lie some 200m apart and then very close to the N of an isolated rock. Just short of the point it passes between two more groups of rocks 150m apart the S group being larger with several long low above water rocks. Once past the island keep to the bearing though there are no nearby dangers.

Note There are other passes between these two islands which can be used in good weather provided an experienced lookout is available to con the yacht through the rocks. Pay careful attention to cross currents.

Ile Ratino – Ile Cavallo pass

A narrow pass between unmarked rocks for use in good weather only with a forward lookout posted.

From W Follow the coast on an E course at ¼M from Cap Pertusato towards the S end of Ile Cavallo passing outside Le Prêtre beacon, BRB two balls topmark. When the headland of Pointe Cappiciolo is in line with the W side of Ile Ratino change to a 035° course and bring the E side of Poraggia into mid passage keeping equidistant between Ile Ratino and Ile Cavallo while going through the pass.

From E From a position 300m to SE of Ile Poraggia approach the pass between Ile Ratino and Ile Cavallo and proceed on a 215° course equidistant between the two islands. When the lighthouse on Cap Pertusato appears course can be altered towards the W passing outside Le Prêtre beacon, BRB two balls topmark.

Passage de la Piantarella

This is the usual inshore passage for yachts by day and in normal weather. It cannot be used at night or in bad weather.

Rear leading mark on Pointe Sprono Le Prêtre beacon   *Ile Cavallo*

Passage de la Piantarella looking E

Leading marks

Passage de la Piantarella. Leading marks 228°

Passage de la Piantarella. Tignosa di Ratino beacon

Ile Poraggia   *Ile Cavallo*   *Leading marks*

Passage de la Piantarella looking W

From W Approach the S point of Ile Cavallo on an E course passing some ¼M off the coast of La Corse and outside Le Prêtre beacon, BRB with two balls topmark. When the headland of Pointe Cappiciolo is in line with the small islets to the W of Ile Ratino, change to 010° course and pass equidistant between these islets and Ile Piana. When the white wall (front) leading mark on Ile Piana bears 225° change to 048° course leaving Tignosa di Ratino beacon, N cardinal BY ⚑ topmark, 150m to starboard. The rear leading mark, also a white wall, on Point Sprono will soon appear. Keep these in line astern. When Ile Poraggia is reached it is necessary to make about 100m to NW of the leading line which passes very close to this group of islands.

From E Navigate to a position where the Ile Poraggia group of islands lie 300m to SE and proceed on a course of 228°. The two white wall leading marks will be seen and should be brought into line and followed. This course passes some 150m to N of the Tignosa di Ratino beacon, BY ⚑ topmark. When this beacon is 200m to E turn onto a course of 190° pass-

ing equidistant between Ile Piana and the offlying rocks of Ile Ratino. When the lighthouse on Cap Pertusato appears course may be altered towards the W.

Ile Piana and the Corsican coast passage

This passage is only for use by craft drawing less than 1m (3ft) in fair weather and with a lookout forward sounding carefully. The passage follows the mainland coast at 150m from Pointe Sprono around the bay and along the coast in a NE direction.

Anchorages

Anchorages on the mainland coast of La Corse are given at page 185. Around Iles Lavezzi, page 193, and around Ile Cavallo, page 196. In addition there is an anchorage 250m to NE of Ile Piana in 7m sand and another 250m to NW of the Tignosa di Ratino in 13m sand. These anchorages are exposed from NE–E–S–SW.

3·18 Iles Lavezzi

Position 41°20′·5N 9°15′·5E
Minimum depth   in the entrance 4m (13ft)
                 in the harbour 2·5m to 1m (8·2 to 3·3ft)
Width of the entrance 50m (164ft)
Population None
Rating 1–3–5

General

A delightful, almost bare, group of rocky islands which offer three beautiful anchorages with crystal clear water over a white sandy bottom. The islands are deserted though in the season tourists are brought over by motor boat from La Corse in their hundreds and many yachts use the anchorages. The approach and entrance require some care due to offlying rocks and shallows. The various anchorages offer good protection from wind and sea though it may be necessary to change anchorage if the wind direction should alter.

Data

Charts

Admiralty *1213*
French *7024*
ECM *1008*

Magnetic variation

0°10′W (1990) decreasing by 7′ each year.

Currents

An E-going current of up to 2 to 3 knots may be experienced during and after a NW–N gale. Weaker W-going currents may be encountered after strong winds from NE–E especially during winter months when there is a W-going current of a semi-permanent nature.

Lights

Pointe de Becchi (Iles Lavezzi) Oc(2)WRG.6s27m15-11M Square tower, red band and white house. 053°-W-111°-G-237°-W-278°-G-334°-W-346°-R-053°.   Partially obscured 138°-218°.
Ecueil de Lavezzi Fl(2)W.6s18m9M BRB topmark 2 balls.

Buoys

Ecueil de Lavezzi S cardinal light buoy, YB ⍗ topmark, Q(6)+LFl.15s, is situated just over ½M S of Ecueil de Lavezzi beacon.

Beacons

The SW point of Iles Lavezzi is marked with a conspicuous memorial tower *La Sémillante*.

Warning

In bad weather especially from the NW the seas and winds can be considerably increased by the funnel effect between the high hills of La Corse and Sardinia.

Lighthouse   Cala Lazarina   Cala di Greco   Ile Piana

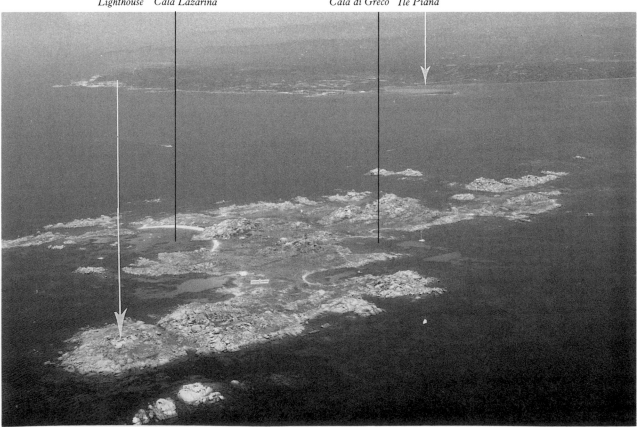

Iles Lavezzi looking NE Cala di Giunco and Cala di Greco

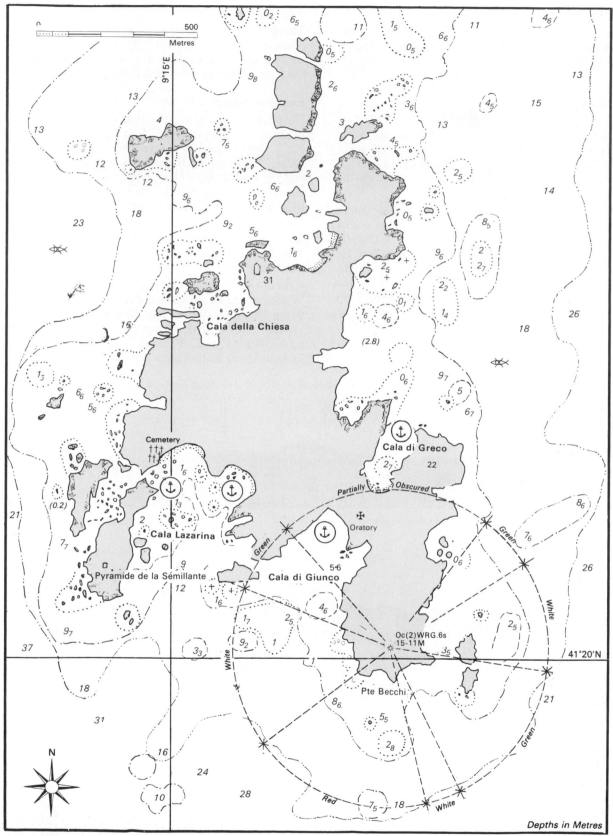

500
Metres

9°15'E

13

13

13

4

12

12

18

23

9₈

0₂

6₅

11

1₅

6₆

11

4₆

13

2₆

3

3₆

4₅

15

4₅

2₅

14

7₅

2

6₆

9₆

9₂

5₆

1₆

31

0₅

8₅

2

2₇

Cala della Chiesa

2₅

2₂

26

16

1₅

6₆

5₆

1₆

4₆

0₁

1₄

18

(2.8)

0₆

9₇

5

6₇

Cemetery
†††
††

Cala di Greco

2₇

22

1₆

1₃

8₆

(0.2)

21

2

7₇

9

Cala Lazarina

Pyramide de la Sémillante

12

Green

5·6

Oratory

Cala di Giunco

7₆

26

0₆

1₆

4₆

2₅

Green

White

9₇

1₇

2₅

1

Oc(2)WRG.6s
15·11M

2₅

37

3₃

9₂

1

3₅

41°20'N

18

Pte Becchi

21

31

8₆

5₅

Green

N

16

24

28

Red

7₅

18

White

10

2₈

Depths in Metres

Iles Lavezzi

Restrictions
A large part of the area around these islands is a nature reserve and all forms of sport which destroy animals, fish, birds and vegetation etc. are forbidden.

Approach by day
From W Round the high white cliffs of Cap Pertusato with its conspicuous lighthouse and signal station and set an ESE course towards the SW point of Iles Lavezzi which has a pyramid-shaped tower *La Sémillante* on the point which will be seen in the closer approach.

From NE From the wide and deep Golfe de Santa Manza round the prominent Pointe Cappiciolo onto a SSE course. Leave the small group of rocks Ile Poraggia ½M to starboard and pass between Ile Cavallo and Ile Perduto leaving a W cardinal light buoy, YBY topmark, VQ(9)W.10s, just to E. Then on a SSW course towards the lighthouse on the S tip of the Iles Lavezzi which should be rounded at 400m.

Approach by night
Though there are adequate navigational lights for a night approach to the area a close approach to this island would be hazardous due to the number of off-lying rocks and shallows and is not advised.

Entrance by day
Cala Lazarina Make a position where the memorial pyramid *La Sémillante* is NW 300m and proceed on a NNE course leaving a series of small above water rocks 75m to port. One small rock has a metal hook and the next group a short white post (missing 1980). Round this white post at 20m onto a NNW course into the anchorage. A bow lookout is advised.

Cala di Giunco From a position where the lighthouse bears NE 300m make a N course leaving the shore 50m to starboard to the head of the *cala* where the anchorage lies.

Cala di Greco Approach the N half of the island on a W course and in the close approach identify the small white building and wall around the cemetery. Approach it on a SSW course leaving a small isolated rock 30m to port. Proceed with care and a bow lookout to the anchorage at the head of the *cala*.

Sémillante memorial — *Pointe Becchi lighthouse*

Iles Lavezzi. Approach looking E. Sardinia in the distance

Sémillante memorial

Iles Lavezzi. Cala Lazarina entrance

Anchorage — *White post (missing 1980)*

Iles Lavezzi. Cala Lazarina entrance

192

Lighthouse   *La Semillante memorial*

Iles Lavezzi. Cala Lazarina, Cala di Giunco looking SW

Rock   Cemetery

Iles Lavezzi Cala di Greco looking S

Anchorages

Cala Lazarina Anchor in 2m sand 50m from the sandy beach in an area not much larger than 100, by 100m. Shallow draught craft may anchor further SW or with care to E. Anchorage open to S.

Cala di Giunco Anchor in 2m sand at the head of the *cala* with the white-walled cemetery bearing NE and some 25m from the sandy beach. Anchorage open to S–SW. Take special care when anchoring due to cables in this *cala*.

Cala di Greco Anchor in 2m sand 30m from the head of the *cala*. Anchorage open to NE.

Moorings

There are some private moorings in these *calas* which could be used if not required by their owners. Some are used by the daily ferry boat.

Formalities

Customs officers may make snap inspections of yachts.

Cemetery   Pte Becchi lighthouse

Iles Lavezze Cala di Guinco entrance looking NE

Iles Lavezzi Cala di Greco looking N

Facilities

None.

Beaches A number of small sandy beaches in the many inlets around the island.

Visits The two cemeteries and the memorial tower can be visited. Plaques give details of the shipwreck of the frigate *Sémillante* on 15th February 1835 while taking reinforcements from Toulon to the Crimea. All of the 750 crew, passengers and troops were drowned. Alphonse Daudet in his *Lettres de mon Moulin* used this disaster as the basis of one of his stories.

There are many donkeys on the island some of which are very tame. A small house and some ruins are all that remains of a settlement of fishermen.

3·19 Ile Cavallo

Position 41°21'·0N 9°13'·0E
Minimum depth in the entrance 3m (9·8ft)
in the harbour 3 to 1m (9·8 to 3·3ft)
Width of the entrance 50m (164ft)
Population 50 (approx)
Rating 2–4–3

General

A rocky island with a certain amount of low scrub and small trees which has been developed as a high class holiday area by an Italian consortium. It has five possible anchorages which need some care in the approach and entrance. Shelter from winds from all directions is possible. Facilities ashore are very limited and the house owners do not like visitors. An airfield has been built for small private planes and an anchorage provided for large yachts. A small private harbour has been built to S of Cala di Palma without permission and the owner has been told to remove it.

Data

Charts

Admiralty *1213*
French *7024*
ECM *1008*

Magnetic variation

0°10'W (1990) decreasing by 7' each year.

Beacons

Le Prêtre BRB topmark 2 balls. SW of Pointe Sprono.
Tignosa de Ratino BY topmark. NW of Ile Ratino.

Currents

An E-going current of up to 2 to 3 knots may be experienced during and after a NW–W gale. Weaker W-going currents may be encountered after strong winds from NE–E especially during the winter months when there is a W-going current of a semi-permanent nature.

Warning

In bad weather especially from the NW–W–SW, the seas and wind can be considerably increased by the funnel effect between the high hills of La Corse and Sardinia. A good forward lookout is essential in this are due to many isolated rocks.

Approach by day

From W Round the high white cliffs of Cap Pertusato which has a conspicuous lighthouse and signal station and follow the coast along at ¼M and outside Le Prêtre BRB with two balls topmark on a 4·6m patch. With care and a good lookout forward, on a NE course, pass halfway between the coast of Ile Ratino and the coast of Ile Cavallo. Keep on this course until a SE bearing clears the N side of Ile Cavallo.

From NE Cross the wide and deep Golfe de Santa Manza and round the promontory of Pointe Cappiciolo onto a course just E of S. Leave the Ile Poraggia ¼M to starboard and approach Ile Cavallo on a S course.

Approach by night

Approach and entrance by night are not advised due to the considerable numbers of unlighted offlying rocks and shoals.

Entrance by day

Cala di Palma Entrance to this anchorage requires considerable care for the first visit and slow speed with a bow lookout is essential. Enter from a position where the island is contained between N and W on a NW course. An alternative approach may be made on a W course from a position 100m to S of the SW extremity of the island then keeping close to the N shore. Open from E–S. Sand beach, several small landing pontoons, a slip and an illegally constructed small harbour.

Cala di Zeri Enter on a SW course towards the W corner of the *cala*. The centre and E side is rock filled. Open to NE. A large and a small beach at head of *cala* with a small pontoon (2m) between them.

Cala di Greco Enter on a S course leaving an outlying rock 75m to port and a shallow (1·5m) to starboard. Open to N. Keep in mid-*cala*, landing slip at head of *cala* Pipeline and cable – see chart page 195.

Cala di Giunco Enter on a NE course. Open S–SW. Several small sandy beaches.

Marine (Cala, Anse) di Cavallo Despite its name this is a bay filled with rocks but an anchorage may be found by approaching at slow speed and with a lookout forward on a NE course. Open to S–SW.

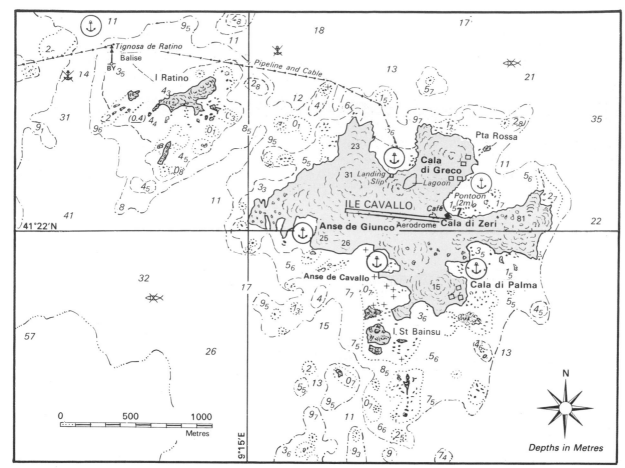

Ile Cavallo

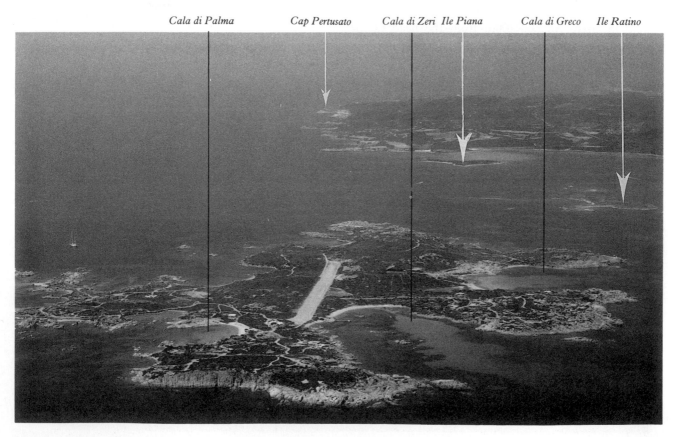

Ile Cavallo. Cala di Zeri looking SW

Ile Cavallo. Cala di Zeri

Ile Cavallo. Cala di Greco

Anchorage

Cala di Palma (L'Anse des Pêcheurs) Anchor off the mouth of the S sub-bay in 4m sand.

Cala di Zeri Anchor 100m from the head of the *cala* close to the NE shore in 3m sand.

Cala di Greco Anchor 100m from the head of the *cala* in 2m sand.

Cala di Giunco Anchor 100m from the head of the bay in 3m sand.

Marina (Cala, Anse) di Cavallo Anchor with great care and after checking the surrounding area for obstructions 100m to S of the W edge of the beach in 2m sand.

Formalities

Customs officers may make snap inspections of yachts.

Facilities

None, but in an emergency assistance might be available from the holiday houses or campsites on the island. There is a small private slip quay and workshop at Cala di Palma.
Beaches Many sandy beaches at the head of the inlets.
Cafés In summer months there is a beach café at Cala di Greco.

Visits The Romans used this island as a quarry and half fashioned pillars, blocks and low relief carvings can still be seen.
Communications A ferry belonging to the holiday homes makes a daily trip to La Corse.

Future development

Plans exist for a yacht harbour to be built in Cala di Greco for 231 berths and 130 apartments and another to SW of Cala di Palma and NE of islet San Bainsu.

Pointe Cappiciolo (Punta di u Cappiciolu)

A prominent point with high cliffs sloping up to a hill (105m) just under 1M to SW of the point stands the Tour Santa Manza (127m). A few close inshore rocks to the S of the point otherwise it is steep-to.

Pointe Cappiciolo looking N

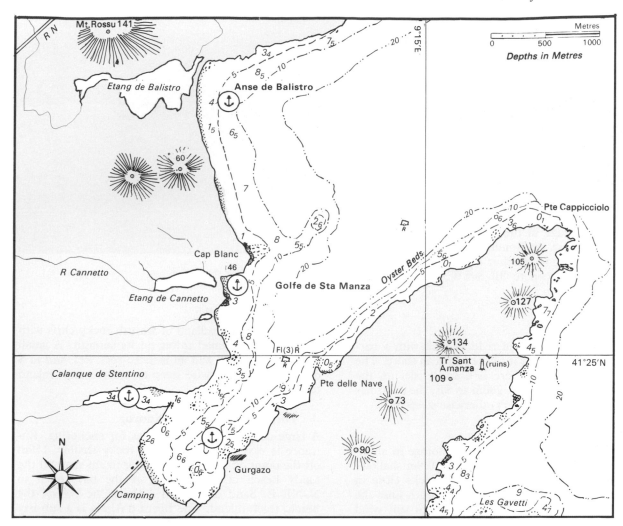

⚓ Golfe de Santa Manza (Sant'Amanza)

A large deep gulf with yellow white cliffs which offer excellent protection but is open to NE–E; it is very easy to enter and the channel is marked by buoys, No 4, small R conical light buoy (Fl.R.2s), ¾M to W of Pointe Cappiciolo and another, No 6, small R conical light buoy (Fl(3)R.6s) located ½M to N of Pointe delle Nave. There are other unlighted buoys which mark the channel to the head of the gulf. Attention must be paid to the many oyster beds which occupy an area 2500m by 500m to SW of Pointe Cappiciolo, and to a 0·6m shallow patch, the buoyed channel by-passes these. The best and most sheltered anchorage lies in the S corner near the village of Gurgazo where there is a landing and where provisions may be obtained, there is also a road here. An alternative anchorage is at the head of the gulf, both anchorages are in 3m sand and weed. Sailing clubs, houses, hotels and summer camps occupy much of the shore along the beach which has caught a lot of flotsam. There is another beach at Balistro to N. The very beautiful Calanque de Stentino should be visited by dinghy and yachts with less than 1·7m draught can anchor here. A deep water anchorage exists in 20m sand ½M to N of Pointe delle Nave. Another

ointe Cappiciolo

⚓ Golfe de Santa Manza looking SW

anchorage lies just S of Cap Blanc. There are plans for a yacht harbour to be built here. There is nothing new in this idea, in 1794 when it was in English hands George III was told that it would make a good harbour and in 1870 Napoleon III was told the same thing.

⚓ Anse de Balistro

An anchorage which is in the corner of a bay, in front of a sandy beach behind which is a lagoon. Anchor in 3m sand and weed, open to NE–E–SE. Main road 1M inland.

⚓ Pointe de Rondinara S

A useful anchorage in the corner of a bay near the isthmus of Pointe de Rondinara. Rocky sides with close in rocky heads. Anchor off sandy beach in 3m sand and weed, open to SE–S–SW. Track to main road. Deserted.

Pointe de Rondinara

A large round headland of reddish rock with a narrow isthmus connecting it to the Corsican shore. The top is scrub covered, there is a small islet on the point and an isolated rock 200m to SE, the coast has many close in rocky dangers otherwise steep-to.

⚓ Port de Rondinara

Not a real port but an excellent anchorage in an almost landlocked sandy bay, there are 0·8m shallows in the middle of the bay and some rocks close in along the NW beach. A white sandy beach lines the sides of the bay. Anchor in 3m sand to suit wind direction. The bay is open to NE–E–SE. The Club Nautique de Glénans has a base here. There is a road to the main road.

⚓ Port de Rondinara looking SW

Pointe de Sponsaglia

A small hooked headland of whitish rocky cliffs with a conspicuous ruined tower on its summit. A small islet lies 50m to E and an isolated rock lies 90m to S of this point, otherwise steep-to, a track runs inland to the coast road.

⚓ Port Nuovo (Golfe de Nuovo)

A large deep bay with two areas for anchoring. Entrance is easy but note a 0·8m rocky shallow 150m off the point on the S side. Anchor in 3m sand off the sandy beach at the W end of the bay, open to N–NE–E. Sand dunes and a lagoon lie behind the beach, track inland. The Bocca d'Alesia is a sub bay on the S side of Port Nuovo with rocky sides and close inshore rocky dangers, it is shallow on the W side. Enter with care, anchor off sandy beach in 3m sand, shell and weed, open to N–NE–E. Deserted.

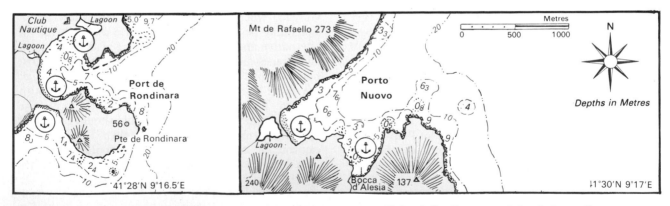

Pointe de Rondinara looking NNE

Pointe de Sponsaglia

Pointe de Sponsaglia looking S

⚓ Golfe de Santa Giulia looking W

⚓ Port Nuovo looking SW

⚓ Golfe de Santa Giulia looking N

Golfe de Santa Giulia

A large semi-landlocked bay surrounded by low scrub covered hills. A white sandy beach runs around the shore with a river mouth in the S corner. There are a number of shallows and several groups of rocky islets surrounded by covered rocks. Enter with care using a bow lookout and continuous sounding. Anchor on N or S side of the bay in 3m sand, open to NE–E–SE. There is a large Club Méditerranée base on the N side of the bay, also a jetty and a road runs to the main road.

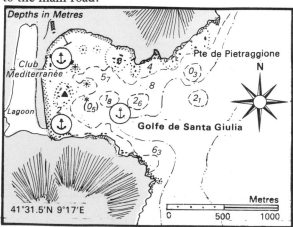

Ile du Toro

A 40m high rock lying 4·5M off the coast surrounded by three rocks islets and some awash and covered rocks. ½M to E of the Ile du Toro lies a 2·6m shallow, the Danger du Toro, which has a S cardinal light buoy, YB ▼ topmark, Q(6)+LFl.15s, is on its S side.

⚓ Pointe d'Aciajo W (Capau d'Acciaju)

An anchorage off the sandy beach lying on the S side of the Pointe d'Aciajo. This point has rocky islets and rocks lying up to 200m to SE–S. If rounding it keep well clear. Anchor off the beach in 3m sand, open to E–SE–S. Housing estate ashore road and tracks.

⚓ Anse de la Folaca (Folacca)

A wide bay with rocky islet Ile de la Folaca in the centre, it has rocky heads close to it. Anchor in the SW corner in 3m sand off the sandy beach, open to NE–E–SE. Housing estate and roads ashore.

199

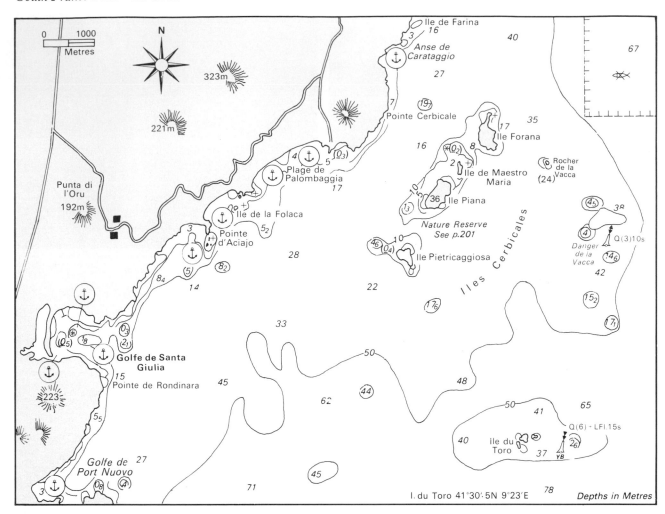

Depths in Metres

I. du Toro 41°30'.5N 9°23'E

⚓ Anse de la Folaca looking W

⚓ Plage de Palombaggia (Anse d'Acciajo)

A long thin bay with a popular sandy beach. The points at each end of the beach have offlying rocks extending 200m. There are also a few rocks extending 250m from the centre of the bay. Anchor off beach at either end of the bay in 3m sand, open to NE–E–SE–S–SW. Some houses ashore also a road.

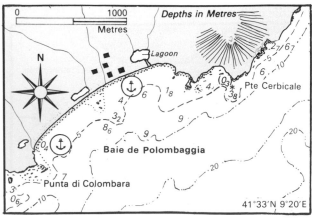

⌁ Baie et Plage de Palombaggia N and S looking S

⌁ Baie et Plage de Palombaggia N and S looking N

Pointe Cerbicale (Caja Cavallu)

A headland which is not conspicuous unless coasting close in. It slopes up to a 145m hill which is scrub covered. There is a good view from here of the coast and islands. The coast is free from obstructions with the exception of a rocky projection to SW.

Iles Cerbicales

Four of these islands lie in a 2M NE–SW line about 1M SE of Pointe Cerbicale. The fifth island lies ½M further E. At the NE end Ile Forana (34m) is sloping with one peak, Ile Maestro Maria (7m) is flat and has good beaches. Ile Piana is the largest with 34m and 31m peaks, Ile Pietricaggiosa (10m) at the S end, Ile de la Vacca (21m) which is ½M to E is high and pointed. The Danger de la Vacca with 4·0 and 4·5m shallows lies 1½M to E of Ile Piana and is marked by an E cardinal light buoy, YB ⬧ topmark, Q(3)10s. Passages are available between all the islands with minimum depth of 9m except for the passage N of Ile Piana where there is a 1·4m submerged rock. There are several shallow patches and an isolated rock on the W side of the islands, which are best

seen from the chart. The islands are a nature reserve and landing without permission is forbidden between 1st April and 31st August.

Ile de la Vacca is sometimes used as a target for naval firing practise. Should this occur close the Corsican coast and keep within a ¼M of it.

⌁ Anse de Carataggio (Piccovaggio)

A small sandy bay with white sandy beach and rocky sides. Anchor in 3m sand and weed near the centre of the bay, open to NE–E–SE–S. Track to road inland S, deserted.

⌁ Anse de Carataggio looking NW

⌁ Baie de Bona Matina

A useful anchorage in a small bay tucked away on the S side of Pointe de la Chiappa, unfortunately the bay is now surrounded by large housing estates. The white sandy beach has beach cafés and is crowded in summer. Rocky dangers extend 100m S from the S point of Pointe de la Chiappa, there are also rocks close inshore on the sides of the bay. Anchor off the beach in 3m sand and weed, open to E–SE–S. Simple requirements available ashore and a road to Porto Vecchio. There is a large nudist camp here.

Signal station and lighthouse *Golfe de Porto Vecchio*

Top of Pointe de la Chiappa looking W

Pointe de la Chiappa

A major headland on the S side of the mouth of the Golfe de Porto Vecchio, steep whitish grey rocky cliffs, scrub covered top 44m high. A conspicuous lighthouse on the summit with white square tower, red lantern on white building (Fl(3+1)W.15s65m 24M RC), also a red and white banded radio mast. A signal station stands 250m to W. The point is steep-to except for some rocky dangers which extend 100m to S of the S point.

Roches de la Chiappino and beacon

300m to N of the main point of Pointe de la Chiappa lies a small group of rocks marked by a masonry beacon tower Tourelle Chiappino with BRB ⁞ top-mark 12m high (destroyed 1989 base just visible). The passage inshore of the beacon has a minimum depth of 11m.

⚓ Baie de Bona Matina and Pointe de la Chiappa looking NW

Signal station   *Lighthouse*

⚓ Baie de Bona Matina and Pointe de la Chiappa looking NW

Section D – Porto Vecchio to Bastia

The coast

The sixty-five mile section of coast northwards from Porto Vecchio to Bastia covers the larger part of the E coast of La Corse and is in general quite different from the rest of the island's coasts.

The high ranges of hills and mountains draw further and further back from the coast as progress is made towards the N and even the foothills cease near Solenzara where a flat sandy plain commences and reaches as far as Bastia. From Campoloro to the N, the foothills are again in evidence but stand back from the coast.

As would be expected on a flat sandy coast good sheltered anchorages are not to be found and natural harbours are only at the mouths of rivers and in salt lakes (*étangs*).

From Porto Vecchio to Solenzara some 14M to N there are six anchorages which are described, these are in various bays where the foothills come down to the coast. The remaining 41M has only the artificial harbour of Campoloro wherein yachts can seek shelter. It is expected that more artificial harbours will be built on this section of coast and the *étangs* of Urbino and Diane are obvious choices for conversion.

The coast is not deserted and there are many holiday houses. Inland, vast areas of fruit, cereal and vines are under cultivation. A main road parallels the coast at a varying distance usually about 2M. Between Porto Vecchio and the lighthouse at Alistro local magnetic deviations of the order of up to 5° may be encountered.

3·20 Port de Porto Vecchio

20137 Corse du Sud

Position 41°35'·49N 9°17'·25E
Minimum depth in the entrance 3·5m (11ft)
in the harbour 3·5 to 1m (11 to 3·3ft)
Width of the entrance 20m (66ft)
Number of berths 430
Maximum length overall 30m (98ft)
Population 8738
Rating 2–2–3

General

A modern yacht harbour and a commercial harbour at the head of a large and beautiful gulf, easy to enter in most weather conditions and offering complete shelter in the harbour. Adequate facilities for yachtsmen and everyday requirements can be obtained from an attractive walled town close by. There are several very attractive anchorages around the gulf and many places including a river to explore. This is a very popular harbour and during the season it becomes very overcrowded.

Data

Charts

Admiralty *1425, 1992*
French *6911, 6929*
ECM *1108*

Magnetic variation

0°05' W(1990) decreasing by 7' each year.

Marine radiobeacon

Pointe de la Chiappa CP (— · — · / · — — ·) 308 kHz 100M every 6 minutes. Grouped with Ile de la Giraglia (GL).

Port radio

VHF Ch 9.

Weather forecasts

Posted twice a day at the *Bureau de Port*. Recorded forecast (French) (☎ 95 21 05 81 and 95 20 12 21).

Lights

Pointe de la Chiappa Fl(3+1)W.15s65m24M White square tower, red lantern. RC and signal station.
Pécorella Fl(3)G.12s12m6M. White tower, green up-pointed cone on top.
Pointe Saint Cyprien Fl.WG.4s26m11/9M White square tower, black lantern. 220°-W-281°-G-299°-W-072°-G-084°.

Porto-Vecchio. Note: Fire fighting seaplanes use this area

Punta de Fozzoli DirOc(2)WRG.6s10m15-13M. White tower, black top. 258°-G-271·7°-W-275·2°-R-288·2°.

Commercial harbour DirIso.WRG.4s9m11-9M White metal framework tower, red top. 208·5°-G-223·5°-W-225·5°-R-240·5°.

Yacht harbour DirIso.WRG.4s9m11-9M.

Digue Est head Fl(2)R.6s5m6M White tower, red top. Vis 212°-302°.

Digue Nord-Est head Fl.G.4s4m5M White tower, green top. Vis 200°-302°.

Beacons

Tourelle Pecorella White tower, green top, green name (Fl(3)G.12s) topmark. Located on a rock in the mouth of the gulf.

Tourelle Chiappino, BRB beacon tower with topmark 2 balls located off Pointe de la Chiappa on a small group of rocks (Destroyed 1982). Base still visible.

Ecueil de la Cioccia, R truncated beacon tower (Fl.R.2s) marks the channel to the yacht harbour.

Buoys

Danger du Toro S cardinal light buoy, YB ⚡ topmark, Q.Fl(6)+LFl.15s, marks a rock awash to E of the Iles du Toro.

Danger de la Vacca, E cardinal light buoy, BYB ⚡ topmark, Q(3)10s marks 0·4m shallows to SE of Ile de la Vacca.

Benedetto G pillar light buoy with ▲ topmark, Fl(4)G.15s, off Pointe de l'Arena where leading lines changes.

Four G buoys with up-pointing cone topmark, mark the starboard side of the entrance channel. They have green reflecting strips.

Four R buoys with cylinder topmarks and red reflecting strips mark the port hand side of the entrance channel.

A G buoy (Q.G) marks the bifurcation of the channel to the commercial and to the yacht harbours.

Warning

The shallow sandy area to N of Pointe de l'Arena is slowly extending. Do not attempt to cut this corner. For a first visit follow the marked channels carefully, do not attempt to follow local yachts which are making use of large areas of deep water with un-marked dangers.

Fire-fighting planes

Large flying boats may land in the Golfe de Porto Vecchio to load water to fight fires. Important, see page 33.

Restricted areas

A nature reserve is established 2½M to E of Pointe de la Chiappa which is 3M long in a N–S direction and 1M wide in an E–W direction. Fishing, subaqua diving and anchoring in the area is forbidden.

The whole of the area around the Iles Cerbicale including the outlying islets and shallows are also a nature reserve and the same restrictions apply between 1st April and 31st August and include landing on any island or islet.

Approach by day

From S Follow the coast in a NE direction from the deep wide Golfe de Santa Manza passing through a ¼M wide, 16m deep channel between the Iles Cer-

Tourelle Chiappino (destroyed 1982) base visible   Tourelle Pecorella

Porto Vecchio. Entrance to gulf from S

Pointe Saint Cyprien lighthouse

Porto Vecchio. Entrance to gulf from N looking WSW

Porto Vecchio. Pointe Saint Cyprien lighthouse looking N

bicales and the mainland of La Corse to Pointe de la Chiappa which can be recognised by a large holiday estate on its SE side and the conspicuous lighthouse, signal station and radio masts on top. Round this point very close in passing between it and Chiappino BRB beacon tower with two balls topmark (destroyed in 1982 but is still visible).

From N Follow the coast to S about ¼M offshore across the wide Golfe de Pinarellu which has an isolated island in its mouth. 1½M further to S, cross the deep Golfe de Saint Cyprien (Baie de San Cipiranu) outside the low rocky Ile Cornuta and pass equidistant between Pointe Saint Cyprien which has a squat lighthouse tower white, black top (Fl.WG.4s26m11/9M) and the Pecorella G beacon tower (Fl(3)G.12s).

Approach by night

The following lights assist in the approach:

Isola Razzoli Fl.WR.5s77m13/9M Truncated conical tower. 022°-W-092·5°-R-106·5°-W-237°-R-320°.

Isola Santa Maria Fl(4)W.20s17m10M Tower on white 2-storey house. 173°-vis-016°.

Harbour pilotage

By day Give the Tourelle Pecorella, W tower, G top, a 200m berth and set a course down the centre of the outer part of the Golfe de Porto Vecchio to a point halfway between Pointe d'Arena a rounded rocky tree-covered promontory and Pointe de Benedetto a lower tree-covered headland ¾M to the N. In this area Benedetto, G pillar light buoy with up-pointed cone topmark (Fl(4)G.15s) will be found. Now set a SW course between a series of G buoys with up-pointed cones and R buoys with cylinder topmarks towards a group of large metal sheds painted white at the RoRo terminal. When the small conical tree-covered Ile Ziglione (13m) is abeam, a small G light buoy (Q.G) ▲ topmark will be seen ahead. Round this buoy on to 255° leaving it to starboard. ¾M ahead will be seen a small R beacon tower, Fl.R.2s, Ecueil de la Cioccia. Leave this tower close to port and the two light towers at the yacht harbour entrance will be seen ahead.

Porto Vecchio Benedetto light buoy looking SW (next buoys arrowed)

By night Enter the outer part of the Golfe de Porto Vecchio and make for a point near its centre. Course should be set to avoid the dangers around the beacon towers of *Chiappino* off Pointe de la Chiappa and *Pecorella* (Fl(3)G.12s) off the Pointe Saint Cyprien (Fl.WG.4s). The directional light Fozzoli (DirOc(2)WRG.6s) will then be seen. Navigate into the white sector and follow it on a 273° course until

Porto Vecchio channel buoys looking SW (arrowed)

Porto Vecchio Bifurcation light buoy looking SW

Porto Vecchio. Bifurcation light buoy looking WSW

the commercial harbour light (DirIso.WRG.4s) is seen. When in the white sector of this light turn to 224° and follow it. After 1¼M a small buoy (Q.G) must be rounded onto 225° leaving it to starboard. The course is now towards a Fl.R which is left to port then towards a Fl(2)R.6s and Fl.G.4s at the entrance to the yacht harbour.

Anchorage in the approach

There are numerous anchorages around the Gulf details of some are given below.

Marine d'Arghi A small sandy bay open to N–NE–N with an anchorage 200m off the beach in 3m sand. A

Salines (salt pans)

Porto Vecchio. Anchorage Marine d'Arghi looking S

Porto Vecchio. Anchorage Baie de Stagnolo looking N

few houses, a large salt pan and the road behind the beach. There is an uncompleted harbour for dinghies and small fishing boats on the W side of the bay.

Marine Vizza A deserted anchorage 150m off the small beach in 3m sand open to the NW–N–NE but otherwise well protected.

Ile Ziglione Anchorage between the island and the coast in 3m sand well protected but open to N. There are some private moorings in the area, a landing stage and houses on the shore. Sound carefully.

Baie de Stagnolo (Saint Agnolo) Anchor in 3m sand off the E side of the bay, well protected but strong winds from SW send in short waves. There is a Touring Club de France base here and summer camps.

Anse de Timbro le Machie (Tramulimacchia) A shallow bay open to SE–S–SW. Anchor 100m off the beach at the N side of the bay in 3m sand. Due to shallows, approach this anchorage on a NW course sounding carefully.

Bay to W of Pointe Saint Cyprien (Punta San Ciprianu) A very small bay open to S–SW. Anchor near the moorings sounding carefully at the head of the bay. Houses around the bay. Many rocks at the SE corner.

Golfe de Saint Cyprien (Baie de San Ciprianu) A superb sandy bay deserted except for a housing development with shop and restaurant on the W side. Approach on a NW course and anchor equidistant between the Ile de Saint Cyprien and the coast in a NNW direction in 3m sand. Attention to an isolated rock 180m to NNW of this island.

⚓ Ile Saint Cyprien   Ile de Cornuta

Porto Vecchio. Anchorage Golfe de Saint Cyprien looking N

Entrance to yacht harbour

Porto Vecchio. Ecueil de la Cioccia beacon tower

Porto Vecchio. Yacht harbour looking E–SE

Entrance

By day Approach the entrance on 242° from Ecueil de la Cioccia R beacon tower and round the head of Digue Nord-Est at 15m to avoid shallows onto a NW course entering between the two *digue* heads.

By night Approach Fl.G.4s on 242° and when close divert to round it at 15m leaving Fl(2)R.6s to port onto a NW course.

Berths

Secure to head of Digue Nord-Est close to the fuelling berth and report to the *Bureau de Port* on the W side of the harbour for the allocation of a berth. Then secure stern-to quay or pontoon with mooring chain from the bow. This chain is attached to a nylon line which is connected to the pontoon or quay.

Formalities

Bureau de Port (☎ 95 70 17 93) at W side of harbour open summer 0800–2000 hours, winter 0830–1200 and 1400–1730. *Affaires Maritimes* (☎ 95 70 26 31), customs (☎ 95 70 07 36) in the same building.

Charges

There are harbour charges. There is no charge for a 3 hour visit.

Facilities

Slip A slip in the S corner with only 1m of water.
Cranes Three mobile cranes, 4, 7 and 30 tonnes.
Fuel Pumps for petrol and diesel *(gasoil)* at the head of the Digue Nord-Est (☎ 95 70 21 41). Open 0900–1900.
Water Water points on the pontoons and quays.
Electricity 220v AC outlets on the quays and pontoons.
Provisions Many excellent shops in the old town and a small shop behind the harbour.
Ice In season ice is delivered daily by lorry to the harbour.
Garbage Rubbish containers on the quays and pontoons and sold from shop at S of the harbour.
Chandlery Four shops one to SW, one to S of the harbour and others in the town.
Repairs Several workshops with mechanics for engine repairs and three small yards outside the town. A sailmaker outside the town.
Post office A modern PTT just outside and to W of the old town.
Hotels Four ★★★, four ★★, two ★ and six unclassified.
Restaurants Many good restaurants and many café/bars.
Yacht clubs There are several sailing school/clubs around the golfe and some dinghy clubs including the Yacht Club de Porto Vecchio (☎ 93 70 00 56), Baie du Stagnole and Cercle Nautique de Porto Vecchio at the *Bureau de Port.*
Showers Showers and WCs available at the *Bureau de Port.*
Information office The Syndicat d'Initiative has an office at the town hall *(mairie)* (☎ 95 70 09 58).
Lifeboat An inflatable inshore rescue craft is kept here.

Porto Vecchio looking WSW

Medical Doctors and hospital available.

Visits In addition to the many attractive anchorages around the Golfe de Porto Vecchio the old town with its walls, which are almost complete, and bastions, are well worth seeing. Visits can also be made to the several prehistoric sites in the area. These include *torres* from 3000 BC to *Statue-Menhirs* of later dates. There is about 2·9m for some 400m in the Rivière Stabiacciu and dinghies can ascend about 1M further depending on the amount of water in the river.

Beaches Numerous sandy beaches around the whole gulf.

Communications Bus service to Bonifacio and Bastia. Airport at Figari. Car ferries to Palau.

Future development

Extra facilities are to be provided for yachtsmen and tourists. A small yacht harbour may be constructed to N of existing harbour.

History

This ancient Genoese walled town with its small fishing harbour below was probably built on the site of a prehistoric settlement, because the area has been in occupation since 3000 BC and the town is located on the best natural defensive site. Porto Vecchio means 'old port' in Italian.

The town never expanded greatly due to the unhealthy marshy *salines* at the mouth of the Stabiacco river where malarial mosquitoes used to breed.

The Golfe de Porto Vecchio has been praised since Roman times, Diodorus Siculus called it a most beautiful port and even Boswell said that it may vie with the most distinguished harbours in Europe. In recent times due to the extermination of the mosquito and to the tourist trade the area is expanding and becoming more prosperous.

Roches de Pecorella and beacon

Near the centre of the mouth of the Golfe de Porto Vecchio lies a shallow area 500m long by 200m wide awash and covered rocks 2·0 to 2·6m deep. A tower, *Tourelle de Pecorella*, stands near the middle of the dangers, it is a masonry beacon G over W with a ▲ topmark. There are four wrecks on the W and N sides of the beacon.

Pointe d'Araso (Punta d'Arasu)

A rounded headland at the N side of the entrance to the Golfe de Porto Vecchio. Two islets of red rock Ile de Cornuta (11m) 500m to S of the point and Ile St Cyprien (Ile San Cipriano) (23m) 400m to SW. These islands have foul ground extending 150m to N. A passage 4m minimum depth equidistant exists between the islands and the point but care is needed to avoid a lone awash rock in the passage lying N of Ile St Cyprien.

⚓ Pointe Capicciola W (Punta Capicciola)

A pleasant deserted anchorage behind the Pointe Capicciola, rocky cliff sides to high scrub covered hills. Small sandy bay with rocks at NE end at head of bay, anchor in 3m sand and weed off this beach, open to E–SE–S.

Pointe Capicciola

A 46m hill which slopes to the coast where a reddish tongue of rock 30m high projects 500m. One small rock stands close to the point.

Ile de Pinarellu

A very conspicuous and prominent rocky-cliffed island 500m by 400m and 51m high, lying at the S point of the Golfe de Pinarellu. A small detached islet on its N side and a group of rocks extending 100m S from its S side. A conspicuous square tower stands on the scrub covered top.

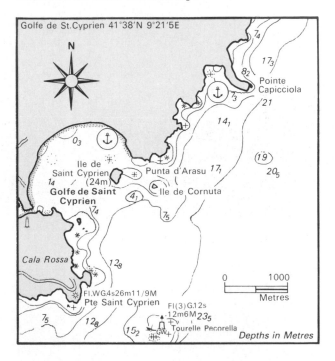

Ile de Pinarellu looking W

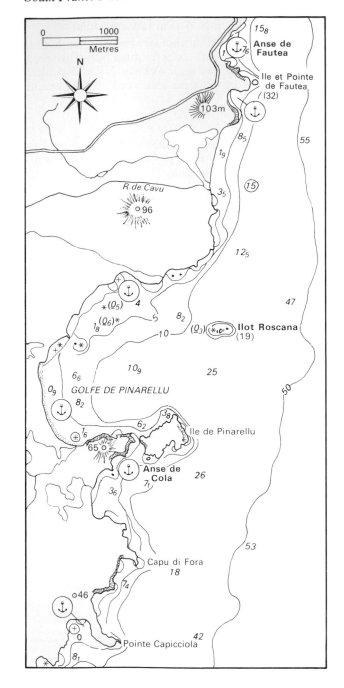

⚓ Anse de Cola

A nice little anchorage hidden away behind Ile de Pinarellu, which has a square tower on top, surrounded by rocky cliffs sloping up to scrub covered hills 65, and 51m high. A patch of rocks lies on the S side of the Ile de Pinarellu extending 100m S. Anchor in 5m sand and weed near the corner of the bay, open to E–SE–S. On the S side of the bay are sand dunes, caravans, beach huts and summer campers.

⚓ Golfe de Pinarellu

A large gulf with a white sandy beach 1·5M long at its head. Ilot Roscana, a bare reddish rocky islet 20m high is located near the centre of the entrance to the gulf, at certain angles and light this island looks like a face with long hair. Rocky dangers extend 100m to E and W of this islet. The whole of the NW side of the bay has rocky dangers which extend up to 500m from the shore but with a good lookout these rocks can be seen in the clear waters making careful navigation in the area possible. Anchor in 3 to 5m sand with some weed off the sandy beach, open to NE–E–SE–S. Near the centre of the head of the bay are large red apartment blocks and many houses, there are more to the N side of the bay. There is a launching slip to S of the red apartment buildings. Mechanic at Lecci 3M inland.

⚓ Golfe de Pinarellu looking SW

⚓ Anse de Cola looking NW

Ile de Pinarellu   *Ilot Roscana*

⚓ Golfe de Pinarellu looking SW–W–NW

⚓ Pointe de Fautéa SW

A small anchorage just behind the Pointe de Fautéa on the W side with a sandy beach at its head. Anchor off the beach in 2·50m sand and weed, open to E–SE–S.

Ile et Pointe de Fautéa

A small roundish rocky scrub covered promontory sloping up hill to 79m with a conspicuous round tower on its point. The coast road runs behind this feature. Off the point and almost joined to it is a small-pyramid shaped islet the Ile de Fautéa 32m high.

Ile et Pointe de Fautéa looking S

⚓ Anse de Fautéa looking W

⚓ Anse de Fautéa

An open bay between rocky cliffs with a white sandy beach at its head behind which runs the coast road, a conspicuous road bridge with three round tunnels lie at the N end of the beach, a housing estate is under construction W of the bay. Anchor off the beach in 3m sand, open to NE–E–SE.

⚓ Anse de Fautéa looking W

⚓ Anse de Tarco (Anse de Tarcu)

A small bay with sandy beach at its head and landing slip protected by a small breakwater. The coast road runs behind the beach where there is a large apartment block and a group of houses at each end of the beach, a housing estate is being built up the river valley further inland. There is a high road bridge over the river at the S end of the beach which has three arches. Anchor off the beach in 3m sand, open to NE–E–SE. The PTT and TV towers 1M inland to S are conspicuous.

⚓ Anse de Tarco looking SW

⚓ Anse de Tarco looking SW

⚓ Anse de Favone looking SW–W–NW

⚓ Anse de Favone

A bay with a 800m long sand beach at its head and the coast road running behind it. There are many houses scattered around the area. Beach restaurants/cafés, an hotel and some shops. Anchor in S part of bay in 3m sand off the beach, open to N–NE–E.

⚓ Anse de Tanone

A small V-shaped bay rocky sides with rocks close in. Coast road behind stony beach. Anchor in 3m sand, open to NE–E–SE.

⚓ Anse de Cannella

A small bay with stony beach and reddish cliffs and coast road running behind, two houses and beach café. Anchor in 3m sand in N corner, open to NE–E–SE.

⚓ Anse de Favone looking W

⚓ Anse de Cannella looking W–NW

⚓ Anse de Cannella looking W–NW

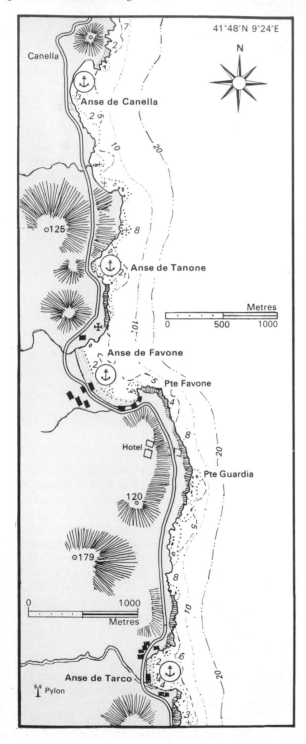

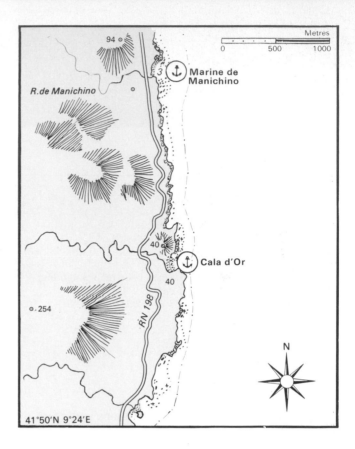

⚓ Marine de Cala d'Or (Marin de Cala d'Oro)

A very small bay with a white stony beach and coast road behind. A house on the S side of the bay and a housing development behind. The bridge over a river is conspicuous. Anchor in 3m sand and weed. Open to NE–E–SE.

⚓ Marine de Manichino (Marine de Manichinu)

A very small bay with a stony beach at its head and the coast road behind. The N side of the bay has rocky shallows. Enter near the S point and anchor off beach in 3m sand, open to NE–E–SE. Housing estate to N of the bay.

⚓ Marine de Manichino looking W

3·21 Port de Solenzara

20145 Corse du Sud

Position 41°51′·45N 9°24′·30E
Minimum depth   in the river entrance 1 to 2m (3·3 to 6·6ft)
in the harbour entrance 4m (13ft)
in the harbour 3 to 1·5m (9·8 to 4·9ft)
Width of the entrance 20m (66ft)
Number of berths 500
Maximum length overall 30m (98ft)
Population 500 approx
Rating 3–4–4

General

An artificial yacht harbour with pontoons and quays S of the mouth of a river where there is a bar which is constantly changing. Entry to the river is only possible in calm weather because the seas break on the bar with any onshore wind, but once inside excellent protection is available. Facilities are limited but everyday requirements can be met. The village and area are quite pleasant but become very crowded with holidaymakers and campers in the season. The new yacht harbour has all facilities and is easy to enter except with strong SE winds.

Data

Charts

Admiralty *1999*
French *6855*
ECM *1007*

Magnetic variation

0°05′W (1990) decreasing by 7′ each year.

Weather forecasts

Posted twice a day at *Bureau de Port*. Recorded forecast (French) (☎ 95 21 32 71 and 95 20 12 21).

Air radiobeacon

Solenzara airfield (41°56′N 9°24′E) SZA (···/---··/·-) 349 kHz 80M.

Lights

Leading lights (intended) Front Oc(2)WRG.6s. White stripe on black square on white post with black top. 213°-W-357°-R-015°. Rear Oc(2)W.6s. Black stripe on white square on white post.
Yacht harbour Digue de Large head Oc.W.6s (band). Elbow F violet from a white tower.
Quai d'Accueil Oc.R.12s (band)

Buoys

A group of 4 large white mooring buoys with E cardinal light buoy, BYB ♦ topmark, Fl(3)10s, to seaward of them lies off the coast some 2M to N where there is an oil terminal for the airfield.

Approach by day

From S From the wide and deep Golfe de Porto Vecchio towards the N, the coast has two large gulfs, those of Saint Cyprien and Pinarellu, and a number of smaller bays. The conspicuous tower on the Ile and Pointe de Fautéa and the wide Anse de Favone which has some houses around the bay can be recognised. In the closer approach the large blocks of flats located just inland of the harbour will be seen.

Entrance

Port de Solenzara. Approach from S

From N The coast from Campoloro to the S has few easily identifiable features. The lighthouse Alistro on a hill inland is easily seen and the small jetties at the entrance to the *étangs* of Diane and Urbino will be identified if coasting close in. A very tall water tower some 2M inland from the mouth of the Tavignano river and the airfield at Solenzara with its offlying buoys may also be recognised. In the closer approach the houses and blocks of flats at Solenzara will be seen. Keep at least 500m from the coast near the airfield it is foul with rocks inshore.

Approach by night

The lights given below allow an approach by night to be made to the area but until the new lights are installed at Solenzara a close approach would be dangerous without a previous visit in daylight.
Pointe de la Chiappa Fl(3+1)W.15s65m24M White square tower and house marked *Chiappa* in red.
Alistro Fl(2)W.10s93m22M Grey 8-sided tower, red house, black lantern.

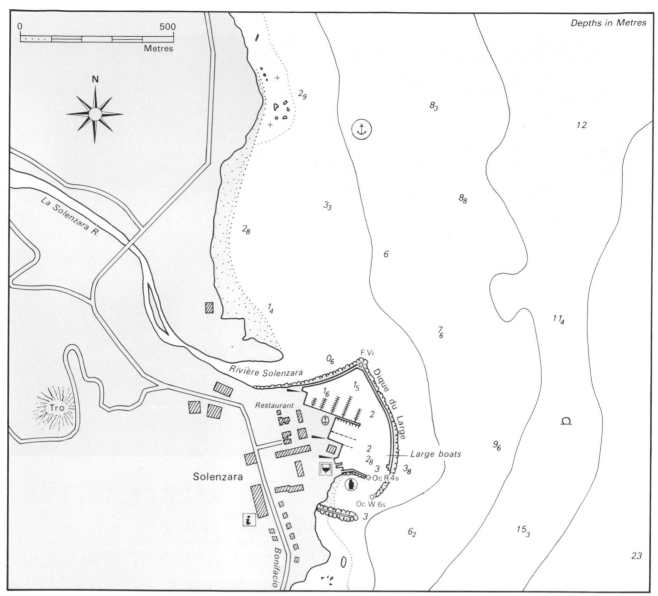

Port de Solenzara

Head of Digue du Large

Port de Solenzara. Entrance

Anchorage in the approach

Anchor ½M due N of the river entrance in 5m sand open to NE–E–E.

Entrance

By day Approach the head of Digue du Large on a NW course round it at 20m into the harbour.

By night Approach Oc.W.6s (band) on a NW course and enter between it and Oc.R.12s (band) into the harbour.

Berths

Secure to fuel quay on port hand inside the entrance and await instructions or obtain them from *Bureau de Port*. Berths are on pontoons with 'fingers'.

Formalities

Bureau de Port (☎ 95 57 46 42). Open winter 0800–1100 and 1400–1700. Summer 0800–2000. *Affaires Maritimes* and customs at Bonifacio.

215

Solenzara looking W.

Charges
There are harbour charges.

Facilities
Slips A slip in SW corner of the harbour. Two more on W side of harbour.
Hard Hard standing for yachts on W side of the harbour.
Crane A 4-tonne mobile crane is available.
Travel-hoist A travel-hoist of 25 tonnes available on W side of the harbour.
Fuel A petrol pump near the river quay, another in yacht harbour. A service station in the village where diesel and petrol are obtainable. Open 0700–1200 and 1300–2100 hours.
Water From taps on pontoons and quays.
Electricity 220v AC points on pontoons and quays.
Provisions Shops in the village including a supermarket.
Ice From the *Bureau de Port*.
Chandlery Two shops.
Repairs Engine and hull repairs possible.
Post office A PTT in the village.
Showers Four showers and WCs.
Hotels One ★★★, three ★ hotels and five unclassified.
Restaurants Many restaurants and many café/bars.
Yacht club Club Nautique de Solenzara (☎ 95 57 40 01).
Information office The Syndicat d'Initiative has an office in the village (☎ 95 57 43 75).
Visits The archaeological site at Aléria which lies 14M to N is one of the most important on the island and the nearby museum has a splendid collection of Greek and Roman ceramics, probably the best in the world. There are traces of the original Roman road from beyond Aléria to near Bonifacio. This road was mentioned in the *Itinerary of Anton Minus*.
Medical A doctor is available.
Beach Excellent beach to N.
Communications Bus service along the coast.

Future developments
Improvements and extra pontoons are planned.

History
There is little recorded history of this harbour. Because it was on the N to S route it was probably a small settlement with fishing craft working out of the river mouth. Recent tourist development has enlarged the village considerably.

Rivière Solenzara
The mouth of this river is close on the N side of the Port de Solenzara the harbour breakwater forming its S bank. There is a sand bar at its mouth and deep water is usually found close to the breakwater (1 to 2m). This river should only be attempted in calm weather with prior visit in a dinghy to find the deepest water. In spate the river flows out at 3 knots. Above the sand bar 1·6m is usually found. Secure to quays on the S bank. See Port de Solenzara page 214 for facilities.

Aérodrome de Solenzara

A military airfield located N of the Travo Rivière and 4M to N of Solenzara. A forbidden area runs for 2M to N of the river and extends 500m from the coast. This area is shallow and has many dangerous covered rocks, give it a wide berth. There is a line of trees between the runways and the coast and only a radio beacon tower, the control tower, some hangers and a cistern can be seen from the sea.

Foce di u Fium Orbu and wreck (mouth of the river Fium Orbu) and wreck looking SW-W

Aérodrome de Solenzara looking W

Offshore fuel terminal Solenzara

This terminal is located 700m from the shore near the centre of the runways. There are four white mooring buoys, a black conical buoy with yellow band. On the seaward side is a E cardinal light buoy, BYB ♦ topmark, Q(3)10s.

Foce di u Fium Orbu (mouth of the river Fium Orbu)

This river mouth has a conspicuous white house with a tower, Tour de Calzarello just to S. ½M further S is a conspicuous wreck, it is forbidden to approach within 200m of it. Just over 1M to N from the mouth of the river a 0·5m submerged rock lies 200m from the shore.

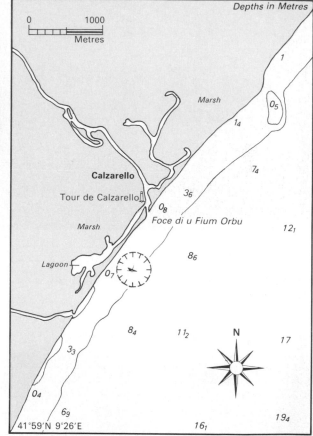

Control tower

Foce di u Fium Orbu

217

Etang d'Urbino

A large lagoon of squarish shape with about 1·5M sides with an island and projections. There is an entrance canal with two projecting training walls, the channel tends to silt up. This lagoon is only suitable for shallow draught craft and a dinghy should be used to sound the channel before attempting to enter. The coast road runs along the NW side of the lagoon. The lagoon is used for the cultivation of oysters and mussels and the beds must not be disturbed. A black tower stands on the coast ¾M to N of the entrance.

Etang d'Urbino

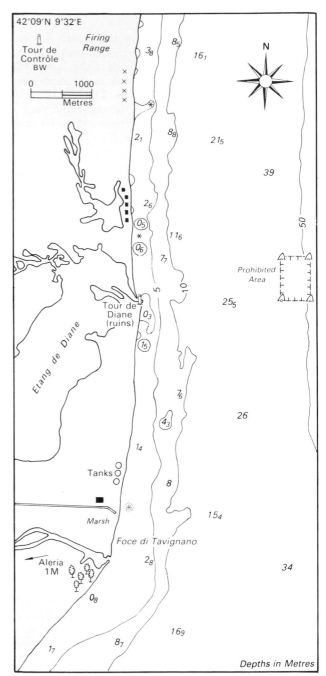

Etang d'Urbino looking W

Foce de Tavignano Fleuve (mouth of the Tavignano river)

Dark green trees mark the S side of the entrance and a group of huts the N. It is a large river with a complex sand bar across its mouth. Boats can enter in calm weather (1 to 2m) especially after a period of calm when the river digs a deep channel. Boats can then ascend 1M to Aléria where there is a village on a bluff and an excellent museum in a nearby fort. Aléria was an important Greek and Roman commercial town and port and many remains can still be seen. Before attempting the entrance use a dinghy to sound out the deepest channel.

Foce de Tavignano Fleuve (mouth of the river Tavignano) looking W

Foce de Tavignano Fleuve

Port Etang de Diane

A similar *étang* to that of d'Urbino now used for
cultivation of mussels and oysters. It was originally
the naval harbour, used by the Greeks and Romans.
The ruined Tour de Diane and a short training wall
marks the entrance. If approaching from the S the
wine tanks just N of the Tavignano Rivière will be
identified and the entrance found 1½M further N. If
approaching from the N the four large crosses of the
firing range will be seen 2M to N of the entrance.
Sound out the entrance using a dinghy before entering because it is subject to silting. The depths are
usually 2 to 3m. Approach the entrance on a SW
course because it is shallow to E, SE and S of the entrance. The entrance is frequently dredged. Do not
interfere with the beds of shell fish.

Port Etang de Diane

Port Etang de Diane looking SW

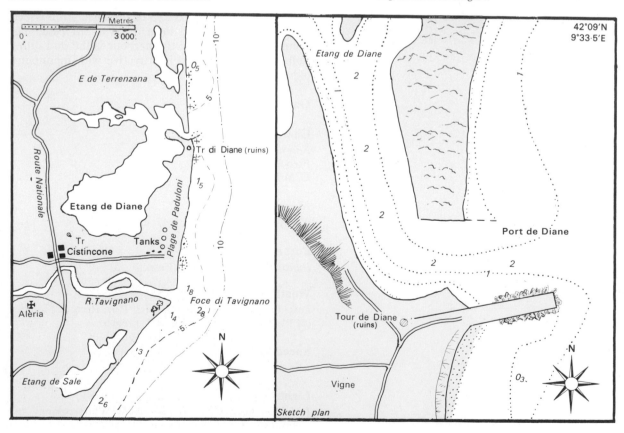

Sketch plan

Phare d'Alistro (lighthouse) looking NW

Champ de tir de Diane (firing range)

A firing range is located N of the Port Etang de Diane and S of the ruined Tour de Bravone. There are four very large crosses like Xs on the coast and control tower black and white chequers is visible just under 1M inland.

Phare d'Alistro

An important light situated ¾M inland on a hillock, it has a grey 8-sided tower black lantern and red house and is surrounded by dark green trees and other houses (Fl(2)W.10s93m22M)

3·22 Port de Campoloro

20221 Haute Corse

Position 42°20'·56N 9°32'·55E
Minimum depth   in the entrance 4m (11ft)
            in the harbour 3·5 to 1m (11 to 3·3ft)
Width of the entrance 60m (197ft)
Number of berths 500
Population 13 (approx)
Rating 3–2–3

General

This modern yacht harbour has been built on the coast some distance from any town or village. Approach and entrance are easy but would become difficult and dangerous with heavy swell and winds from NE–E. Facilities are fair at the moment but plans exist for the construction of more shops and additional facilities. Provisions have to be obtained from a local supermarket or villages located 1M to 2M away. The immediate area around the harbour is flat and rather dull but the hinterland is attractive with mountains, old villages and forests.

Data

Charts

Admiralty *1999*
French *6823*
ECM *1007*

Magnetic variation

0°05'W (1990) decreasing by 7' each year.

Port radio

Bureau de Port VHF Ch 9 (French)

Weather forecasts

Posted twice a day at the *Bureau de Port*. Recorded forecast (☎ 95 36 04 96 and 95 20 12 21) (French).

Speed limit

3 knots.

Lights

Jetée Est head Oc(2)WR.6s7m9/6M White column, red top. 184°-W-342°-R-184°.
Jetée Nord head Fl.G.2s3m2M Green and white tower. 334°-unintens-064°.

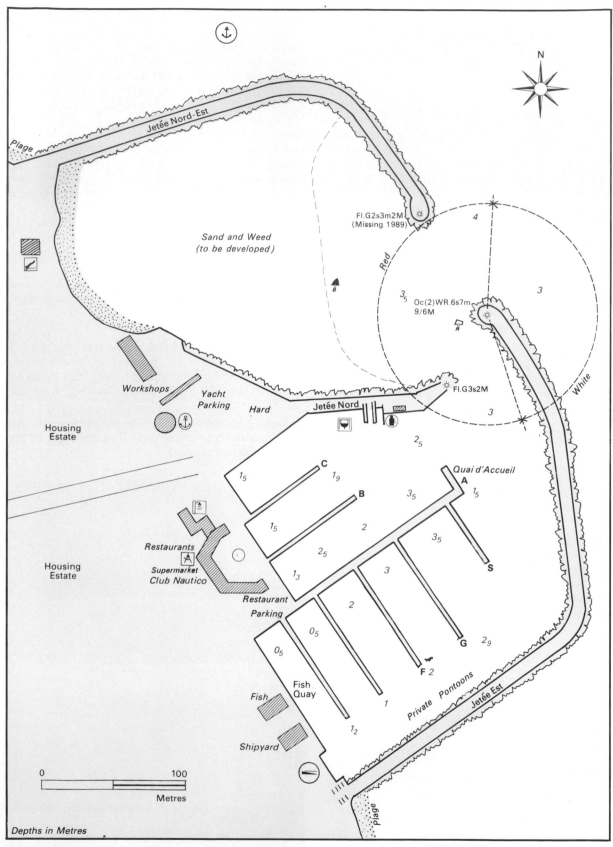

Jetée Nord-Est

Plage

Sand and Weed
(to be developed)

Fl.G2s3m2M
(Missing 1989)

Red

N

4

3

B

3₅

Oc(2)WR.6s7m
9/6M

R

White

Workshops

Yacht
Parking

Hard

Jetée Nord

Fl.G3s2M

3

Housing
Estate

2₅

1₅

C

1₉

Quai d'Accueil

A

1₅

Housing
Estate

Restaurants

Supermarket
Club Nautico

1₅

B

3₅

2

3₅

2₅

3

S

Restaurant

Parking

1₃

2

G

2₉

0₅

F 2

Fish
Quay

0₅

1

Private Pontoons

Jetée Est

Fish

1₂

Shipyard

Plage

0   100

Metres

Depths in Metres

Port de Campoloro

Warning

Due to silting the depths in this harbour may not be as shown on the chart. The harbour is dredged when necessary. Rocky feet extend from some quays and pontoons.

Approach by day

From S The coast from Solenzara is low, flat and sandy. It has few identifiable features but it is possible to recognise the airfield at Solenzara with its silver painted fuel tanks and the oil pipe terminal offshore marked by buoys. An E cardinal light buoy, BYB ♦ topmark, Q(3)10s marks the outer side of the area. There is also a very tall water tower 2M inland behind the mouth of the Tavignano river. The short jetties at the *étangs* of Urbino and Diane will be seen if coasting close inshore. The lighthouse on a small hill inland at Alistro and the town of Cervione on a mountain spur are conspicuous. An isolated house *Maison d'une Nuit* stands on a low hill behind this harbour. The harbour itself is not conspicuous and will not be seen until close-in, but the new workshop is conspicuous.

Maison d'une nuit

Campoloro. Approach from S

Entrance   *workshops*

Campoloro. Approach from N

From N From Bastia the coast is low, flat and sandy and has a few recognisable features. The E cardinal light buoy, BYB ♦ topmark, Lucciana Fl(3)5s, lying outside some mooring buoys of an oil pipe terminal, may be identified together with some black painted oil tanks ashore. There is a large white domed build-

ing (Aero RC Poretta) with some other buildings and a 'T'-shaped pontoon at Les Residences des Iles. There are two training walls at the mouth of the Fiume Alto river. The isolated *Maison d'une Nuit* on a small hill lies behind this harbour. The harbour itself is difficult to see from far but the new workshop is conspicuous.

Approach by night

The following lights may be used but the only effective light is that of Alistro:

Bastia, Jetée du Dragon head
Fl(4)WR.12s16m15/12M Grey tower, red lantern. Red sector covers coastal shallows.

Alistro Fl(2)W.10s93m22M Grey 8-sided tower, on red house black lantern.

Anchorage in the approach

Anchor in 3m sand 100m to N of the entrance in calm weather or in greater depth further out to sea.

Entrance

By day Approach the head of the Jetée Est on a W course and round it at 20m leaving it to port and head of Jetée Nord Est to starboard, then on to a S course leaving the head of Jetée Nord 20m to starboard.

By night Approach Oc(2)WR in the white sector on a W course divert to round it at 20m leaving it to port and Fl.G.2s to starboard.

Campoloro looking SW

Berths

Secure to the 'L'-shaped head of the pontoon immediately ahead on entry and report to the *Bureau de Port* for berthing instructions. Secure in the allotted berth with stern-to the pontoon and bow-to mooring chain which is secured to the pontoon by a light chain to enable it to be picked up.

Formalities

The *Bureau de Port* (☎ 95 38 07 61, 95 38 04 50 and 95 38 07 46) at NW of the harbour. Customs (☎ 95 31 00 48) and *Affaires Maritimes* (☎ 95 31 64 24) offices in the same building. Open 0800–1200 hours, and 1400–1800 hours out of season. In season 0700–2100.

Charges

There are harbour charges.

Facilities

Slip The small slip in the S corner has only about 1m of water.
Hard A large hardstanding to NW of the harbour.
Crane 15 and 20-tonne mobile cranes.

Travel-lift A 50-tonne travel-lift available.
Fuel Petrol and diesel are available from pumps at the N end of the harbour. Season 0700–1200 and 1500–1900. Out of season 0800–1200 and 1500–1700 (☎ 95 38 00 03).
Water From points on the pontoons.
Electricity Outlet points from 220v AC on the pontoons.
Provisions From the village shops at Moriani Plage 2M to N or Prunette 1M to S. Shops to be built at the harbour in the future.
Ice Ice available at the harbour in the season.
Garbage Rubbish containers on the pontoons.
Chandlery At the workshops and on main road to S.
Repairs A shipwright who works in wood or GRP and engineers also electronic experts.
Laundrette To W of the harbour.
Post office PTT at Moriani Plage 1½M.
Hotels At Moriani Plage one ***, two **, three * and two unclassified.
Yacht club Yachting Club Campoloro (YCC). At *Bureau de Port*.
Restaurants Two restaurants to NW of the harbour and more at Moriani Plage 1M and Prunette ½M.
Showers Showers and WCs to W of the harbour.
Information office Some local information kept at the *Bureau de Port*. The Syndicat d'Initiative has an office at Moriani Place (☎ 95 38 41 57).
Medical Doctor and dentist at Moriani Plage.
Lifeboat A lifeboat is to be established here.
Visits The old town of Cervione should be visited. This was the summer residence of the Romans from Aléria and the seat of the Bishop of Aléria. There is a 16th century church and another outside the town dating from 11th century. Some 14M to the S lies Aléria which is one of the most important archaeological sites on the island and the nearby museum has probably the largest collection of Greek and Roman ceramics in the world.
Beaches Excellent beaches stretch for miles in either direction.
Communications Bus service along the coast, two in morning and two in afternoon, airport is 15M to N.

Future development

The provision of extra facilities are planned plus dredging to keep depths 4·5m in the entrance and 3·8m inside the harbour.

History

The name of the ancient *pième* (parish) of Campulori, now Campoloro, means *champ de lauriers* (a field of laurels).

Bureau de Port

Quai d'Accueil

Campoloro. Inside the harbour looking SE–S–SW–W

Résidence des Iles, Dome and Aero RC beacon looking W

Résidence des Iles, Dome and Aero RC beacon

A group of apartment blocks and very distinctive and conspicuous dome with an Aero RC Beacon No. 4086 Bastia. BP (—···/·——·) 369 kHz located here. In summer a T-shaped floating pontoon is installed in front of the buildings.

Foce di Fium Altu

The mouth of the Rivière de Fium Altu which is ½M to N of the dome. Too shallow to enter.

Foce di u Fium Altu (mouth of river Fium Altu) looking W

Lucciana mooring buoys off airfield

Foce di Ciavattone

The mouth of two rivers, Le Golu Fleuve and the Rivière de l'Olmi. The mouth has a sand bar and the deep water channel changes. In calm weather sound carefully from a dinghy before approaching and entering.

Lucciana Offshore Fuel Terminal – Aérodrome de Bastia-Poretta

Eight white mooring buoys with one YB conical buoy ½M off the coast and an E cardinal light buoy, BYB ♦ topmark, Q(3)5s is moored further offshore.

Punta di Arcu

Not really a point more a bend in the low flat coast.

⚓ Punta du Arcu N

An open anchorage in 20m sand and mud ¾M from the coast and 4M to NNW of the Lucciana fuel terminal, open to N–NE–E–SE. Village of Pineto ashore.

Offshore Fuel Terminal-Bastia

A fuel terminal lies 500m offshore and 2M to S of Bastia. There are four white mooring buoys and two BY conical buoys. A E cardinal light buoy, BYB ♦ topmark, Q(3)10s, is moored on the seaward side. Note underwater cables come ashore 600m to N of this terminal where there are four yellow beacons.

⚓ Anse de Porto Vecchio

An anchorage in a small bay with a popular beach of sand and stone. Behind the beach are roads and the buildings of Bastia, anchor in 2·5m sand and mud, open to NE–S–SE–S. A deeper open anchorage is 400m SE further out in 20m sand and mud. For facilities see Port de Bastia. Page 164.

224

Appendix

I. GLOSSARY

French	English
abri, abrité	shelter, sheltered
accastillage	ship chandlery
aigu, -é	pointed, sharp
aiguille	needle
algue	seaweed
amer	landmark, beacon
amont	upstream, landward
appontement	landing stage
anse	bay, cove
argile	clay
arrière-port	inner port
asséchant	drying
aval	downstream, seaward
azur	blue
baie	bay
bal, balise	beacon
banc	bank
barre	bar
bas, -se	low
basse	shoal
bassin	basin, dock
batterie	battery
blanc, -che	white
bleu, -e	blue
bois	woods
bouche	mouth of a river
boue	mud
bouée	buoy
brisant, brisants	shoal, breakers
brise-lames	breakwater
bureau de port	harbour office
butte	knoll, mound
câble aérien	overhead cable
calanque	cove, inlet
cale	ramp, slip, hard
canal	canal, channel
canot de sauvetage	lifeboat
cap	cape, headland
capitainerie	harbourmaster's office
carburant	fuel, petrol
carré, -e	square
carénage	scrubbing berth
carrière	quarry
champ-de-tir	firing range
chantier	dockyard
château	castle, mansion
chaussée	bank, causeway
chenal	channel
clocher	steeple, belfry
col	neck, mountain pass
colline	hill
conduite	pipeline
corps mort	mooring
côte	coast
courant	current, stream
couvent	convent
crête	ridge, crest
crique	creek
crochet scellé	ringbolt
croix	cross

French	English
darse	basin
débarcadère	wharf, landing place
détroit	strait, narrow
déversoir	weir
digue	mole, breakwater
douane	customs
draguer	to dredge
droit	right-hand
dur, -e	hard
eau	water
écluse	lock (of a canal basin)
écueil	rock, reef
église	church
enceinte militaire	military area
épave	wreck
épi	short mole, spur
est	east
estuaire	estuary
étier	navigable creek
falaise	cliff
feu	light
fleuve	river, stream
forêt	forest
fosse	ditch, a deep
galets	shingle
gare	station
gauche	left-hand
golfe	gulf
goulet	inlet
grand, -e	great
gravier	gravel
grève	sandy beach
gris, -e	grey
gros, -se	coarse, large
grue	crane
guérite	watch-tower, turret
guet	watch-house
halage	towing
hampe	pole beacon
haut, -e	high, tall
haut-fond	a shoal
havre	harbour
huître	oyster
hutte	hut, cottage
interdire	to forbid
interdit	forbidden
île	island, isle
îlot	islet
jaune	yellow
jetée	jetty
lac	lake
large	broad, wide
maison	house
marais	swamp, marsh
marée	tide
mât	mast
mécanicien	mechanic
mer	sea

French	English
méridional, -e	southern
milieu	middle
môle	mole, pier
mont, montagne	mount, mountain
morte-eau	neap tide
mouillage	anchorage
moulin	mill
mur	wall
musoir	mole or pierhead
neuf, -ve	new
nez	nose, promontory
noir, -e	black
nord	north
nouveau, -el, -elle	new
occidental, -e	western
oriental, -e	eastern
ouest	west
parcage, parking	car park
passe	passage, pass
pertuis	opening or strait
petit, -e	small
phare	lighthouse
pic	peak
pierre	stone
pieux	stakes, piles
pignon	gable
pin	pine or fir tree
piscine	bathing pool
plage	shore, beach
plaine	plain
plat, -e	flat, level
plongeoir	diving stage
pointe	point
pompage	pumping station
pont	bridge, deck
pont dormant	fixed bridge
pont mobile	moving bridge
pont tournant	swing-bridge
port	port, harbour
presqu'île	peninsula
prise d'eau	water point
projeté	intended
pylône	pylon
quai	quay, wharf
rade	road, roadstead
récif	reef
redoute	redoubt, fort
réservé	reserved
rivière	river
roche	rock
rocher	rock, generally above water
rond, -e	round
rouge	red
roux, rousse	reddish
ruisseau	rivulet
sable	sand
sablon	fine sand
saline	salt water lagoon/salt works
septentrional, -e	northern
sommet	summit
sud	south
terre-plein	levelled ground, platform
tertre	hillock, knoll
tête	head
torchère	flare
torrent	stream, torrent
tour	tower
tourelle	small tower, turret
travaux projetés	works in progress
traverse	shallow ridge or bar
vagues	waves
val	narrow valley
vallée	valley
vasière	mudbank, mudflat
vedette	ferry
vert, -e	green
vieil, vieille, vieux	old, ancient
village	village
ville	town
vive-eau	spring tide
voilier	sailmaker

In the town

French	English
banque	bank
bibliothèque	library
bijouterie	jeweller
blanchisserie	laundry
boucherie	butcher
bureau de poste, la poste, (PTT)	post office
charcuterie	butcher (cooked meats)
chemin de fer (SNCF, SNRP)	railway
coiffeur	hairdresser
cordonnier	shoemaker
crémerie	dairy
drapier	draper
droguerie	chemist
epicerie	grocer
fruits et légumes	greengrocer
gare	railway station
gendarmerie	police station
Hôtel de Ville	town hall
Agencie immobilière	estate agent
journaux	newspaper
laverie	laundrette
librairie	bookshop
magasin	shop
marché	market
mairie	town hall
meubles	furniture

French	English
papetier	stationer
pâtisserie	cake shop
Syndicat d'Initiative (SI)	information office
tabac	tobacconist (also sells stamps)
tailleur	tailor
taxi	taxi
vins	wine shop

Note Many of these titles are preceded by *marchand, agent, bureau, chez,* etc.

II. CONVERSION TABLES

metres–feet

m	ft/	ft
0·3	1	3·3
0·6	2	6·6
0·9	3	9·8
1·2	4	13·1
1·5	5	16·4
1·8	6	19·7
2·1	7	23·0
2·4	8	26·2
2·7	9	29·5
3·0	10	32·8
6·1	20	65·6
9·1	30	98·4
12·2	40	131·2
15·2	50	164·0
30·5	100	328·1

centimetres–inches

cm	in/cm	in
2·5	1	0·4
5·1	2	0·8
7·6	3	1·2
10·2	4	1·6
12·7	5	2·0
15·2	6	2·4
17·8	7	2·8
20·3	8	3·1
22·9	9	3·5
25·4	10	3·9
50·8	20	7·9
76·2	30	11·8
101·6	40	15·7
127·0	50	19·7
254·0	100	39·4

metres–fathoms–feet

m	fathoms	ft
0·9	0·5	3
1·8	1	6
3·7	2	12
5·5	3	18
7·3	4	24
9·1	5	30
11·0	6	36
12·8	7	42
14·6	8	48
16·5	9	54
18·3	10	60
36·6	20	120
54·9	30	180
73·2	40	240
91·4	50	300

kilometres–statute miles

km	M/km	M
1·6	1	0·6
3·2	2	1·2
4·8	3	1·9
6·4	4	2·5
8·0	5	3·1
9·7	6	3·7
11·3	7	4·3
12·9	8	5·0
14·5	9	5·6
16·1	10	6·2
32·2	20	12·4
48·3	30	18·6
64·4	40	24·9
80·5	50	31·1
120·7	75	46·6
160·9	100	62·1
402·3	250	155·3
804·7	500	310·7
1609·3	1000	621·4

kilograms–pounds

kg	lb/kg	lb
0·5	1	2·2
0·9	2	4·4
1·4	3	6·6
1·8	4	8·8
2·3	5	11·0
2·7	6	13·2
3·2	7	15·4
3·6	8	17·6
4·1	9	19·8
4·5	10	22·0
9·1	20	44·1
13·6	30	66·1
18·1	40	88·2
22·7	50	110·2
34·0	75	165·3
45·4	100	220·5
113·4	250	551·2
226·8	500	1102·3
453·6	1000	2204·6

litres–gallons

l	gal/l	gal
4·5	1	0·2
9·1	2	0·4
13·6	3	0·7
18·2	4	0·9
22·7	5	1·1
27·3	6	1·3
31·8	7	1·5
36·4	8	1·8
40·9	9	2·0
45·5	10	2·2
90·9	20	4·4
136·4	30	6·6
181·8	40	8·8
227·3	50	11·0
341·0	75	16·5
454·6	100	22·0
1136·5	250	55·0
2273·0	500	110·0
4546·1	1000	220·0

Index